IN SEARCH
OF A
RESPONSIBLE
WORLD SOCIETY

In Search of a Responsible World Society

THE SOCIAL TEACHINGS
OF THE WORLD COUNCIL OF CHURCHES

BY
PAUL BOCK

THE WESTMINSTER PRESS
PHILADELPHIA

Copyright © 1974 The Westminster Press

Book Design by Dorothy Alden Smith

Published by The Westminster Press®
Philadelphia, Pennsylvania

PRINTED IN THE UNITED STATES OF AMERICA

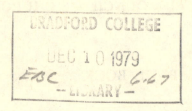
Library of Congress Cataloging in Publication Data

Bock, Paul, 1922–
   In search of a responsible world society.

   Bibliography: p.
   1. Church and social problems.   2. World Council of
Churches.   I. Title.
HN31.B68   261.8   74–9986
ISBN 0–664–20708–1

To Eve,
My Helpmate

Contents

Foreword

BY JOHN C. BENNETT

Professor Bock's book enables us to perceive the cumulative effect of decades of corporate thinking and teaching within the ecumenical community. There is no other book that makes available the substance of the most significant reports and pronouncements from the Stockholm conference almost to the present. Emphasis is on the World Council of Churches, but the work of ecumenical bodies that preceded the World Council and the work of the International Missionary Council, which was united with the World Council, are also included. The author knows well all the processes out of which this thinking and teaching have come. He does an excellent job of comparing and interpreting and of providing some knowledge of the context of the documents, but he does not get between the reader and the materials studied. He includes many extracts from the documents and this adds greatly to the usefulness of the volume, since these are not to be found together anywhere else.

The Roman Catholic Church in its encyclicals and in the reports of the Second Vatican Council has given expression to a great deal of social doctrine, but corporate thinking within the worldwide Christian community apart from the Roman Catholic Church has come from the work of the ecumenical bodies represented here. The results of such thinking are for the most part addressed to the churches, and their authority rests upon their intrinsic worth. They have come out of much conflict and out of struggles to deal with crises and catastro-

phes and with many baffling and unprecedented problems.
There was a considerable change of presuppositions between
Stockholm (1925) and Oxford (1937), and there has been a
great change in what has been seen to be important between
the period dominated by the churches of Europe and North
America and the present period, in which it can be said that
among other things the World Council of Churches is a sound-
ing board for the churches of the Third World.

It is one of the most remarkable experiences of church history that during these decades—a time of wars and revolutions,
of the passing of old empires and the emerging of new nations,
of racial conflicts and fresh awareness of both the destructive
hostilities and the injustice of "racism," of cold war and the
nuclear threat to survival—the churches of most nations have
been in fellowship with each other, and their representatives
have been in continuous discussion of the very social issues that
have been most divisive. This book is a clear and fair and con-
cise record of that discussion. The reader is not provided with
a consensus of social doctrine, but, in spite of the conflicts and
the dynamism of the times, it is possible to find here many
continuities and many widely shared convictions about the relation between Christian faith and social justice and peace that
transcend most of the barriers of culture and national experience. There is here an invaluable and too much neglected
source of Christian guidance for the churches today.

Preface

It is generally known that in the Roman Catholic Church there are social teachings which provide guidance to church members on social questions, and that the primary source of these is the series of papal encyclicals beginning with *Rerum Novarum* by Pope Leo XIII in 1891. It is less well known that in recent decades the non-Roman churches have also been developing a body of social teachings. Such teachings could not develop on a world scale while these churches were as fragmented as they were prior to the twentieth century. But with the emergence of the ecumenical movement, and particularly through the establishment of the World Council of Churches in 1948, it was possible to develop a universal body of social teachings comparable in some respects to the encyclicals. The process began in 1925 in Stockholm, at the conference of the Life and Work movement, one of the movements antecedent to the World Council.

It is the purpose of this book to provide an introduction to these teachings, to give some background for understanding them, and to include many of the teachings themselves. Thus far one book has appeared dealing with this topic and, interestingly enough, it was written by a Jesuit. *The Social Thought of the World Council of Churches*, by Edward Duff (1956), covers the developments to 1954.

Some very important things have happened since that time, notably: (1) the Third World churches have increased their influence in the World Council of Churches, emphasizing social responsibility in a world of rapid social change, and (2) dialogue has opened between the Roman Catholic Church and the non-Roman churches. Discussion of social teachings has been included in this dialogue, and the 1970's find the Roman Catholic Church and the World Council of Churches working together in several areas such as world development and the search for peace.

It has become apparent that in the dialogue with the Roman Catholics the churches of the WCC have been both learners and contributors. Some concepts that appear within World Council statements show similarities to ideas expressed earlier in papal encyclicals. At the same time it is obvious that some of the ideas of the encyclicals of Pope John XXIII and Pope Paul VI and some of the statements of the Second Vatican Council are much like those expressed several years earlier by the WCC. Such a contribution could be made in the 1960's because of the prior decades of struggle by Protestants, Anglicans, and Orthodox to find a social ethic for themselves. Particularly in the light of this new cooperative relationship among major Christian bodies of the world it is fruitful to review the history of the search for an ecumenical ethic in the churches belonging to the WCC. There is also another reason for reviewing this history. The year 1975 marks the fiftieth anniversary of the Universal Christian Conference on Life and Work held in Stockholm.

It is important to recognize that this book deals with only one aspect of the World Council's activity, namely, its work in the area of social thought. It does not deal with the other equally important areas of endeavor such as youth work, evangelism, faith and order, interchurch aid, and service to refugees.

A central thread running through the World Council's teachings is the concept of "the responsible society," which was expanded in the 1960's to "the responsible world society." At the World Conference on Church and Society held in Geneva in 1966, W. A. Visser 't Hooft, former general secretary of the

WCC, said that "our present understanding of our watchword must be 'Responsible men participating responsibly in a world society in which all accept responsibility for the common welfare.' "

Heidelberg College   **P.B.**
Tiffin, Ohio

Acknowledgments

I wish to express appreciation to:

Heidelberg College, Tiffin, Ohio, for granting a sabbatical leave which made possible the research for this book.

The Aigler Fund of Heidelberg College, and Dean Arthur Porter, for support given to the research project.

Staff members of the World Council of Churches, Geneva, Switzerland, especially the Rev. Paul Abrecht, director of the Department of Church and Society, and the Rev. Ans J. van der Bent, librarian, for their guidance, criticisms, and bibliographical suggestions.

Scholars at the University of Heidelberg, in Heidelberg, Germany, especially H. E. Tödt, Professor of Christian Social Ethics, and Karl-Heinz Dejung, doctoral student, for sharing with me their thinking on ecumenical social ethics.

Professors John C. Bennett and Walter G. Muelder, for criticisms of the manuscript.

My wife Eve, for her help in revising the manuscript.

Elaine Knutson, Emmarie Knieriem, and Vickie Barker, for typing.

I

The Nature and Purpose
of World Council Pronouncements

An appropriate place to begin is with the question, Why? Why seek an ecumenical social ethic? Prior to that is the question, Why should there be a Christian social ethic? There is no more controversial issue in the Christian churches in any part of the world than the question as to how or why Christianity should be applied to social issues. Many argue that the Christian faith is personal and that it has nothing to do with economics or politics. Others acknowledge that it has some bearing on social questions but disagree as to what that is. People also disagree as to whether the church as an institution should be involved in such issues, and whether church statements should be taken seriously by individual Christians.

Why a Christian Social Ethic?

The Christian, responding in gratitude to the undeserved love of God expressed most fully in Jesus Christ, manifests love toward his neighbor. Much of it is expressed in personal care and in direct, face-to-face relationships. But love goes farther. It includes people whom one does not know but who are in need of help, and it expresses itself through support of caring agencies—hospitals, schools, orphanages, and homes for the aged. Yet love goes still farther. It goes beyond personal care and social service to social action—that is, to action that reforms social structures.

If one loves his neighbor, he cares whether that neighbor

lives in an orderly society or in a state of anarchy, whether he lives in a world at peace or a world at war, whether he has economic security or lives in poverty, whether he is given equal opportunity or is discriminated against, whether he has freedom of speech and religious liberty or whether he is persecuted. This is all a part of caring for one's neighbor. Social structures can be helpful or injurious to man. Thus one helps or hurts his neighbor by improving social structures or by ignoring social problems.

In the past century there has been a growing awareness in churches of the need for a social ethic as people have faced the problems and possibilities emerging from the industrial revolution. There have been sharp conflicts over capitalism vs. socialism, democracy vs. totalitarianism, racism vs. civil rights. But the church has been interested in social ethics from its beginnings.

Admittedly, the New Testament has only the embryonic form of a social ethic. It was written at a time when Christians were a persecuted minority with little influence over the affairs of state, and when there were widespread expectations of a near end of history. The New Testament ethic is, for the most part, an ethic of the Christian community, showing Christians how to care for each other. But social questions do appear, as in Rom., ch. 13, where Paul teaches Christians to obey the state, even a pagan state, because it is an instrument of God to bring about order. There are social teachings also in Revelation, where John calls for resistance to a state that has become demonic in its demands for emperor worship.

Theories about social ethics became much more fully developed after A.D. 313. Christians then became a favored religion under Constantine and constituted a majority. From then on Christians clearly had the opportunity to shape the civilization of Europe. Scholars such as Augustine and Aquinas worked out Christian positions on private property, the state, war, the family, and other topics. The Reformers rejected some of this medieval Catholic social ethic but accepted much of it in a revised form or new context. They continued, for example, to accept the just war theory originally formulated by Augustine. One of the ideas that they did reject was the belief that the monastic life of poverty, chastity, and obedience was a superior form of Christian life. The Reformers called Christians to live their vocations as Christians in the world of business, farming, politics, and other areas of endeavor.

The more radical wing of the Reformation, as exemplified by the Mennonites and the Quakers, completely rejected the medieval ethic and called Christians to a communal life based on the Sermon on the Mount, a life that included conscientious objection to war. Thus Protestantism from its very beginnings had a diversity of approaches to social ethics.

At any rate, the concern for a social ethic is not a new one. He who claims that the church has no social responsibility is rejecting much of the Christian heritage. Learning from previous efforts of the church to be socially responsible, the church is called upon to develop a social ethic that is pertinent to the twentieth century as well as faithful to the Christian heritage.

WHY CHURCHES TAKE POSITIONS

It can be argued that each individual Christian should arrive at his own social ethic and that the church should restrict itself to "spiritual" activity such as worship, Christian education, and pastoral care. But Christianity, from the beginning, has not been an individualistic affair. It has been a community, a body of Christ in which each member contributes to and benefits from the whole.

Obviously not everyone has an opportunity to study all the social problems or the Biblical and theological foundations for social action. Each person is, of course, ultimately responsible for his own decisions and actions on social issues. But if he does understand Christianity to be communal and not individualistic, he will welcome the best insights of his fellow believers who have devoted their time and skills to the finding of responsible Christian positions on particular issues. Christian social teachings need to be thought of as communal guidance and help to churches and individuals.

In the light of the Christian understanding of the sinfulness of man, it should be recognized that individuals have a strong tendency to apply the Christian label to positions that happen to be in their own economic and social interest. One likes to find Christian support for his biases. In view of this, an individual needs to be challenged by the larger community to see if he has really taken into account the full picture, if he has really placed himself in the shoes of other groups in society to see how particular policies affect them.

Why an Ecumenical Social Ethic?

It became quite apparent to a number of Christian leaders in the early twentieth century that the problems of social justice and peace were so great that a fragmented church could not begin to deal with them. The problems growing out of industrialization (unemployment, child labor, long hours, recessions, unsafe working conditions) had already aroused Christian leaders in several countries in the late nineteenth century, and they sought contact with each other. Then there arose peace movements in the nineteenth century and the early twentieth century, and again the Christian leaders of different nations reached out toward each other.

World War I showed Christian leaders how divided and weak they were. Their attempts to help avert war were of little consequence. In the war itself the churches in effect became tools of their governments. Germans, using the slogan *"Gott mit uns,"* proclaimed God to be on their side. Americans fought a crusade to make the world safe for democracy and sold war bonds in churches.

It was apparent that if the church was to perform a prophetic function in the modern world, that is, if it was to serve as a conscience to nations, classes, or races—rather than to be an uncritical supporter of any—it would need to have a more universal as well as a more historical perspective.

Christians of one nation, in considering a problem, would need to learn how Christians in other nations see it. Members of one race would need to see how things look to members of another race. Christians from one denomination would need to learn from those of another. This would help to raise the sights of Christians and to enlarge their outlook. Looking at Christianity in a universal perspective, one might be less inclined to identify it with the American way of life, the Japanese way of life, the Western way of life, or the white man's way of life. One might be more inclined to see that Christianity, properly understood, transcends all other loyalties.

There are both theological and practical considerations that lead to an ecumenical ethic. Theologically, the Christian faith affirms that the church is one, that it is responding to a God who loves the world, and that its members are to be one in manifesting God's love.

Practically, it is evident that the world has become one, and that the problems of one part of the world directly affect other parts. Few problems are purely domestic. Thus, to deal with any social problem, one needs a worldwide scope. Neither the Waldensian Church in Italy nor The United Methodist Church in the United States is large enough in scope to deal with worldwide revolutions. This requires all the resources and perspectives of a universal Christian body.

W. A. Visser 't Hooft, general secretary of the World Council of Churches during most of its history, wrote:

> The experience of these years shows how difficult it is for all Churches to rise above the necessarily limited viewpoint of their national and social environment, but it has also shown that it is precisely through the ecumenical encounter that the necessary mutual correction can take place so that the Churches can arrive at a more objective judgment concerning the road to true peace and real justice.[1]

THE AUTHORITY OF ECUMENICAL TEACHINGS

Out of the sharing of insights and experiences of Christians of many different backgrounds, studies have emerged, the essence of which has been expressed in ecumenical meetings in the form of social pronouncements. From the very beginning the question has been raised as to what authority these pronouncements have.

It was obvious long ago that, particularly for Protestants, ecclesiastical statements would never have the authority of papal statements. One of the factors in the Reformation was rebellion against hierarchical authority. Though the Reformers sought to preserve a communal consciousness whereby the whole church lived under the authority of the Word of God which in turn was interpreted by its pastors, modern Protestantism has often fallen into a kind of individualism wherein each man interprets the Bible as he sees fit and develops an ethic to suit himself. Individualists sometimes have little respect for church leadership—either denominational or ecumenical. Movements for church renewal in recent years have sought to restore a sense of community. Insofar as this is realized, people might be willing at least to give a hearing to the social teachings of their church and to the councils to which it belongs.

Ecumenical leaders have never claimed that their statements are binding on member churches or on individuals in those churches. At the same time they have urged their churches and their members to take them seriously. They are, after all, the product of careful deliberation by a council of Christians of different denominations from all over the world, and their findings might therefore be expected to carry considerable informal authority for the churches. The nature of their authority is expressed in this statement from the World Council of Churches' First Assembly, which was held in Amsterdam in 1948:

With respect to public pronouncements, the Council regards it as an essential part of its responsibility to address its own constituent members as occasion may arise, on matters which require united attention in the realm of thought or action. Further, important issues may arise which radically affect the Church and society. While it is certainly undesirable that the Council should issue such pronouncements often, and on many subjects, there will certainly be a clear obligation for the Council to speak out when vital issues concerning all churches and the whole world are at stake. But such statements will have no authority save that which they carry by their own truth and wisdom. They will not be binding on any church unless that Church has confirmed them, and made them its own. But the Council will only issue such statements in the light of God's revelation in Jesus Christ, the Lord, and the living Head of the Church; and in dependence on the power of the Holy Spirit, and in penitence and faith.[2]

Its constitution states clearly that when the World Council of Churches makes pronouncements it does not have constitutional authority over constituent churches and does not have the right to speak for them. The Assembly and the Central Committee speak for the WCC. The Assembly, which is held every six or seven years, consists of delegates appointed by the member churches. The Central Committee, a smaller, but representative body, is elected by the Assembly and meets yearly to carry on the work of the WCC. At WCC assemblies, statements or pronouncements are almost never "adopted"; they are "received" or "approved" for circulation in the churches. The use of these terms is in the first instance an invitation to comment and discussion rather than endorsement.

Committees or commissions may speak in their own name and may also make recommendations to the World Council of Churches. At times the WCC calls study conferences such as the World Conference on Church and Society held in Geneva in 1966, but such conferences are unofficial. They speak to the churches and to the WCC but not for the WCC.

It is apparent then that the authority of WCC pronouncements does rest largely in the authority of "their own truth and wisdom." When a statement is adopted by the WCC, it is still open—not only for endorsement by member churches but for concrete actions by them. The unity of the churches in social action lies in the reception process. Only as the churches act together on them do the ecumenical statements become instruments of unity. This united action can be seen in a number of areas: in efforts to support world development, in programs to combat racism, and in action to support disarmament.

The Making of the Statements

The statements issued by the WCC at its assemblies and Central Committee meetings are the product of previous study and discussion by Christian leaders all over the world. Study documents are prepared and discussed within countries and denominations before delegates from churches participate in the assemblies.

Consistently the WCC has sought to involve not only theologians but also laymen with direct knowledge of the economic and political world in the preparation of study materials and statements. One of the ecumenical leaders who stressed the importance of lay involvement was J. H. Oldham of England. In a book prepared for the Oxford conference of 1937 he wrote:

Only those who have to act can reach a responsible decision. Advice divorced from responsibility is dangerous. It is a healthy thing that the expert be exposed to criticism. But it is not good for society that the judgment of the trained statesman or the experienced civil servant or the practical business man be replaced by the opinions of well meaning amateurs. What lay at the root of the ineffectiveness of the church in the Middle Ages, as Dr. Lindsay points out, is that the condemnation of evil practices in economic and political life "came from people who lived outside the practical difficulties. One set of men, the clergy, were laying down rules for another set of men, instead of inspiring these men to lay down rules for themselves." [3]

The involvement of lay people in ecumenical conferences on social issues reached a peak in Geneva in 1966. Participants in the World Conference on Church and Society were predominantly church lay people who were experts in various social and scientific fields.

It is also important to note that ecumenical leaders did not assume that the issuance of statements was the heart of social action. What was much more important was direct action by laymen in their professions and in their exercise of citizenship.

In developing guidelines for Christian social ethics, ecumenical leaders have had a number of considerations. Underlying everything is their concern to be true to the Biblical faith, to understand the God of the prophets, of Jesus, and of Paul, to see how He is working in today's world, and to find His will for today. They also want to understand the present world, different in many ways from the Biblical one, and to be open to truth about this world from many sources—science, history, philosophy, etc. Furthermore, they desire to learn from previous Christian experience. Christians have had centuries of experience in relating their faith to life in the world. In the ecumenical movement there has been a desire to learn from all traditions. The Quaker experience is different from the Lutheran, and the Eastern Orthodox experience is different from the Reformed. Each group can learn from the others while being true to its own heritage.

Christians have something to contribute to each other not only from their denominational or confessional heritage but also from their national experience. A Christian who engaged in the resistance movement against Hitler learned something that Christians who have not faced totalitarianism directly need to understand. A Christian who lives in a nation politically but not economically free from colonialism has a perspective on problems of social justice that Christians in industrially highly developed nations need to understand. Encounters of this kind can contribute to the making of a universal Christian ethic.

Yet there are also irresolvable differences here. Quakers will certainly disagree with most other churches about war. Most Protestants will disagree with Eastern Orthodox Christians about birth control. German Lutherans will disagree with American Methodists about the theological foundations of social ethics. Thus, amid the agreements, there are continual disagreements, and there is always tension. But it is a creative tension. Positions become sharpened and clarified by being challenged.

In a WCC-sponsored Consultation on Theological Issues of Church and Society held at Zagorsk, U.S.S.R., in 1968, the participants struggled with the problems involved in making common approaches to ethical issues while having differing theological views. Their struggle is reflected in this quotation from the report:

> Christians in recent decades have also found that they were able to reach consensus on many ethical questions, without achieving full agreement on confessional or theological teachings. This suggests that the living experience of church fellowship in the one spirit of Christ may be, in modern conditions, more important than agreement in theological opinion regarding social ethics.
>
> However, this common practical commitment is becoming less and less satisfactory. The question of whether we are dealing with an agreement among individual Christian consciences or with a consensus among churches cannot be avoided. . . . Moreover, present procedures for dealing with such weighty issues as technological development or revolution must be re-examined in order to find a more vital relationship between our social practices and our theological understanding of man and his calling to participate in God's creation.[4]

While the World Council of Churches is committed not to impose upon its member churches any particular view of church or society, there have been times when its actions have appeared to be more in accord with the approach of one church tradition than another. Churches and individual Christians have been free to follow or not to follow, and they have always been free to criticize the actions taken. There have been a number of debates within the WCC about its pronouncements. It has been accused of being too much oriented toward Western thinking, and it has responded to the criticism by seeking to correct the bias. While some have said that the pronouncements are too vague and general to be useful, others have said that they have been too specific. The WCC has been accused of advocating specific policies when it should be enunciating general principles and leaving specific policies to statesmen.[5] This inner criticism has been of great help to the ecumenical movement.

The great diversity of world experience and the rapidity of social change add to the difficulties of consensus. Can a world ecumenical body say something that will apply in a highly developed industrial society and also in a tribal agricultural society, that will apply to Christians living in Communist countries and to Christians living in capitalist countries? In view of rapid social change, will not the teachings become outdated almost as quickly as they are completed? These are some of the problems involved in the search for an ecumenical social ethic.

COMPARISONS WITH ROMAN CATHOLIC DOCUMENTS

Perhaps some comparisons with Roman Catholic documents will help to clarify the nature and authority of WCC pronouncements.

WCC statements are products of a council representing many confessions; papal encyclicals are produced by the leader of one church and his advisers. In the Second Vatican Council, however, a statement entitled "Pastoral Constitution on the Church in the Modern World" was produced by bishops of the whole world.

Laymen have been more directly involved in the preparation of WCC statements than in the preparation of Roman Catholic documents—both encyclicals and Vatican II utterances.

WCC statements are generally produced more quickly than papal encyclicals or, e.g., the statements of Vatican II. This is due to the fact that WCC assemblies do not last more than two weeks. However, a process of worldwide study precedes the actual conference.

WCC statements do not bear the same authority. Their authority rests on their inherent truth or wisdom. Papal en-

cyclicals, while they are not in the category of infallible teachings, carry great weight because they are issued by the "Vicar
of Christ," whose teaching authority is doctrinally established.

Commenting on the authority of Vatican statements, Ronald
Preston of England has observed a trend toward conciliarism
and shared authority not only in Vatican II but also in the
worldwide debate following Pope Paul's issuance of the encyclical *Humanae Vitae,* dealing with birth control. Preston
wrote, "Perhaps it will be seen more clearly that in the end
the influence of papal documents depends upon their cogency
being generally evident to the people of God, and the extent
to which they draw upon the life of that people has a direct
relation to the cogency being recognized." [6]

There may, then, be some convergence in the procedures
taken by the two bodies and in the response of lay people to
the documents. In subsequent chapters it will become apparent
that there is considerable similarity in content.

The Usefulness of Pronouncements

What has been said thus far about ecumenical pronouncements is well summarized by Ronald Preston in this statement
about their usefulness:

If conclusions are properly arrived at they do not unchurch those
who disagree. What they do is to put the onus on them to produce
cogent reasons for disagreeing with the consensus, rather than the
onus being the other way around. They are extremely useful for at
least six reasons.
1. As a help to the individual Christian in his own decisions.
2. As a link between those of different confessions.
3. As a potential link between Christians and those of other faiths
   and none.
4. As a dissolver of the division between the parson and the layman,
   for the experience of both is needed to formulate them.
5. As a stimulus to creating a bad conscience when society, and perhaps the church as a whole, is complacent.
6. In helping the church to achieve some purchase over events and
   not lag behind them.[7]

It is helpful to keep these points in mind whenever one examines ecumenical social pronouncements. Essentially they are guidelines for social action provided by the world Christian community.

II

Trends in Ecumenical Social Thought, 1925–1970

The modern search for an ecumenical social ethic has been taking place for at least half a century. It is appropriate to begin with the Universal Christian Conference on Life and Work which was held in Stockholm in 1925, and also to recognize the preparatory meetings in the previous five years. The Stockholm conference might be considered to be the culmination and the convergence of previous efforts and the beginning of a series of ecumenical meetings concerned about a universal Christian social ethic. It is important to note that the Life and Work movement, which sponsored the conference, was one of the antecedents of the World Council of Churches.

In this chapter an attempt will be made to give an overview of the development from Stockholm onward, pointing up key trends. The time span under consideration has been divided into five periods.

A. Discovering a Common Social Task, 1925–1929

It is understandable that the period immediately after World War I was conducive to the inauguration of a world Christian movement for justice and peace. The world war, with its enormous destruction of life and property and its alienation of peoples, was generally viewed as a great catastrophe for mankind and for Christianity. Thus this period is characterized by the awareness of an urgent need for joint

church action. There was not time to wait until the churches
had solved their doctrinal differences.

The Stockholm conference represented a convergence of
Christian movements in various countries which were devoted
to social justice and/or world peace. The movements for social
justice came into being in the late nineteenth and early twentieth centuries as responses to the problems raised by industrialization. In the United States in 1908, the Federal Council
of Churches adopted the "Social Creed of the Churches." The
social gospel movement in the United States had its counter-
parts in a number of European countries. These included the
Christian Social Union in England, the *Evangelisch-Sozialer
Kongress* in Germany, the *Association protestante pour l'étude
pratique des questions sociales* in France, and a similar Christian social movement in Switzerland.

Of the movements primarily concerned with peace one of
the most important was the World Alliance for Promoting
International Friendship through the Churches, which was
founded in 1914. One of its supporters was the Church Peace
Union, an American foundation made possible by a gift from
Andrew Carnegie.

There is a direct connection between this World Alliance
and the Life and Work movement, which sponsored the Stockholm conference, because Nathan Söderblom, Swedish archbishop and leading theologian, was for a time the leader of
both. The Alliance did not officially represent churches, though
it drew together persons from the churches. Archbishop Söderblom now felt that in addition to the Alliance-sponsored meetings, there was a need for a conference sponsored by an ecumenical council of churches—a council which should be able
to speak on behalf of Christendom on the religious, moral, and
social concerns of men. He was convinced that churches should
not have to wait until they have achieved unity in doctrine
and church organization before they cooperate on moral and
social issues. As he envisioned the council it would not infringe
upon the autonomy of individual churches. It would exert

influence only by virtue of the spiritual authority of its judgments.

Thus in the plan for the international Christian conference, it was distinguished from the World Alliance. The new endeavors developed into the Life and Work movement. From 1920 to 1925 committees worked to prepare for the great event.

In the first planning meeting of 1920, tension was very great. French delegates declared that they would not participate unless the German delegates confessed the war guilt of Germany. The Germans, however, were unwilling to make a confession for themselves alone. The meeting was in danger of breaking up. Ernesto Giampiccoli, moderator of the Waldensian Church in Italy, told the conference that he had lost a son in the war, but that he nevertheless was trying to maintain a spirit of Christian charity toward representatives from the formerly hostile nations. He invited everyone to pray the Lord's Prayer, putting stress on the petition "forgive us our trespasses as we forgive those who trespass against us." Giampiccoli saved the conference and perhaps the young ecumenical movement from foundering on the rocks of nationalism.

One of the problems the planners had to consider was how inclusive the conference should be. Nathan Söderblom insisted that the invitation be sent to all churches, including the Eastern Orthodox and the Roman Catholic. Otherwise, he said, it would not be an ecumenical conference. He did not expect the Roman Catholic Church to accept the invitation but he felt that the decision should be made by Rome, not by the conference planners. The possibilities of participation by the Orthodox were good. Söderblom had made special efforts to keep in touch with them and some participated in the planning. Thus from the beginning there was a partial Orthodox involvement in the ecumenical movement but no official Roman Catholic involvement.

In August 1925 more than 600 delegates from 37 countries gathered in Stockholm for the Universal Christian Conference on Life and Work. The differences in perspective were at times painfully obvious. German Lutherans reacted negatively to statements by some British and Americans about building the Kingdom of God on earth. This was a traditional conflict, not only between Lutheranism and Calvinism (the latter had been consistently more activistic) but between Lutheran orthodoxy and the liberal social gospel as it was being expressed at that time. Many German theologians felt that the Anglo-Saxon theologians tended to place too much confidence in human achievement.

The Stockholm conference did not make pronouncements in the way that subsequent conferences did. It produced only a brief message summarizing the central concerns. It contained expressions of penitence for the failure of the churches to do their duty, affirmed the obligation resting on the churches to apply the gospel "in all realms of human life—industrial, social, political and international," but limited the mission of the church, which "is above all to state principles, and to assert the ideal, while leaving to individual consciences and communities the duty of applying them with charity, wisdom and courage." It also looked beyond the church to allies in the pursuit of justice, particularly to youth and to workers. A key section in the message is the following:

> The sins and sorrows, the struggles and losses of the Great War and since, have compelled the Christian churches to recognize, humbly and with shame, that "the world is too strong for a divided Church." Leaving for the time our differences in Faith and Order, our aim has been to secure united practical action in Christian Life and Work. The conference itself is a conspicuous fact. But it is only a beginning.[1]

The slogan of Life and Work at this time was "Doctrine divides, but service unites." Special effort was made to avoid doctrinal discussions, leaving them to the other movement, called Faith and Order. But this did not always prove to be possible, as was evident in the conflicts between Anglo-Saxons and Germans.

The greatest weakness of the conference was the small number of delegates from the younger churches (i.e., of Asia, Africa,

Latin America). Only six delegates were present from India, China, and Japan. This was due partly to travel costs but partly also to the assumption that the younger churches were in the domain of the International Missionary Council. At any rate, it was clearly a Western conference.

The great value of the Stockholm conference was that it was a beginning. It established contacts between Christians who had been on different sides in the war; it brought about fellowship across denominational and national lines; it laid foundations for the future. The conference established a continuation committee to carry on studies in different areas. In 1930 this committee became the Universal Christian Council for Life and Work.

While the Life and Work movement was getting started and was concentrating its full attention on social ethics, another ecumenical agency, the International Missionary Council (IMC), which had been fostering international Christian cooperation in missions since 1921, was finding that issues of social ethics also emerged in its program. The missionary work was greatly affected by war, and missionaries were constantly confronted by the effects of economic and political policies of foreign nations upon the people to whom they ministered.

The International Missionary Council meeting held in Jerusalem in 1928 included such problems as missions and race conflict, missions and industrialism, and missions and rural problems. In some respects the meeting was like the Stockholm conference, reflecting a social gospel approach but applying it more directly to the problems faced by Christians of the younger churches. It also involved many more people from Asia, Africa, and Latin America than was the case at Stockholm. The IMC was a direct outgrowth of the historic World Missionary Conference held in Edinburgh in 1910.

After the Jerusalem meeting a close working relationship developed between the Department of Social and Economic Research of the IMC and the Universal Christian Council for Life and Work, both of which had their headquarters in Geneva.

This first phase of the search for an ecumenical social ethic might be called an international social gospel phase. The search at this time was under strong Anglo-Saxon influence and was based on a liberal theology. Discussions centered on the applications of the principles of love, brotherhood, and justice to the social order. The church was to be a central spiritual community, asserting these principles and applying them to all realms of experience. The church was to convert men to social responsibility and thus imbue a Christian spirit into all of society, thereby humanizing society. It was a time of hopefulness, and many Christians believed that by working with secular institutions—reform movements, governments, labor unions, and the League of Nations—they could bring life on earth close to the Kingdom of God.

B. FINDING DEEPER THEOLOGICAL FOUNDATIONS
FOR SOCIAL CONCERN, 1930–1945

The second period under consideration is a time of great advance in ecumenical social ethics, highlighted by the conference at Oxford in 1937. It is characterized by a deeper understanding of theological foundations, a clearer awareness of the church's unique contribution to society, a greater realism, and an honest confrontation with secularism, especially in its totalitarian forms.

In the early 1930's it became apparent that the optimistic hopes of the 1920's were not being realized. A worldwide depression and consequent large-scale unemployment shattered much of the confidence people had in their economic systems. The League of Nations appeared impotent as military action in Ethiopia, Spain, and Manchuria threatened the peace. The rise of totalitarianism in Italy and Germany, especially the latter, posed a whole set of problems concerning the nature of the church and its relation to the secular community and state.

Meanwhile, there were important changes in the theological climate. Dialectical theology, expressed forcefully by Karl

Barth and Emil Brunner, Swiss Reformed theologians, challenged the tendency of the liberal social gospel to identify the Kingdom of God with an ideal social order, and its optimism about the possibility of changing man through education and improvement of his environment. In Germany the Confessing Church resisted Nazi pressures, and its struggle to be a church faithful to Christ contributed much to ecumenical thinking.

At its meeting in 1934 the Universal Christian Council for Life and Work decided upon the theme "Church, Community, and State" for the ecumenical conference to be held in 1937. In the words of the editor of the Oxford conference report, "The essential theme of the Oxford Conference, as was stated in the first announcement of it, was the life-and-death struggle between the Christian faith and the secular and pagan tendencies of our times." [2]

The meeting of 1934 witnessed a change of direction in Life and Work. Stockholm (1925) had focused on unity in service in the hope of contributing to the unity of the churches. The preparation for Oxford focused on the relationship of the church to the world. The person appointed to lead the preparation of the study documents was J. H. Oldham, a layman with considerable experience in the International Missionary Council. In subsequent years he exerted much influence on ecumenical social thought, perhaps more than any other individual.

The worldwide study done in preparation for Oxford surpassed anything in previous church history. The volumes prepared by scholars from several countries were widely circulated and discussed. When the conference convened in July 1937, there were 425 persons from 120 churches in 40 countries participating.

Hitler did not permit the German Evangelical Church delegation to come. Martin Niemöller and several other expected delegates were under guard or in prison. Two Baptists and a Methodist who had remained aloof from the controversy were allowed to attend. There were forty representatives from Orthodox and other Eastern churches. This time there were forty participants from the younger churches as compared with six at Stockholm. But it was still a predominantly Western conference.

The crusading motto of the conference was "Let the Church Be the Church." It was clear that the church everywhere had compromised itself and had become a tool of national, class, economic, and racial interests. The message said, "We do not call the world to be like ourselves, for we are already too like the world." The church's task was to be supranational, supraclass, supraracial. It was not to identify itself with any social system, but to carry out a prophetic critique of all of them.

Tremendous emphasis was placed on the role of the laity in shaping the thought and performing the social task of the church. J. H. Oldham particularly emphasized this theme.

The change in theological climate was apparent at Oxford. An American exponent of the view called Christian realism was Reinhold Niebuhr. During his pastorate in Detroit, Michigan, he had been led, by the pressure of social and economic issues, to a recovery of Reformation teaching on justification by faith and to the Augustinian-Lutheran understanding of sin. Because Christian realism was increasing in influence in America, the gap between Europeans and Americans was not as great as it had been at Stockholm. One did not now need to choose between utopian activism and pessimistic passivism. There was the option of realistic activism.

In keeping with this theological trend the Oxford report stressed a Christian view of justice derived from the love commandment. It took a realistic view of man and his sinfulness and did not anticipate a utopian society but rather one in which power had to be used to assure justice. The Kingdom of God was viewed not as a realizable goal in society but as a concept of the perfect rule of God, which draws men forward but which also judges all of men's achievements.

An important contribution of Oxford was the development

of guidelines for evaluating a particular social order. These came to be known as "middle axioms," and the conference report defines them in this way:

Such "middle axioms" are intermediate between the ultimate basis of Christian action in community, "Thou shalt love thy neighbor as thyself"—which though for Christians unassailable, is too general to give much concrete guidance for action—and the unguided intuition of the individual conscience. They are at best provisional and they are never unchallengeable or valid without exception or for all time, for it is in a changing world that God's will has to be fulfilled. Yet as interim principles they are indispensable for any kind of common policy.[3]

The Oxford conference produced some guiding principles of a just society in regard to the political and economic order, world order, race relations, etc. These will be examined in later chapters.

J. H. Oldham, originator of the "middle axioms," also placed them in context when he wrote about "an ethic of inspiration" and "an ethic of ends," advocating the former and rejecting the latter. He believed that the Christian is not asked to live in obedience to fixed norms or to a moral code such as that provided by natural law, but is called instead to respond to the living Christ. The ethic of ends, he believed, was too static.

Thus it appears that the middle axiom theory seeks to remain within a Biblically centered approach stressing response to God's action in history and yet to provide some guidelines as to what that response might be. The results seem in many cases to be similar to the guidelines Roman Catholics derive through reason, that is, through natural law approaches. The middle axiom approach, however, claims to be based as much on revelation as on reason, claims to be more tentative and more flexible. One reason Protestants have shied away from natural law thinking is that they see evidences of inflexibility, the most striking example being that of Catholic thought on birth control.

The Oxford conference was later viewed as a landmark in

ecumenical social ethics. Subsequent meetings of the World Council of Churches built upon the foundations laid at this meeting.

In view of Life and Work's increasing interest in theological foundations it is understandable that at the Oxford conference it was agreed that Life and Work should merge with Faith and Order, another branch of the ecumenical movement, which had been studying agreements and disagreements in doctrine, worship, ministry, and polity. The latter body agreed to the merger in its meeting in Edinburgh in the same year. Thus in 1938 at Utrecht, the Netherlands, Life and Work united with Faith and Order, bringing into being the new Provisional Committee of the World Council of Churches in Process of Formation.

The lack of adequate participation of the younger churches at Oxford was partly compensated for by the meeting of the International Missionary Council in Tambaram, near Madras, India, in 1938. There half of the delegates were from the younger churches. Even though China and Japan were at war, there were delegates from both countries.

World War II followed soon upon the close of these conferences, and the IMC and the provisional WCC were challenged to put into practice their understanding of the church as a supranational institution. The IMC did significant work in securing funds for German missions in Africa and elsewhere, which had been cut off from their source of financial support and leadership. The provisional WCC maintained contacts between Christians on both sides of the war, helped victims of war and persecution, prepared churches to work for peace, and, at the end of the war, took steps to renew and to restore broken relationships. The Oxford teaching about the universal church was especially meaningful in such a time.

It is gratifying to note that the young ecumenical movement survived the war. This became apparent at a meeting in Stuttgart, Germany, in October 1945, when a delegation of American, British, Dutch, French, and Swiss churchmen met with the new Council of the Evangelical Church in Germany. At the very beginning of the meeting the German churchmen expressed their penitence for not having done enough to prevent the rise of totalitarianism, and their desire to work for the renewal of the church and for the restoration of ecumenical movement. Thus fellowship of churchmen from hostile countries was restored. War guilt, which poisoned interchurch relations for more than a decade after World War I, was approached in a different manner, and the handling of it led to restoration of Christian unity.

C. IDENTIFYING THE MARKS OF A RESPONSIBLE SOCIETY, 1946–1954

In the post-World War II period the World Council of Churches amplified and applied the teachings of Oxford as it sought to establish the marks of a political and economic order compatible with Christian ethics, to transcend the East-West conflict, and to speak to both sides pertinent words of justice and peace, and as it faced new challenges of the post-war world such as racial conflict and the problems of newly independent nations.

At World Council of Churches assemblies, issues of social ethics were a part of the agenda along with issues of faith and order, evangelism, etc. They were not given full time as at Stockholm and Oxford. Nevertheless, very intense preparatory study was done for both the Amsterdam and the Evanston Assembly and social questions received their share of attention. The background of knowledge and experience gained at Oxford carried over into these conferences.

The Provisional Committee meeting in 1946 chose as a theme for the Amsterdam Assembly "Man's Disorder and God's Design." It divided the topic to be worked upon by commissions. Section III on "The Church and the Disorder of Society" and Section IV on "The Church and the International Disorder" were in the realm of social ethics.

The preparation for Section IV was carried on by the newly formed Commission of the Churches on International Affairs, an agency jointly sponsored by the WCC and the IMC. Its purpose was to advise the parent bodies concerning world order issues, to represent them at the United Nations and other international organizations, and to clarify the ecumenical conscience on matters involving intergovernmental relations.

The World Council of Churches officially began in August 1948 when 351 delegates representing 147 churches in 44 countries assembled at Amsterdam. While a number of delegates from Orthodox churches were present, the Russian Orthodox Church issued a statement denouncing the World Council as "imperialistic" and calling the ecumenical movement "political and antidemocratic." The Anglican Church sent a delegation, as did most Protestant bodies of the world, including some from Communist countries. Protestants not participating were mostly conservative or fundamentalist. The younger churches from the Third World were better represented than at previous conferences.

The Amsterdam Assembly took place in the early stages of the cold war. Manifesting the desire to transcend the East-West conflict, the planners invited a churchman from the West and another from the East to give addresses on international affairs. John Foster Dulles of the United States spoke for the West and Josef Hromádka of Czechoslovakia spoke for the East.

An important contribution of the Assembly was its statement about a responsible society. The Assembly recognized, as had the Oxford conference in 1937, that there is no Christian social order, and that no social order should be identified with the Kingdom of God. On the other hand, it was convinced that there are some marks of a just society which Christians should seek to achieve in their countries, while recognizing that the specific forms would be different in various parts of the world. Drawing upon the guidelines developed at Oxford, the Amsterdam Assembly developed a definition of the responsible society which brought about a balance of freedom, order, and justice.

The most controversial statement at Amsterdam asserted that "the Christian Churches should reject the ideologies of both communism and laissez-faire capitalism, and should seek to draw men away from the false assumption that these extremes are the only alternatives." [4]

In the realm of international affairs important statements were made on disarmament, aid to refugees, and religious liberty. The essence of the WCC statement on religious liberty was incorporated later in 1948 into the United Nations' Universal Declaration of Human Rights.

After the formation of the World Council of Churches in 1948 it was possible to launch a systematic study of social questions. The Study Department, supervised by Nils Ehrenstrom of Sweden, initiated an inquiry into "Christian Action in Society" and in August 1949 invited Paul Abrecht from the United States to direct the work. Two important study conferences took place in Asia within four years after the Amsterdam Assembly. Increasingly, Third World Christians felt that the concept of the responsible society was being defined too much in Western terms.

When the Second Assembly of the WCC was held in Evanston, Illinois, in 1954, it used the theme "Christ—the Hope of the World." There were 502 delegates from 161 member churches present.

At Evanston three sections were devoted to social issues. One dealt entirely with racial injustice and discussed the importance of the church's work for a nonsegregated church in a nonsegregated society. Another section refined further the concept of the responsible society and raised questions for Christians in Communist lands. The third, an international affairs section, called upon nations to pledge to refrain from the use of nuclear weapons and press for the cessation of nuclear testing. Furthermore, it provided some guidance to nations for living together in a divided world without war.

Even in the absence of the churches of China, the articulate delegates from Africa and Asia provided a constant reminder that hundreds of millions of people on those continents had awakened and were demanding recognition. The alienating of Chinese Christians from the ecumenical movement had been hastened by the WCC Central Committee statement of 1950 supporting United Nations action in the Korean war. At that time, T. C. Chao, one of the five presidents of the WCC, resigned his position.

D. Facing Rapid Social Change, 1955–1961

In the late 1950's the churches moved from an overemphasis on the concerns of the western world to an equal concern for the eastern and southern parts of the globe. It is unfortunate that the ecumenical movement did not really come to grips with the problems of these areas until the decolonization movement was well under way. This is partly due to the fact that prior to this time few Third World churches were members of the WCC. Their contact with the ecumenical movement was largely through the IMC, a world body of mission agencies. Being mission churches, they were customarily represented in the WCC through a parent church in another land. Thus their participation was indirect.

Paralleling the movement of colonies for independence from imperial powers was the movement of mission churches for independence from mother churches. Once independent, many of them joined the World Council of Churches. This gave them status equal to the older churches, and a chance to give as well as to receive within the fellowship of a universal church body.

Yet within their own regions they had little contact with each other. They knew more about the mother churches in foreign lands than about the sister churches on their own continent. Thus the first need was to develop a regional ecumenical consciousness. Asian churches led the way in this respect, and churches in Africa and Latin America followed their example.

The Evanston Assembly in 1954 and the preliminary study conferences in Asia pointed to the need for new directions in WCC social thought. Meeting in Davos, Switzerland, in 1955, the new working committee for the Department on Church and Society proposed a comprehensive program in support of churches facing issues of rapid social change in Africa, Asia, and Latin America. The proposal was approved shortly thereafter by the Central Committee, and a strong team was assembled to provide leadership.

Over the next five years the team worked with groups in the countries involved. A climactic point in this study program was the International Ecumenical Study Conference on Social Change, held in 1959 in Thessalonica, Greece.

The trend of thinking of the younger churches is well summarized by Paul Abrecht:

In contrast with the familiar ecumenical emphasis on gradual social change and reform, the inquiries in the new nations pointed to the rapid breakdown of old social systems and traditions and the need for political and economic systems supporting rapid development. In contrast with western Christian thought which despite all its preoccupations with secularization was based on assumptions of a society still greatly influenced by Christian values and institutions, Christian social thinking in the new nations tended to emphasize the Christian contribution to a pluralistic social ethic which would promote human values in a national perspective. In contrast with the extremely critical attitude manifested toward nationalism in many of the Western Churches, the "younger Churches" stressed the creative role of the new nation-states in the work of development and in creating a new sense of dignity and self-respect. In opposition to the Western Churches, which still placed great confidence in the traditional structures of world political and economic relations, Christians from the new nations pointed to their inherent biases, and challenged the assumption of an "international law" developed by the western powers and imposed on the rest of the world.[5]

While the WCC sought to implement the Evanston Assembly's concern for the developing countries, it also sought to implement its strong stand on racial segregation. This placed the WCC in opposition to apartheid in South Africa. As tension increased there, WCC leaders held consultations with South African churches, but even so, in 1960 three Dutch Reformed churches in South Africa withdrew from the WCC. In that same year the WCC established a secretariat on race relations within the Department on Church and Society to strengthen ecumenical witness in race relations.

In view of these emphases it is small wonder that the Third Assembly of the WCC (1961) was held in New Delhi, India, thereby providing the delegates direct exposure to the problems of the Third World. The main theme was "Jesus Christ —the Light of the World." Now there were two hundred member churches. The majority of the twenty-three new ones were from Africa, Asia, and Latin America, including two Pentecostal churches from Chile. Several other important ecumenical developments took place in this assembly. The Russian Orthodox Church as well as several other eastern European Orthodox churches joined the WCC. The IMC merged with the WCC. For the first time there were Roman Catholic observers at a World Council Assembly. Their participation was authorized by Pope John XXIII, who later reciprocated by inviting Protestant, Anglican, and Orthodox observers to the Second Vatican Council.

The New Delhi statement on service called Christians to act as "servants of the Servant-Lord" in the world, "manifesting the Kingdom of God and the Lordship of Jesus Christ in all human relations and all social structures." Servanthood was then applied to rapid technological and social change, the problems of responsible use of technology, the threat of the arms race, the need for a more flexible approach to the responsible society, the struggle for racial equality, and the need for more imaginative forms of Christian service.

E. CONFRONTING REVOLUTION, TECHNOLOGY, AND SECULARISM, AND WORKING TOGETHER WITH ROMAN CATHOLICS, 1962–1970

In the 1960's the WCC became more truly universal in its membership, for it added more churches from the Third World and from the Communist world to its roster. This provided new possibilities but also created new tensions. The 1960's were a time of "rising expectations," as submerged people of the Third World and nonwhite people of the developed and developing countries demanded their rights. A theology of revolution was widely discussed. The more positive approach to the secular world, already apparent in the 1950's, was strengthened. New opportunities for cooperation among Catholics, Protestants, and Orthodox came into being as the Second Vatican Council sought to update the Roman Church and to reach out to the separated brethren.

Anger and violence in racism increased in both the United States and southern Africa. The WCC Secretariat on Racial and Ethnic Relations conducted consultations in many parts of the world.

Following the New Delhi Assembly there was a feeling that a world Christian conference should be called to deal exclusively with social issues. In 1966 such a conference met in Geneva, Switzerland, and most of the participants were church laymen qualified in some social, political, or technological field. Prior to the conference four volumes were prepared by representative scholars from all over the world. The World Conference on Church and Society was a study conference, not an official WCC Assembly, but its report was presented to the next Assembly. There was a strong representation from the Third World. In an opening address Visser 't Hooft said: "In Amsterdam the emphasis was too largely on economic justice *within* each nation. We have come to see far more clearly that the crucial issue now is that of *international* economic justice." [6]

Calling for an enlarged concept of the responsible society, he said, "I come therefore to the conclusion that our present understanding of our watchword must be 'Responsible men participating responsibly in a world society in which all accept responsibility for the common welfare.' " [7]

The conference gave much attention to the north-south gap in the world, that is, to the widening gap between the rich nations, largely from the northern hemisphere (including the Soviet Union) and the poor nations, largely from the southern hemisphere. The conference made the issue of world economic development a major issue for the churches. Revolution was a topic of central importance, and several speakers talked about a theology of revolution. The harsh realities of the race issue were dramatized by the fact that Bishop Alpheus Zulu of South Africa was denied a passport and Martin Luther King of the United States was prevented from coming by a race riot in Chicago. Nevertheless, millions of Europeans heard King's sermon on television.

Much credit for the growing interest in a theology of revolution can be given to the Latin Americans, a segment of world Christendom which (except for one Mexican delegate) was not represented at Oxford. Their experience of living under systems subjecting vast numbers of poor to a handful of privileged and wealthy has convinced many of them of the necessity of revolution as a means of attaining social justice. Whether this could be done without violence was a debatable point. A leading exponent of a theology of revolution was Richard Shaull, a professor at Princeton Theological Seminary who had spent much time in Latin America.

Besides considering social revolution, the conference gave attention to technological revolution. In his address, E. G. Mesthene of Harvard emphasized the need for the church to take a positive attitude toward technological change and to help direct it toward human betterment. Mesthene and Jacques Ellul of France debated the place of technological change in relation to the struggle for human betterment.

Some leaders from developing countries pointed out the inherent conflict between these two revolutions. They asserted that without the social revolution the technological revolution would simply make the rich nations richer faster and widen the gap between the rich and poor countries. One working group said, "It would be wrong for every North American child to have an electric toothbrush before every Latin American child has a daily bottle of milk." [8]

Related to the social problem was the problem of armaments, since much of the world's resources needed for development was being diverted toward armaments. Thus the conference made some recommendations regarding multilateral disarmament.

Pope Paul's encyclical *Populorum Progressio,* issued in 1967, supported goals of world development similar to those espoused at Geneva, and opened the door to new possibilities for common Christian action. In April 1968 a joint meeting of the WCC and the Pontifical Commission on Justice and Peace was held in Beirut, Lebanon. The agenda centered around the theme of World Cooperation for Development. This was the first international conference jointly sponsored and financed by Roman Catholic, Protestant, and Orthodox bodies. Continued cooperation has been assured through the formation of SODEPAX—exploratory Committee on Society, Development, and Peace.

Robert McAfee Brown, a Protestant observer at Vatican II, has noted a convergence in Vatican and World Council thinking. He points out that both are recognizing that the church should take a positive attitude toward "the world," that the church's role is not to dominate the world but to be a suffering servant in it, and that the church is living in a time of revolution. He goes on to say, "If Martin Luther started a revolution in the sixteenth century that drove Catholics and Protestants apart, Martin Luther King, Jr., started a revolution in the twentieth century that is drawing them back together again." [9] It might also be noted that the slogan of the 1920's, "Doctrine divides, but service unites," seemed again very appropriate in the 1960's to describe cooperation in social action, not only among people of different churches and religions but also among socially concerned Christians and secular persons.

The World Council of Churches' Fourth Assembly met in Uppsala, Sweden, in the summer of 1968 with 904 delegates from 235 member churches in attendance. Its theme was "Behold, I Make All Things New." It did not have time to deal with all the recommendations of the Geneva study conference, but it did have a section on development that gave enthusiastic endorsement to the Geneva proposals on this subject. The section on Justice and Peace in International Affairs also undergirded a number of Geneva statements. The conference as a whole took steps to further Vatican-WCC cooperation.

Calling for courageous action and worldwide social concern, the conference report on World Economic and Social Development said:

> If our false security in the old and our fear of revolutionary change tempt us to defend the status quo or to patch it up with half-hearted measures, we may all perish. . . .
>
> The church is called to work for a world-wide responsible society and to summon men and nations to repentance. . . .
>
> Churches are called, in their preaching and teaching, including theological education, to set forth the biblical view of the God-given oneness of mankind and to point out its concrete implications for the worldwide solidarity of mankind and the stewardship of the resources of the earth.[10]

The report on "Justice and Peace in International Affairs" urged further steps toward disarmament, took a strong stand on racism, gave wholehearted support to the United Nations, and came out in favor of selective conscientious objection.

In August 1969 the World Council of Churches took one of its most controversial actions. Its Central Committee approved a "Plan for an Ecumenical Program for the Elimination of Racism." Black leaders from the United States and from Africa were among the participants in the deliberations. The WCC voted to contribute funds to the battle against racism to be used for action such as economic sanctions as well as for education. Also it decided to make financial grants to liberation movements in several parts of the world, including southern Africa. Clearly the church had come a long way from the time when Martin Luther endorsed the suppression of the peasant revolt in Germany.

During the 1960's the theological perspective known as Christian realism fell into decline. Though there was no clear unifying theological pattern in this decade, a new humanism or a theology of secularization came into considerable prominence. The church was asked to take a positive stand toward the world. While the 1930's and 1940's stressed the dangers of secularism, especially the totalitarian forms, the 1960's stressed the positive aspects of the secular world. No one expected, as some had in the 1920's, to make the world over into the Kingdom of God, but there was a great interest in working with secular forces such as civil rights movements and the United Nations to bring about humanization.

During this period there were changes in ethical thinking. Contextual or situation ethics received wide support while the ethics of principles, including middle axioms, declined in influence. According to contextual ethics, the Christian community needed to find what God was doing in each historical situation and to respond to his actions. It would be difficult to find general principles valid for all parts of the world.

Thus the proximate theological and ethical consensus of the previous period seemed to dwindle. Polarization was taking place between people of rich nations and people of poor nations, members of black and members of white races, advocates of reform and espousers of revolution, believers in situation ethics and believers in principle ethics, theologians with traditional theological perspectives and theologians with contemporary ones.

It must be pointed out that the earlier theological and ethical consensus was possible because the ecumenical movement had been predominantly Western and predominantly Protestant. But when in the 1960's the Russian Orthodox Church and many younger churches of the Third World joined the WCC, bringing along different viewpoints, the tensions of a revolutionary world became reflected in the social thinking of the WCC. Thus in the 1960's the WCC was undertaking a more difficult task than in the 1940's, and the increased tension needs to be seen in relation to the increased challenge.

In 1969 the WCC launched a new series of studies designed to come to grips with "Technology and the Future of Man." Studies were projected for the early 1970's on three aspects of this theme: Science, Technology and the Quality of Life; The

Political and Economic Choices in a Technological Era; and the Images of the Future.[11]

Thus the search for an ecumenical social ethic goes on. It continues to be a struggle as it always has been, and the possibility of consensus may be remote. But, as in the past, the dialogue, the search, and the common action bring people closer to each other as they seek to serve God in the world.

To review quickly, it is apparent that ecumenical social thought has moved in the past half century from a Western-oriented to a universal movement; from a cooperation without agreement on theological foundations to a cooperation with considerable agreement, then back to cooperation with only limited agreement; from a somewhat humanistic social gospel to an orthodox theological foundation and back in the direction of humanism; from an optimistic view about the world to rather bleak views of secularism and back to more hopeful views of the secular world; from a responsible society to a responsible world society; from nonparticipation of the Roman Catholic Church in the ecumenical movement to dialogue and a close working relationship.

III

The Political and Economic Orders

During its history Christianity has existed in all kinds of social systems, and it continues to exist in many different kinds today. Obviously, the Kingdom of God goes beyond social systems and is not to be identified with any of them. What are some guidelines to the type of society Christians should seek?

Ecumenical leaders in the twentieth century have not been facing this question anew. They were able to build upon centuries of Christian social thought expressed in the writings of men such as Augustine, Thomas Aquinas, Martin Luther, John Calvin, and Walter Rauschenbusch.

The heritage of twenty centuries provides a whole spectrum of Christian approaches to the state and the economic order. The idea that Christians should support democracy is relatively modern—that is, about three centuries old. Its major roots are in the Anglo-Saxon left-wing Calvinist tradition, in which the struggle for religious freedom was closely associated with Parliament's struggle against the King and the people's fight for freedom of expression and freedom from arbitrary arrest. The thinking of the Enlightenment contributed much to the development of democracy.

Eighteenth- and nineteenth-century pietism and revivalism placed much confidence in individual conversion. It was widely believed that the religious task was to produce good men, who, in turn, would produce a good society. Also the belief spread that the economic order should not be controlled by the state. It was assumed that if each man worked for his self-interest, certain economic laws such as the law of supply and demand would bring results that would be for the common good. This principle seemed to work while private enterprise operated on a small scale, but after the industrial revolution all of the prevailing assumptions were called into question.

Social gospel leaders of the late nineteenth and early twentieth centuries were dealing basically with the economic order. They accepted democracy as the correct expression of Christianity in politics, but they did not see the competitive economic order as a proper expression of Christian ethics. They found child labor, unsafe working conditions, depressions, great inequality of incomes, and the profit motive wholly incompatible with Christian ethical principles. In effect, they were calling for a return to medieval and Puritan views when they declared that the economic order ought to come under greater control of the state in order that it might work for the common good. However, unlike the Puritans, they had a very optimistic view of man and expected to realize God's Kingdom through social reform.

HUMAN VALUES ABOVE PROPERTY VALUES

The Stockholm Life and Work conference of 1925, with which this study begins, followed in the spirit of the social gospel. Convinced that the prophets and Jesus had given mankind social teachings about the sacredness of personality, the superiority of service to profit-seeking, and the importance of concern for the poor, Christian social leaders sought that ideal social order which would be compatible with these teachings. The conference said:

We have declared that the soul is the supreme value, that it must not be subordinated to the rights of property or to the mechanism of industry, and that it may claim as its first right the right of salvation. Therefore we contend for the full and free development of the human personality. In the name of the Gospel we have affirmed that industry should not be based solely on the desire for individual profit, but that it should be conducted for the service of the community. Property should be regarded as a stewardship for which an account must be given to God. Co-operation between capital and labour should take the place of conflict, so that employers and employed alike may be enabled to regard their part in industry as the fulfillment of a vocation. Thus alone can we obey our Lord's command, to do unto others even as we would they should do unto us.[1]

Perhaps of greater value than the Stockholm teachings were the studies of various social problems carried on in subsequent years by the Universal Christian Council for Life and Work. The constitution of the Council stated as its chief objective "to perpetuate and strengthen the fellowship between the churches in the application of Christian ethics to the social problems of modern life." In 1929 a research project was conducted in regard to unemployment. At that time there were over twenty million unemployed in Western countries alone. A conference held in 1932 issued a report on the Churches and the World Economic Crisis that attracted widespread attention. It dealt with issues such as tariffs, war debts, the role of government in restoring a healthy economy, and the problem of fair distribution of income and resources.

Meanwhile, the International Missionary Council also came to grips with the problems of the social order in its 1928 conference in Jerusalem. It pointed to a number of injustices in Asia and Africa and Latin America, such as the employment of forced labor. The conference urged that fair employment practices that were being put into effect in Europe and America be applied to the other parts of the world. The Jerusalem meeting, after making proposals concerning working hours, minimum wages, proper standards of health, elimination of child labor, and better conditions for women, asked for a "system of inspection competent to supervise the application of such legislation." In so doing, the delegates were clearly expressing support for the work of the International Labor Organization. The conference also manifested a great interest in the economic and social problems of rural areas, and advocated education and community development programs for elevating the life of rural people. Like Stockholm, the Jerusalem conference attacked the evils of the economic systems of the dominant nations of the world. It said:

> We acknowledge with shame and regret that the churches everywhere and the missionary enterprise, coming as it does out of an economic order dominated almost entirely by the profit motive (a motive which itself stands under Christian scrutiny), have not been so sensitive of those aspects of the Christian message as would have been necessary sensibly to mitigate the evils which advancing industrialization has brought in its train, as we believe that our failure in this respect has been a positive hindrance—perhaps the gravest of such hindrances—to the power and extension of missionary enterprise.[2]

In the early 1930's the subject of the Christian and the State became a matter of central importance. The Nazi regime with its ideology of "blood and soil" helped stir the churches to face this issue. Thus in the summer of 1933 the Research Department of the Universal Christian Council for Life and Work invited the churches to share in a thorough study of the authority and function of the state in its relation to the individual, the community, world order, and the church. A conference held in Paris in 1934 brought together such eminent thinkers as Nicolas Berdyaev, a Russian philosopher living in Paris; Emil Brunner, a Swiss Reformed theologian; Max Huber, a Swiss statesman; and J. H. Oldham, a British ecumenical leader.

Out of these studies and conferences emerged the plan to hold the 1937 Oxford conference on the theme of Church, Community, and State. The Oxford conference was a meeting of great import for ecumenical social thought. Its thinking about the political and economic order provided the foundations for the later development of the concept of the responsible society.

JUSTICE THROUGH THE RESPONSIBLE USE OF POWER

As has been noted earlier, the theological approach known as Christian realism exerted considerable influence on Christian thought. Reinhold Niebuhr, an exponent of this view, has observed that an important contribution was made by the Anglican natural law approach as expressed in the writings of Archbishop William Temple. Niebuhr appreciated the Anglican stress on the state as an instrument of justice as a counterbalance to the Lutheran emphasis on the state as an instrument of order.

Like the Protestant Reformers, Niebuhr stressed the sinfulness of man, but his understanding of man led him to a positive attitude toward the state. Because of man's tendency to injustice, the state was needed as a check over powerful groups in society. While using its power to realize justice, the state itself needed to be controlled by the citizens because no power should be unchecked. Thus the state should be an instrument for justice as well as for order without being expected to bring about the ideal society. Niebuhr criticized the social gospel theologians for being too idealistic in their expectations and the continental Lutherans for being too pessimistic to do anything about the state.

In this particular time nations were suffering from depression and needed state action to help resolve it. On the other hand, in parts of the world the state was already totalitarian. It seemed that the ecumenical theologians had to fight on several fronts—against the conservative "laissez-faire" attitude toward the state, against the liberal utopians, and against totalitarian solutions.

The Oxford report manifested an ecumenical and balanced view of political authority, drawing upon both the positive and the negative views of the state. It said:

> We recognize the existing states as historically given realities, each of which in the political sphere is the highest authority, but which, as it stands itself under the authority and judgment of God, is bound by his will and has the God-given aim of upholding law and order, of ministering to the life of the people united within it or of the peoples or groups so united, and also of making its contribution to the common life of all peoples.
>
> At the same time we recognize that the state as a specific form and the dominating expression of man's life in this world of sin, by its

very power and its monopoly of the means of coercion often becomes an instrument of evil. Since we believe in the holy God as the source of justice, we do not consider the state as the ultimate source of law but rather as its guarantor. It is not the lord but the servant of justice. There can be for the Christian no ultimate authority but very God.[3]

These sentences were to be quoted often in subsequent ecumenical documents.

Oxford clearly distinguished between state and nation. The state could not claim to be the nation, but only its servant. It was to protect the natural communities in the nation, not overwhelm them. Oxford also called attention to distinctive functions of church and state:

The church as the trustee of God's redeeming gospel and the state as the guarantor of order, justice and civil liberty have distinctive functions in society.[4]

With a clear reference to the problems of churches in totalitarian countries, Oxford made the following statement on religious liberty, a statement that was to have a significant influence on subsequent World Council of Churches documents.

In a state which acknowledges a liberal doctrine of rights it is equally evident that the church like other associations should have the liberty which its function requires. In countries where the church finds in the theory and constitution of the state nothing on which to base a claim to right, this does not absolve the church from its primary duty to witness. This duty must then include a witness against such a denial of fundamental justice. And if the state tries to hinder or suppress such witness, all other churches have the duty of supporting this church and giving it the utmost succor and relief in their power.

We recognize as essential conditions necessary to the church's fulfillment of its primary duty that it should enjoy: (*a*) freedom to determine its faith and creed; (*b*) freedom of public and private worship, preaching and teaching; (*c*) freedom from any imposition by the state of religious ceremonies and forms of worship; (*d*) freedom to determine the nature of its government and the qualifications of its ministers and members and, conversely, the freedom of the individual to join the church to which he feels called; (*e*) freedom to control the education of its ministers, to give religious instruction to its youth and to provide for adequate development of their religious life; (f) freedom of Christian service and missionary activity, both home and foreign; (g) freedom to cooperate with other churches; (h) freedom to use such facilities, open to all citizens and associations, as will make possible the accomplishment of these ends: the ownership of property and the collection of funds.[5]

This is a very inclusive statement on religious liberty. In working in this area, the Universal Christian Council for Life and Work benefited from earlier work done by the International Missionary Council and also by the World Alliance for Promoting International Friendship through the Churches. Going back farther, it profited much from men like Roger Williams and from churches that from their inception have affirmed the necessity of religious liberty, namely, the Anabaptists, the Baptists, the Congregationalists, and the Quakers.

The Oxford conference insisted that the church can serve the state best by being the church, and the state can serve the church best by allowing it to be the church.

The Church in differing historical situations may be called to take differing positions of cooperation, criticism, or opposition, and this both in its corporate capacity and as a fellowship of witnessing Christians acting as individuals or as groups.[6]

In regard to the relationship of the church to national feeling or loyalty, Oxford expressed both appreciation and warning:

Every man is born into a specific national community and is united to it by strong ties. The church regards this fact of nationality, in spite of its infection by human sinfulness, as essentially a gift of God to mankind. The love of the Christian for his people should therefore be part of his gratitude to God for the riches which are his through the community into which he has been born. . . .

As with every divine gift, the gift of national community has been and is being abused by men and made to serve sin. Any form of national egotism whereby the love of one's own people leads to the suppression of other nationalities or national minorities, or to the failure to respect and appreciate the gifts of other people, is sin and rebellion against God, who is the Creator and Lord of all peoples. Even more, to see in one's own nation the source and standard of saving revelation, or in any way to give the nation divine status, is sin. This is to be utterly repudiated and irreconcilably opposed by the

Christian conscience in the name of God and for the sake of the nation it is called to serve.[7]

The meaning of these words was apparent to those involved in the church struggle against Nazism. But the temptation to deify nationalism was not restricted to Germany. In 1935 a book appeared in the United States entitled *The Church Against the World*. In it three American scholars—H. Richard Niebuhr, Francis P. Miller, and Wilhelm Pauck—critically examined the blending of church with nationalism and capitalism, and pleaded for the independence of the church from captivity to any secular culture. They saw the tendency of American Protestantism to deify the American way of life, and expressed the hope that the participation of American churches in the ecumenical movement would help in developing a perspective wherein the church would be seen as a divine-human community transcending nation, race, and class.

The Oxford conference, like the earlier Jerusalem conference, saw secularism as the underlying problem of modern society, and viewed the new forms of totalitarianism as pagan expressions of this secularism, as idolatries designed to fill the vacuum left by weakened religion. While making it clear that Christians cannot give their full loyalty to anything less than God, the conference did not give clear guidance about the question of resistance to an unjust state. It seemed to endorse nonviolent resistance or possibly nonviolent noncooperation in certain cases. It left little, if any, room for violent revolution.

Further, it should be insisted that the exercise of force, apart from exeptional instances of extreme urgency, should take place within the framework of generally accepted law and should remain the exclusive monopoly of the organs of the state, in order that it may not become the instrument either of caprice or of the private and collective lust of power.[8]

Church, State, and Education

At Oxford the subject of education was given more attention than in subsequent ecumenical conferences. This was a time when schools in a number of lands were becoming training grounds for totalitarian states. The conference sought to clarify the roles of church and state in regard to education. While recognizing that it is not the church's province "as an organized institution to assume responsibility for the entire conduct of life and education," the conference did concern itself about the church's freedom to carry on its role in Christian education, including youth work, and about the kind of education carried on in the public schools.

> The church is a fellowship of persons freed by the spirit of Christ. She reveres personality, since man is created in God's image and God has revealed himself through men responsive to his Spirit, and his Word became flesh in Jesus Christ.
> She should be opposed to an education which teaches men to subordinate themselves to any human force as the final authority— be it the will of the majority, or of a leader or of an absolute state. That is to violate the sanctity of conscience which must be kept responsible to God alone. In her teaching, governments exist for men, not men for governments. Every human being has unique worth as a child of God, and should be so educated as to encourage him to make his singular contribution to the commonweal.[9]

Oxford laid some important foundations for ecumenical thinking regarding the economic order. Traditionally Christian ethics, because of its understanding of the nature of man, has held to the teaching that private ownership is preferable to public ownership, but it has warned against greed and materialism. In its history Protestantism seems to have had a close relationship to capitalism—an alliance that the social gospel movement had been challenging since the end of the nineteenth century, calling for correction of the social evils stemming from laissez-faire practices. Now in the face of a worldwide depression many traditional ethical and economic theories were being called into question.

The economic theory of Oxford, like its political theory, reflected the influence of Anglican natural law and of neo-Reformation Christian realism. It was felt that one could not apply the Sermon on the Mount directly to society at large, but only to a group of highly committed followers of

Jesus. A social ethic has to be workable for a society of sinful men. To relate love to this situation meant to strive for a society of maximum justice. Men are self-seeking, and collective self-interest is particularly difficult to change. Thus a just economic order would require powerful groups to check each other, the state to check them all, and the citizenry to check the state. In the light of this realism, Oxford was less inclined than Stockholm to denounce the profit motive or to advocate an ideal society.

In its analysis of the world economic situation, the report noted that Christians live in many economic systems. The capitalist age made it possible to overcome the natural scarcity of economic resources by successive technological improvements. It has raised to a considerable degree the general standard of consumption. Through mechanization it has reduced manual labor.

There had been hope that capitalism would not only improve the material conditions of life but also bring about social justice. This has not come about, partly because it has not proved to be true that "each man, seeking his own, would serve the commonweal." The same forces that had produced material progress had enhanced inequalities and insecurity. In the international realm weaker nations had been exploited by technologically stronger ones. Thus socialism and communism arose as reactions to capitalism. In some cases the protest was also against Christianity, which had become too much identified with the privileged classes and with unjust social systems. The appropriate response of the church would begin with penitence.

On the other hand, the report went on to insist that churches must resolutely reject those elements in the actual development of communism which conflict with the Christian truth, namely its utopianism, materialism, and disregard for the dignity of the individual. There was no condemnation of socialism as such—for example, of a democratic form of socialism such as that pursued by the Labor party in Great Britain.

The Oxford conference report went on to point out four

ways in which the capitalistic economic order of that day challenged the Christian understanding of man and society:

(a) The Enhancement of Acquisitiveness.

. . . When the necessary work of society is so organized as to make the acquisition of wealth the chief criterion of success, it encourages a feverish scramble for money, and a false respect for the victors in the struggle which is as fatal in its moral consequences as any other form of idolatry. . . .

(b) Inequalities.

. . . Not only is the product of industry distributed with an inequality so extreme (though the extent of this inequality also varies considerably from country to country) that a small minority of the population are in receipt of incomes exceeding in the aggregate those of many times their number, but—even more seriously—the latter are condemned throughout their lives to environmental evils which the former escape, and are deprived of the opportunities of fully developing their powers, which are accessible, as a matter of course, to their most fortunate fellows. . . .

(c) Irresponsible Possession of Economic Power.

. . . A third feature of the existing situation which is repugnant to the Christian conscience consists in the power wielded by a few individuals or groups who are not responsible to any organ of society. This gives the economic order in many countries some resemblance to tyranny, in the classical sense of the term, where rulers are not accountable for their actions to any superior authority representing the community over whom power is exercised. . . .

(d) The Frustration of the Sense of Christian Vocation.

. . . With regard to the worker and employee, there is the fact that most of them are directly conscious of working for the profit of the employer (and for the sake of their wages) and only indirectly conscious of working for any public good. . . . But even more serious is the constant threat of unemployment. . . .[10]

The report then offered five criteria or middle axioms which could be used in evaluating an economic order. Did it have equal opportunity, practice nondiscrimination, care for disabled and aged, treat labor fairly, and exercise stewardship of the earth's resources? The 1937 statement on stewardship of resources seems most pertinent in the 1970's, when there is great concern for ecology:

The resources of the earth, such as the soil and mineral wealth, should be recognized as gifts of God to the whole human race and used with due and balanced consideration for the needs of the present and future generations.[11]

Earlier it has been noted that loving one's neighbor leads to working for a just society. Yet one needs some concrete notion as to what a just society is. Oxford did not recommend a particular system but provided some criteria for evaluating the society in which one lives. If one takes the above-mentioned guidelines for the economic order plus the previously mentioned guidelines for the state, one has some of the ingredients of the concept of the responsible society which was spelled out several years later at the Amsterdam conference.

In its discussion of property the Oxford conference noted that property rights are relative and contingent since they come from God, and went on to say:

. . . Every argument in defense of property rights which is valid for Christian thinking is also an argument for the widest possible distribution of these rights.

It should further be affirmed that individual property rights must never be maintained or exercised without regard to their social consequences or without regard to the contribution which the community makes in the production of all wealth.

It is very important to make clear distinction between forms of property. The property which consists in personal possessions for use, such as the home, has behind it a clearer moral justification than property in the means of production and in land which gives the owners power over other persons. All property which represents social power stands in special need of moral scrutiny, since power to determine the lives of others is the crucial point in any scheme of justice.[12]

In applying Christian ethics to the social order, the Oxford conference sought to avoid two errors. One is to consider the social order so corrupt that one cannot apply Christianity to it. This approach in effect encourages maintenance of the *status quo* and restricts Christian ethics to interpersonal relations. The other error is to identify some social system with the Kingdom of God.

Every tendency to identify the Kingdom of God with a particular social structure or economic mechanism must result in moral confusion for those who maintain the system and in disillusionment for those who suffer from its limitations. The former will regard conformity with its standards as identical with the fulfillment of the law, thus falling into the sin of phariseeism. The latter will be tempted to a cynical disavowal of the religion because it falsely gives absolute worth to partial values and achievements.[13]

These basic points occurred again and again in ecumenical social ethics: on the one hand, Christianity should not avoid social involvement; on the other hand, it should not be identified with any system.

Finally, the report showed ways in which churches can act. A church can reform its own institutional life and bring its economic practices into line with its ethics, for example, its employment practices, its ways of raising money and administering property. It can develop new machinery for research and action. It can integrate work and worship.

Lay people of the church can act within the existing order to try to change it.

Christians have a particular responsibility to make whatever contributions they can toward the transformation, and if necessary the thorough reconstruction, of the present economic and political system, through their membership in political parties, trade unions, employers' organizations and other groups. In this part of their Christian duty, the same characteristics are called for, though in a different form, as those which Christians are called on to show in all their other activities: readiness to make sacrifices, to take effective action, to forgive those that trespass against them and to love those that seem to be their enemies.[14]

Two meetings of the International Missionary Council took place between the Oxford conference and the First Assembly of the World Council of Churches in 1948. Both had something to say about the political and social order. The first was held in 1938 at Tambaram, near Madras, India, and the second in 1947 at Whitby, Ontario, Canada. Tambaram gave considerable attention to nationalism. Looking at nationalism in relation to the younger churches, Tambaram, like Oxford, saw both the positive and the negative elements. It classified the existing forms of nationalism into three types: self-expressive nationalism, which unites a people, builds self-respect, and is helpful to colonies or young nations; self-satisfied nationalism, which produces complacency, especially in well-established nations; and self-assertive nationalism (such as fascism), which calls for man's total loyalty and fosters idolatry. The church must distinguish among them and bring the appropriate prophetic critique to bear upon them.

Tambaram also gave considerable attention to the subject of religious liberty, refining further the definition given at Oxford. In discussing church and state, it called attention to the importance of the church's contribution to society:

> The history of the younger churches justifies us in recording with thankfulness the part played in national life by Christian statesmen and officials, thus enabling the Christian community to make a contribution often out of all proportion to its members.[15]

THE WEAKNESS OF PIETISM

Many supporters of the missionary movement were pietistically oriented, believing that Christianity should restrict itself to personal salvation. Part of the message was clearly aimed at this constituency.

> As to whether we should center upon individual conversion or upon social change to realize this kingdom, we reply that we must do both. The power of the social order to affect the individual under it is tremendous. In India, for instance, the social order moulds 35,000,000 people every thirty years, each generation, into its own image. In the interests of individual conversion we must demand social change. For we see clearly that evil can be in the individual will and also in the collective will. There is such a thing as an evil soul, but there is also such a thing as an evil system. Shall we rescue the wounded in war and not strike at the war system? Shall we pick up the derelicts of a ruthlessly competitive order and give them charity and yet fail to co-operate with the policies of governments and public bodies when they seek to substitute justice for injustice and opportunity instead of charity?[16]

The Tambaram meeting made it plain that efforts to change the social order are an integral part of the Christian witness in any part of the world.

During World War II the churches of several nations engaged in study and planning for the postwar world. They realized that a war could be won in vain if the war aims were forgotten and the peace was lost. The Four Freedoms of President Roosevelt and the Atlantic Charter stated in general the goals. As the United Nations came into being, leading churchmen of several nations expressed their concern that the United Nations develop a declaration of human rights and that the UN devote its efforts toward their realization. World War I had been fought to make the world safe for democracy. Yet it was followed by the emergence of several new forms of totalitarianism. What would emerge after World War II?

Questions such as this were in the minds of those preparing for the Amsterdam Assembly of 1948. The preparatory papers dealt with a number of issues pertaining to the political and economic order. An article by O. Frederick Nolde, secretary of the Commission of the Churches on International Affairs, pointed to an "immediate and urgent need for the development of the Christian view on human rights in terms which will apply to all men and which can be used in representations to national and international political authorities." [17] It devoted special attention to the need for an inclusive statement on religious liberty. On this freedom there was a clear consensus of the churches expressed at Oxford and at Tambaram, and the Commission felt that it had a clear mandate to realize this goal.

There was an important article in the preparatory material written by J. H. Oldham and entitled "The Responsible Society." It introduced a concept that came into prominence at Amsterdam. Oldham made it clear that he first favored the term "the free society," free not only from totalitarianism, but free also to be human in a technological age that tended to depersonalize and overwhelm man. He was greatly concerned about freedom to obey God and to act in accordance with one's conscience, to pursue and express the truth, to relate meaningfully to other persons through small-group discussion and action.

In the discussions that took place in preparation for Amsterdam, several churchmen criticized the idea of the "free society," pointing out that it was too much Europe-oriented. The problem of the majority of mankind, they said, was not securing freedom against the depersonalizing tendencies of technology but rather securing economic and social justice and security. M. M. Thomas of India was particularly vocal in expressing this. He was supported by H. P. Van Dusen of the United States, who had attended the 1947 International Missionary Council meeting in Whitby, Ontario, where great attention was given to revolutionary changes in the world. Both men felt that a just society was needed as much as a free society. The discussion led to the selection of the term "responsible society," since it comprised both religious and social dimensions (responsibility to God and fellowmen), had inherently no associations with any bloc in the world, and could be so defined as to include both justice and freedom.

By the time of the Amsterdam Assembly the cold war was an important factor in the consciousness of mankind. In several countries of Europe "third force" groups were at work seeking to develop a society that was neither capitalist nor Communist. As the report of the section on The Church and the Disorder of Society shows, the delegates refused to accept either complete state planning or unqualified freedom in economic affairs.

Coherent and purposeful ordering of society has now become a major necessity. Here governments have responsibilities which they must not shirk. But centres of initiative in economic life must be so encouraged as to avoid placing too great a burden upon centralized judgment and decision. To achieve religious, cultural, economic, social and other ends it is of vital importance that society should have a rich variety of smaller forms of community, in local government, within industrial organisations, including trade unions, through the development of public corporations and through voluntary associations. By such means it is possible to prevent an undue centralisation of power in modern technically organised communities, and thus escape the perils of tyranny while avoiding the dangers of anarchy.[18]

The report also said that Christians should reject the extreme ideologies of both communism and laissez-faire capitalism, and "should seek to draw men away from the false assumption that these extremes are the only alternatives."

Charles Taft, an Episcopalian layman from the United States, was responsible for adding the words "laissez-faire" before the word "capitalism" in the resolution. Thus the effect of the statement was to condemn a system that existed in the East—Communism—while simultaneously condemning a system that no longer really existed in the West—laissez-faire capitalism. As the statement pointed out later, much that is characteristic of early capitalism "has been corrected in considerable measure by the influence of trade unions, social legislation and responsible management." Nevertheless, this resolution was widely interpreted as indicting equally the systems existing in the West and in the East. The loudest and angriest criticisms came from business and bank leaders in the United States and Switzerland and from government and church leaders in Moscow.

The Amsterdam statement also had some comments about the problem raised by the existence of Christian political parties in several countries. It advised against the formation of such parties "because they easily confuse Christianity with the inherent compromises of politics." As at Oxford, the stress was placed on Christian influence through the involvement of Christian lay people in political and economic life.

The Church can be most effective in society as it inspires its members to ask in a new way what their Christian responsibility is whenever they vote or discharge the duties of public office, whenever they influence public opinion, whenever they make decisions as employers or as workers or in any other vocation to which they may be called.[19]

THE RESPONSIBLE SOCIETY DEFINED

It was in the midst of this discussion on the "Disorder of Society" that the Amsterdam Assembly worked out the following concept of the "responsible society."

Man is created and called to be a free being, responsible to God and his neighbor. Any tendencies in State and society depriving man of the possibility of acting responsibly are a denial of God's intention for man and His work of salvation. A responsible society is one where freedom is the freedom of men who acknowledge responsibility to justice and public order, and where those who hold political authority or economic power are responsible for its exercise to God and the people whose welfare is affected by it.

Man must never be made a mere means for political or economic ends. Man is not made for the State but the State for man. Man is not made for production, but production for man. For a society to be responsible under modern conditions it is required that the people have freedom to control, to criticise and to change their governments, that power be made responsible by law and tradition, and be distributed as widely as possible through the whole community. It is required that economic justice and provision of equality of opportunity be established for all the members of society.

We therefore condemn:

(1) Any attempt to limit the freedom of the Church to witness to its Lord and His design for mankind and any attempt to impair the freedom of men to obey God and to act according to conscience, for those freedoms are implied in man's responsibility before God;

(2) Any denial to man of an opportunity to participate in the shaping of society, for this is a duty implied in man's responsibility towards his neighbor;

(3) Any attempt to prevent men from learning and spreading the truth.[20]

It becomes clear upon closer examination that the political side of the responsible society concept contains the basic freedoms which have emerged in democratic countries and which have their roots in the Enlightenment and in Christianity. Its economic aspect is less clear but it appears to favor a form of mixed economy, avoiding the concentration of power in a few places, and guaranteeing equal economic opportunity to all citizens.

The concept of the responsible society, which in subsequent years became a crystallization point for ecumenical social thinking, was multidimensional. It included the responsibility of a citizen to society and to God, of society to its members, and of society to norms beyond itself. It was in line with Biblical teachings which view man as the creature called into being to respond to God and to answer to Him for his relations with his fellowmen. While having religious rootage, it is nevertheless a concept usable for Christians working together with non-Christians for a better social order.

The concept has roots in the thinking of the Stockholm conference, which proclaimed that industry and property should be thought of as a social trust before God and the community. But it owed much more to Oxford. There some of the human rights which a state should protect were spelled out and some criteria for evaluating an economic order were established. Oxford saw love and the Kingdom as transcendent ideals, and justice as the central norm.

In working out the responsible society idea, the social ethicists at Amsterdam were following the Oxford pattern by using "middle axioms." The middle axioms for the responsible society were more specific than "Love your neighbor" or "Obey the state," but less specific than particular laws or particular systems. They provided a model or a set of criteria that could be used by Christians in various countries and adapted to their situations. Essentially it was a call to find a social arrangement maintaining in dynamic equilibrium freedom, order, and justice, while barring the way to anarchy and tyranny.

THE IMPORTANCE OF RELIGIOUS LIBERTY

The responsible society, as has been indicated, was one that provided the basic freedoms. This included religious liberty, a definition of which had been developed at the Oxford conference. Already before Amsterdam the Commission of the

Churches on International Affairs was presenting the ecumenical views on religious liberty as well as on other human rights to the United Nations Commission on Human Rights. The declaration on religious liberty agreed upon at Amsterdam contained four major points:

I. Every person has the right to determine his own faith and creed.

II. Every person has the right to express his religious beliefs in worship, teaching and practice, and to proclaim the implications of his beliefs for relationships in a social or political community.

III. Every person has the right to associate with others and to organize with them for religious purposes.

IV. Every religious organization, formed or maintained by action in accordance with the rights of individual persons, has the right to determine its policies and practices for the accomplishment of its chosen purposes.[21]

Amsterdam also pointed out the theological foundations for religious liberty. It said:

While the liberty with which Christ has set men free can neither be given nor destroyed by any government, Christians, because of that inner freedom, are both jealous for its outward expression and solicitous that all men should have freedom in religious life. The nature and destiny of man by virtue of his creation, redemption and calling, and man's activities in family, state and culture establish limits beyond which the government cannot with impunity go. The rights which Christian discipleship demands are such as are good for all men, and no nation has ever suffered by reason of granting such liberties.[22]

The Assembly was interested in other human rights as well as in religious liberty. This is evidenced in the following statement appearing in the report of Section IV on "The Church and the International Disorder":

They [the churches] should press for freedom of speech and expression, of association and assembly, the rights of the family, of freedom from arbitrary arrest, as well as all those other rights which the true freedom of man requires; . . . they should support a fuller realization of human freedom through social legislation; . . . they should oppose forced segregation on grounds of race or colour.[23]

In December of 1948 the United Nations adopted a Universal Declaration of Human Rights. Its statement on religious liberty contained the elements advocated at Amsterdam, thanks to the influence exerted by members of the Commission of the Churches on International Affairs. The UN declaration contains this article:

Everyone has the right to freedom of thought, conscience and religion; this right includes freedom to change his religion or belief, and freedom, either alone or in community with others and in public or private, to manifest his religion or belief in teaching, practice, worship and observance.[24]

The UN declaration as such had no power other than moral influence. Therefore in subsequent years, efforts were made to secure conventions on human rights which would have more force, but there was only limited success in this direction. Nevertheless, it is possible to point to some concrete results from the declaration. A number of nations that have achieved independence since 1948 have incorporated the UN's Universal Declaration of Human Rights into their constitutions.

When the East Asia Christian Conference was convened in Bangkok, Thailand, in 1949 under the joint sponsorship of the WCC and the IMC, one of the main topics of discussion was the rather widespread violation of religious liberty not only by governments but by religions and by Christian churches.

In 1952 a conference was called in Lucknow, India, to study the issues to be discussed at Evanston in the light of the Asian experience. The responsible society and its meaning for Asia was carefully considered. The Lucknow conference considered the agricultural aspects of the social order, dealing with land reform and rural development measures. It underscored the social revolution taking place in Asia, and its report showed a willingness to give the state an important role in development.

The countries of East Asia are committed to the idea of the social planning state as a matter of fundamental social justice and concern

for human welfare. It is one of the conditions of economic development in East Asia that basic and certain key industries must be
nationalized, and at the same time due place must be given to private
enterprise in the development of both large scale and small scale
industries. In the present situation of East Asia, however, it is the
state which can take the initiative and encourage saving and investment by the people.[25]

Thus a note was sounded that was to be heard again and
again. The concept of the responsible society as understood
by Europeans and Americans had to be modified substantially
to be applicable in the countries of the Third World.

The Lucknow conference also stressed the importance of
freedom and self-determination for countries ruled by colonial
powers. Speaking specifically on the issue of the responsible
society, it said:

For us as Christians in East Asia a society is not responsible when—
(1) human rights and freedoms are not effectively promoted for all;
(2) social change and reform are promoted without respect for the
    integrity of the human person;
(3) its people do not possess full sovereignty over their own affairs;
(4) men are discouraged or deterred by official action from freely
    accepting faith in Christ.
For us as Christians in East Asia a society is responsible where—
(1) social justice is actively promoted,
(2) full development of natural resources is pursued,
(3) the fullest share possible of the national wealth is guaranteed to
    all,
(4) human rights and freedoms are effectively guaranteed,
(5) the people have full sovereignty for their own affairs,
(6) the principles of social and political life are in accordance with
    the concept of man as a person called to responsible existence
    in community.[26]

The Evanston Assembly clarified further the Amsterdam
definition of the responsible society and moved in a direction
that was less Western and more worldwide. The title of the
section dealing with social questions was "The Responsible
Society in World Perspective."

To clarify some misunderstandings about the term, Evanston
said:

"Responsible Society" is not an alternative social or political system, but a criterion by which we judge all existing social orders, and at the same time a standard to guide us in the specific choices we have to make. Christians are called to live responsibly, to live in response to God's act of redemption in Christ, in any society, even within the most unfavourable social structures.[27]

FUNCTIONS OF THE STATE

What this meant for political institutions was spelled out as follows:

Christians should work for the embodiment of the responsible society in political institutions by emphasizing the following: (1) Every person should be protected against arbitrary arrest or other interference with elementary human rights. (2) Every person should have the right to express his religious, moral and political convictions. . . . (3) Channels of political action must be developed by which the people can without recourse to violence change their governments. (4) Forms of association within society which have their own foundations and principles should be respected, and not controlled in their inner life, by the state. Churches, families, and universities are dissimilar examples of this nonpolitical type of association.[28]

It was recognized already in the pre-Evanston studies that the Amsterdam report had oversimplified the world conflict by appearing to picture it as a conflict between Communism and laissez-faire capitalism. Actually, a pure laissez-faire economy no longer existed in the world. There were mixed economies, and the debate in non-Communist countries was about the nature of the mixture. It was generally accepted that state intervention in the economic sphere was necessary to some degree. The 1954 Evanston Assembly, using some of the language of the 1937 Oxford conference, stated:

While the state is sometimes the enemy of freedom, under many circumstances the state is the only instrument which can make freedom possible for large sectors of the population. The state is not the source of social justice, but it must be its guardian, ready if necessary to accept responsibility to counteract depression or inflation and to relieve the impact of unemployment, industrial injury, low wages and unfavourable working conditions, sickness and old age.

But in doing so the state remains the servant not the lord of social justice. Therefore we must warn against the danger that the union of political and economic power may result in an all-controlling state. In contradistinction to actions of the state it is the task of nongovernmental sectors in economic life to be the guardian of responsible private action in society. But within the private sector, both employers and employees in all their varied organizations in their turn are the servant, and not the lord, of freedom and welfare. When necessary in the public interest, the state must intervene to prevent any center of economic or social power which represents partial interest from becoming stronger than itself, for the state alone has the power and the authority under God to act as trustee for society as a whole.[29]

In the year before the Evanston Assembly some Europeans who had favored public ownership were seeing its limitations and were in favor of more free enterprise. This was reflected in the report:

The new emphasis on state initiative and international organization in the development of economic life has been accompanied by a fresh recognition of the importance of relative freedom in enterprise and of the regulating role of the price system. Many socialists have come to appreciate the importance of the private sector in the economy and the necessity for the energetic, enterprising and expert businessman as well as being aware of the dangers of centralized government.[30]

The report also placed stress on efficient production as being as important as fair distribution.

Much Christian social thought in the past has tended to ignore the former and stress primarily the latter. Laziness and waste are sins before God no less than selfishness and greed.[31]

Appreciation and concern were expressed for the businessman, the worker, and the farmer. This statement was less one-sided than some earlier documents (such as Stockholm), which had been strongly pro-labor.

The report called attention to the international perspective of a responsible society. It charged Christian citizens to be alert to the effect of national policies on other peoples of the world and to seek to change those policies that disrupt justice and peace.

The Evanston Assembly gave some attention to the family and its place in society, a topic often neglected in ecumenical conferences. The responsible society, it was pointed out, needs to be realized in small groups as well as in large ones. The conference expressed concern about the widespread disruption of family life.

Both Oxford and Amsterdam had stated that the most significant changes in society can come through Christian laymen witnessing daily through their vocations and their citizenship. Evanston had one whole section devoted to "The Christian and His Vocation." It called attention to significant pioneering work done by lay academies, such as the Evangelical Academies in Germany and Zoe in Greece, and stressed the importance of equipping the laity for Christian witness in society.

The report proclaimed:

> The real battles of faith today are being fought in factories, shops, offices and farms, in political parties and government agencies, in countless homes, in the press, radio and television, in the relationship of the nations. Very often it is said that the church should "go into these spheres," but the fact is that the church is already in these spheres in the persons of the laity.[32]

The concept of the responsible society as further refined in Evanston helped many churches in the West in their debates about economic and social policy, especially those churches that were tempted to engage in the self-righteous anti-Communist crusades common in the 1950's. In the United States this phenomenon was known as McCarthyism. However, the Evanston teachings found critical acceptance among Christians in the Third World who felt the need for concepts related more closely to the dynamic social conditions in which they lived.

THE NEED FOR FLEXIBILITY

The Evanston report showed an awareness that patterns appropriate for the industrialized nations were not necessarily applicable to the predominantly agricultural nations of Asia, Africa, and, to some extent, Latin America. It stated:

> The people of these countries have awakened to a new sense of fundamental human rights and justice and they are in revolt against enslaving political, economic, religious and social conditions. There is also the pressure to achieve change rapidly.[33]

The report then summarized the findings of the 1952 conference at Lucknow, India. It was evident to the World Council of Churches at this point that a relevant concept of social ethics, valid for the Third World as well as for the industrialized West, would yet have to be found.

In 1955 the WCC launched a study on "The Common Christian Responsibility Toward Areas of Rapid Social Change." Subsequent WCC social pronouncements reflected the findings of these studies. In this chapter, attention is being given only to the statements describing the kind of society that Christians should work for.

The 1959 ecumenical study conference at Thessalonica, Greece, which was the culmination of a four-year study on social change, reflected the struggles of Third World Christians in seeking a political and economic order appropriate for their situation. The conference report said:

> In the accelerating social, economic and political transitions within the areas of rapid social change, nations are being pulled sharply and painfully between conflicting tendencies in the development of their political institutions. The strong attraction exercised by freedom and justice for the individual and active personal participation in political life, pulls them toward democracy. The sense of great tasks that need to be accomplished quickly, demanding a government strong and decisive enough to deal immediately with the urgent problems of national development, pulls them toward authoritarian, even totalitarian rule.[34]

The uncertainty as to whether to use India or China as a model for development is apparent here.

The report called attention to the carefully balanced statement made by the East Asia conference of May 1959.

Ultimately, a system of government will be tested by its capacity to develop a sense of community among its people, to achieve their deliverance from economic bondage and preserve the basic liberties of individuals and associations. It is our conviction that this balance of objectives will be best preserved only by a democratic system. The challenge before the East Asian countries is to find an indigenous and dynamic form of democracy. It is not necessary to adopt patterns worked out in the different circumstances of Western society; but our forms should provide strong government committed to national integration and national development and, at the same time, a government answerable to the people.[35]

Besides stressing the need for a state that is stronger and more indigenous, the Third World Christians were also pointing to the positive sides of nationalism. Earlier ecumenical documents had pointed out both its positive and negative sides, but had stressed more its negative side, especially during the church struggle with Nazism. The New Delhi Assembly of 1961 had this to say:

Cohesion of new nations, itself a contribution to international stability, is threatened by the reversion of loyalties to old tribal, linguistic, ethnic and religious groupings. "Nationalism" can here be understood as the struggle for an inclusive national culture and a wider sense of solidarity and mutuality, a positive factor, indispensable to the life of the new nations. . . . The strength of nationalism is in uniting a complex society in constructive nation-building. Its weakness is in its possible perversion into policies of antagonism and exclusiveness against other nations.[36]

It also pointed to the need for flexibility in forms of government.

Again, political circumstances of the new states require their own appropriate political solutions rather than patterns established elsewhere. The world knows various forms of government and each is a reflection of basic patterns. The churches' duty is not primarily to favour any one form but to seek the proper protection of human rights and fundamental freedoms for all, political power made responsible by law, government made responsible to the people, and the establishment of those relations between citizens and groups on which alone just societies stand.[37]

In the discussions, the Third World people often questioned some of the traditional assumptions about democracy. Some viewed favorably a "dynamic democracy" as a form of government capable of effecting social changes—even by state-imposed discipline—for the general welfare, but capable also of granting equal opportunity, personal freedom and open criticism of government policy. Such a system may not have the usual Western parliamentary forms and political parties.

Thus one can see in the New Delhi statement an attempt to maintain the essential elements of the responsible society concept while allowing for more flexibility to meet the needs of new and developing nations.

Some of these systems are more authoritarian than those whose outlook has been moulded by the western tradition of democracy would find acceptable for themselves. Yet the difficulty of maintaining order, of avoiding civil strife, of establishing governments strong enough to deal with the desperate need for economic development, may call for new forms of political life.[38]

PRESERVATION OF HUMAN RIGHTS

But if anyone were to gain the impression that the New Delhi Assembly was weakening earlier stands taken in regard to basic human rights, he would see, after reading the following statement, that this is not the case:

Recognition of the limitations under which Christians must live and work in many nations does not mean that one form of government is as good as another, that Christians can be indifferent to the nature of political institutions. It is possible for a Christian to live (or die) with integrity under any political system; it is possible for the Church to obey its Lord in all kinds of external circumstances. But some political structures are more favourable than others for the development of responsible citizens. Mature Christians may grow in grace and in courage under oppressive governments. But under such governments, churches may be rigorously limited in their education of the younger generation, in their opportunity for public witness, and in their pastoral service to the community. Love for the neighbour must move Christians to use whatever opportunities may exist, to work for political institutions which encourage participation by all citizens, and which protect both the person's freedom of conscience and his freedom to express his convictions. No present difficulties justify Christians or churches in acquiescing in either old or new forms of tyranny. Where emergencies may seem to call for temporary authoritarian regimes, let all who support them be warned that power corrupts, and that those who assume it will usually try to keep it. . . . Christians can never give the state their ultimate loyalty.[39]

The New Delhi Assembly adopted a declaration on religious liberty reaffirming what had been said at Amsterdam and amplifying the earlier statement. It stressed more fully than the earlier document the need for freedom to change one's belief. Its greatest contribution was in its explication of the theological foundation for religious liberty.

Christians see religious liberty as a consequence of God's creative work, of his redemption of man in Christ and his calling of men into his service. God's redemptive dealing with men is not coercive. Accordingly human attempts by legal enactment or by pressures of social custom to coerce or to eliminate faith are violations of the fundamental ways of God with men. The freedom which God has given in Christ implies a free response to God's love, and the responsibility to serve fellow-men at the point of deepest need.

Holding a distinctive Christian basis for religious liberty, we regard this right as fundamental for men everywhere.[40]

In the subsequent four years the Second Vatican Council grappled with the issue of religious liberty and expressed itself in ways similar to this, that is, noted the incompatibility of coercion and the redemptive acts of Christ.

In the New Delhi pronouncement on service are several significant sentences that show how the pursuit of religious liberty is directly related to the pursuit of other liberties and to the pursuit of social justice. There is far more involved in the search for religious liberty than the desire of the church to gain protection for its own existence.

The existence of a church may have great indirect effects on the nation's political life, for the Church is the clearest case of an association within a nation which has its own foundation, independent of the state. If the Church is true to itself it will continually seek to remind all rulers and citizens that the state has essential limitations under God. As the Church struggles to preserve or widen its own freedom to witness, it may open the door for freedom of men as men.[41]

Simply by being itself, the church is constantly pointing to a higher reality and a higher loyalty than the state, and is thereby undermining the kind of idolatry characteristic of a totalitarian state which sees no authority beyond itself. By pointing to a higher truth and by witnessing to it, the church helps other communities such as universities which also pursue a truth that is higher than the state. The New Delhi statement points out that when a church collaborates with an oppressive state just to protect itself, it is betraying humanity. The church must "guard persons against the state when the state puts itself in the place of God."

At the Geneva conference on Church and Society held in 1966 there were many delegates from the Third World, and on each topic their voice was heard. In assessing different economic systems, the participants observed that there were roughly three types—free enterprise, mixed economy, and state ownership.

Countries with economic systems corresponding roughly to all three types of organizations have shown themselves capable of rapid economic growth and wide distribution of income.

There is no kind of economic system within which the Christian church is not found, and on the whole Christians tend to support the kind of society in which they live. This fact should not occasion surprise; what is surprising is that Christians have so often argued that only one economic system is Christian. All the above systems can in their various ways, and with varying degrees of success, be employed to support the economic goals mentioned above. Christians should not, however, support these systems as ends in themselves; they are nothing more than means to achieve the ends for which men are made. The role of Christians is to be critical participants in the societies in which they find themselves.[42]

Sometimes the term "critical solidarity" was used to describe the Christian's role in society. In the Geneva report a set of critical questions was provided which a person could use in examining each of the three kinds of economies. The report went on to say:

All these systems are changing, learning from each other, and apparently converging; they already have more in common than the most enthusiastic supporters of any one of them are ready to admit. All must deal with the uncertainties arising from their inability to predict accurately the long-run trends in the fields of population, consumer choices and technology. . . . In all there is some planning. All operate within a framework of government activity; in all, government expenditure absorbs a large part of the national income. But the major issue is where the planning is done and by whom.[43]

The report then includes a much more detailed examination of economic issues.

Another section of the report deals with "The Nature and Function of the State in a Revolutionary Age." Like the social change studies, it manifests a concern for flexibility in government. Some delegates had doubts as to whether an opposition party was needed. They felt that criticism could be expressed in other ways. But the report goes on to say that "we all attach great importance to the constitutional legal rights of the individual."

THE PROBLEM OF VIOLENT REVOLUTION

One of the issues considered was violence versus nonviolence. The report contains these carefully balanced words:

> The clear Christian teaching regarding the respect for persons and love of one's enemy requires the Christian to seek all possible peaceful and responsible non-violent means of action in society. . . .
> But violence is very much a reality in our world, both the overt use of force to oppress and the invisible violence (violencia blanca) perpetrated on people who by the millions have been or still are the victims of repression and unjust social systems. . . .
> It cannot be said that the only possible position for the Christian is one of absolute non-violence. There are situations where Christians may become involved in violence. Whenever it is used, however, it must be seen as an "ultimate recourse" which is justified only in extreme situations. The use of violence requires a rigorous definition of the ends for which it is used and a clear recognition of the evils which are inherent in it, and it should always be tempered by mercy. . . .[44]

The question of the right of revolution was a live issue in the late 1960's. Particularly the Latin American delegates had much to say about it. Some lived in such desperately unjust situations that they saw no way to change them without revolutions.

One question was, Should Christians ever be involved in revolutions? But a more difficult one was, Should Christians ever be involved in violent revolutions? This had been considered before in Christian history. Luther allowed no right of revolution. He dreaded anarchy and supported the suppression of the Peasants' Revolt. Calvin was in general opposed to revolution, but he made an exception. If a parliamentary or legislative body representing the people conducted a revolution against an unjust tyrant, then the revolution would be permissible. The seventeenth- and eighteenth-century revolutions in Scotland, England, and colonial America fall within this exception. From the Middle Ages onward, Roman Catholic thought made certain allowances for tyrannicide, the killing of a tyrant. During World War II some Protestant ministers in Germany also believed in tyrannicide, and on the basis of this belief they participated in the plot on Hitler's life.

But today the "enemy" is often not an unjust individual but an unjust system that keeps itself in power by the use of all kinds of violence. Then the question arises, If violence can be used to preserve injustice, why can it not be used to secure justice?

The question of violent revolution was discussed at the Consultation on Theological Issues of Church and Society held in St. Sergius Monastery in Zagorsk, near Moscow, in March 1968. It was the first conference jointly sponsored by the Department on Church and Society and the Secretariat on Faith and Order of the WCC. Its statement on theology and revolution included this paragraph:

The problem of keeping the means of power and/or violence used in the revolution under moral and responsible control is crucial for the human ends the revolution is seeking. Christians in the revolutionary situation have to do all in their power to exercise the ministry of reconciliation to enable the revolutionary change to take place non-violently or, if this is not possible, with the minimum of violence. But we must realize that some Christians find themselves in situations where they must, in all responsibility, participate fully in the revolution with all its inevitable violence. In such situations they will need the understanding, sympathy, and prayer of their Christian brethren.[45]

The World Council of Churches at Uppsala built on the foundations of the Geneva conference and the Zagorsk consultation, but it was much more cautious than either of these conferences in considering the possibility of the use of violence.

The building of political institutions suitable to national development involves revolutionary changes in social structures. Revolution is not to be identified with violence, however. In countries where the ruling groups are oppressive or indifferent to the aspirations of the people, are often supported by foreign interests, and seek to resist all changes by the use of coercive or violent measures, including the "law and order" which may itself be a form of violence, the revolutionary change may take a violent form. Such changes are morally ambiguous. The churches have a special contribution toward the development of effective non-violent strategies of revolution and social change. Nevertheless we are called to participate creatively in the building of political institutions to implement the social changes that are desperately needed.[46]

A real test of the ecumenical views on nonviolence took place the year after Uppsala, when the World Council voted to help revolutionary movements battling white racism. This will be discussed in a later chapter on racial justice.

The rather constant interest of the WCC in human rights and especially in religious liberty was manifest at Uppsala in the following statements:

The full application of religious liberty to individuals and organizations and the free right of expression of conscience for all persons, whatever their beliefs, for which the United Nations will, as we hope, soon provide a further international Convention, is fundamentally important for all human freedoms. When this convention is adopted it will be for all governments to ratify it and adjust their domestic legislation and administrative practices accordingly. . . .

Violations of human rights in one place may be quickly communicated to all, spreading an evil and destructive influence abroad. Nations should recognize that the protection of fundamental human rights and freedoms has now become a common concern of the whole international community, and should therefore not regard international concern for the implementation of these rights as an unwarranted interference.[47]

SUMMARY

By 1970 it was less clear than it had been in the early 1950's that a responsible society could be defined and that appropriate action for Christians in political and economic life could be clarified in such a way as to be valid universally. Nevertheless, certain trends prevail in the WCC's social teachings.

In developing the concept of the responsible society the ecumenical leaders sought to develop a pattern of civic life showing a balance of freedom, order, and justice. As they saw it, the state would be the most powerful instrumentality in society. However, its power needed to be limited. It would protect the natural communities in a nation, not overwhelm them. Faithful to the democratic tradition, such a state would guarantee basic human rights. The advocates of the responsible society gave special importance to religious liberty, thereby making it clear that there is a higher loyalty than loyalty to the state. While they emphasized the importance of obedience to the state, they recognized the need for resistance for conscience's sake when the state was clearly unjust in its demands. In general they favored nonviolent resistance, though in recent years they have recognized that occasions for legitimate violent resistance might exist.

They recognized both the positive and the negative sides of nationalism and drew a sharp line between imperialistic nationalism and the legitimate aspirations of a people for self-determination.

While the elements of a responsible society in their political aspects sound much like a modern democracy, the churchmen did not intend to sanction a particular form of government or to suggest that one form is applicable in all cases. The rapid social change studies of the 1950's and 1960's suggested that new democracies need not follow the parliamentary forms and the party systems characteristic of the West. Furthermore, there were some specific situations where a strong state was needed to make the changes necessary for the establishment of dynamic democracy. Despite these concessions, the ecumenical consensus continues to insist upon the importance of equality under the law for all groups and peoples, of personal freedom, and of open criticism and discussion of government policy.

In relation to the economic order the WCC taught the value of property—hence the importance of making it available to as many people as possible—but also the limitations of the right of ownership. It emphasized that property is to be used in socially constructive ways. Rejecting laissez-faire capitalism on the one hand and Communism on the other, it opted for a middle way—allowing for a lot of room between a welfare capitalism and a democratic socialism, and suggesting that appropriate systems have to be found for each situation. Concern that not too much power be concentrated in one or a few places led it to favor the mixed economy. Such a system also had the possibilities of realizing the assets of both private and public sectors, the private being particularly strong on production and the public on distribution. The WCC was consistently interested in the groups within society—labor unions, farm groups, etc.—which it viewed as important channels for securing social justice. It placed much emphasis on the idea that Christian laymen should work for social justice through their vocational and political life and through professional groups.

The ecumenical movement has rather consistently held that a church's freedom includes the right to criticize and to influence government policy, but that the state's authority may not similarly interfere with the life of the church. In its understanding of the church's mission in society, it is much less concerned about institutional privileges than it is about the freedom to perform its redemptive work in the world, functioning as a servant people in a secular society.

CORRELATION WITH ROMAN CATHOLIC SOCIAL THOUGHT

Both the WCC and the Vatican have rejected the extremes of Communism and laissez-faire capitalism. Papal encyclicals denounced individualism on the one hand and collectivism on the other. Both have favored labor's right to organize, and both have favored welfare legislation.

WCC thinking about the state has probably been influenced by the Roman Catholic doctrine of subsidiarity. Pope Pius XI expressed this doctrine in *Quadragesimo Anno* in 1931: "It is an injustice, a grave evil and a disturbance of right order, for a larger and higher association to arrogate to itself functions which can be performed efficiently by smaller and lower societies." WCC statements also stressed the distribution of power, the distinction between state and nation, and the responsibility of the state to make possible many groups and activities rather than to control and manage everything.

Among the differences in the two approaches are these: Roman Catholic encyclicals have had more to say about profit-sharing than have the WCC documents. The encyclicals have also said more about the family and its rights. Whereas the Roman Church has supported Catholic political parties, the WCC Assembly at Amsterdam advised against the formation of Christian parties, "because they easily confuse Christianity with the inherent compromises of politics."

There is a difference in the two traditions in regard to their attitude toward socialism. Pope Leo XIII in *Rerum Novarum*, issued in 1891, denounced socialism along with communism, since the right of private property is based on natural law. By contrast, a number of social gospel leaders in the early twentieth century were impressed with democratic socialism. Commenting on the difference, Paul Abrecht of the Department of Church and Society of the WCC wrote:

> It might be argued that, whereas in later years Roman Catholic thinking had to overcome an uncompromising rejection of socialism and Marxism, non-Roman social thinkers were obliged to rid themselves of some of the illusions about man and society which an idealist socialist reading of the Bible had fostered.[48]

Both traditions have battled against the injustices of totalitarianism and have championed human rights. The WCC documents have consistently placed a great stress on religious liberty for all. Roman Catholicism was much slower to recognize the right to religious liberty for other than Roman Catholic Churches, but in 1965 the Second Vatican Council issued a statement on religious liberty quite similar to the 1961 WCC statement at New Delhi. Both of them pointed out that coercion was incompatible with the Christian mission.

Both traditions favor nonviolent forms of social change. Both Pope Paul VI's encyclical *Populorum Progressio* and the Uppsala report of the WCC recognize the desperate situations that drive people toward revolution. While both traditions urge nonviolence, the WCC statements seem to show more sympathy with those who have tried nonviolence and failed and are considering violent methods.

Much of what the WCC thinking has embodied in the term "the responsible society" the Catholic tradition has embodied in the term "the common good." Another related term is "socialization," introduced by Pope John XXIII in his encyclical *Mater et Magistra.* Not to be confused with socialism, this concept recognizes the interdependence of the segments of modern society and the need for strong government as well as strong private groups working together to assure justice, some types of society needing stronger government than others. Pope John's thinking can be correlated with the WCC studies on rapid social change. In both cases a flexible system is sought that will meet the needs of an age of technology; in both cases there is a fundamental concern for preserving human rights.

IV

War and Peace

One of the roots of the ecumenical movement was the peace movement. The Universal Christian Council for Life and Work was in part an outgrowth of the World Alliance for Promoting International Friendship through the Churches. Between the two world wars the two bodies worked closely together. More officially related to the churches than the World Alliance, Life and Work merged with Faith and Order in 1938 to form the Provisional Committee of the World Council of Churches. The World Alliance existed from 1914 to 1940 and during that time made important contributions toward disarmament, protection of religious and national minorities, religious liberty, care of refugees, support of the League of Nations, and mitigation of tensions between nations.

As was noted in the second chapter, questions of war guilt plagued the ecumenical meetings of the early twenties. The question of the justice of the Versailles peace treaty and of the place and value of the League of Nations were also key issues. Despite the efforts of internationalist Americans, the United States did not join the League. Germans opposed it because of its associations with what they considered to be a harsh peace treaty.

In the Universal Christian Conference on Life and Work held in Stockholm in 1925, the delegates had this to say in their message:

We have set forth the guiding principles of a Christian interna-
tionalism, equally opposed to a national bigotry and a weak cosmo-
politanism. We have affirmed the universal character of the Church,
and its duty to preach and practice the love of the brethren. We
have considered the relation of the individual conscience to the state.
We have examined the race problem, the subject of law and arbitration, and the constitution of an international order which would
provide peaceable methods for removing the causes of war—questions
which in the tragic conditions of to-day make so deep an appeal to
our hearts. We summon the Churches to share with us our sense of
the horror of war, and of its futility as a means of settling international disputes, and to pray and work for the fulfillment of the
promise that under the sceptre of the Prince of Peace, "mercy and
truth shall meet together, righteousness and peace shall kiss each
other." [1]

The important effects of the Stockholm conference were the
establishment of links between Christian leaders of various
countries, some of which had been at war with each other,
and the pledge to maintain contact with each other in a common effort to work for world peace.

In the following years, the continuation committee established at the conference carried on several studies and action
projects pertaining to peace, working closely with the World
Alliance. When the Kellogg-Briand Pact for the outlawing
of war was signed in 1928 by 59 nations, many religious
bodies saw it as a decisive step toward a peaceful world.
Desiring to support and implement this pact, several ecumenical church leaders drew up a document urging churches
to take courageous leadership in the direction of peace. Known
as the Eisenach-Avignon Resolution, it was initiated by Bishop
George Bell of England and adopted by the World Alliance
as well as the continuation committee of Life and Work. The
key sentences of the resolution are as follows:

We believe that war considered as an institution for the settlement
of international disputes is incompatible with the mind and method
of Christ, and therefore incompatible with the mind and method of
His Church.

While convinced that the time has come for the revision of existing treaties in the interests of peace, we maintain that all disputes and conflicts between nations, for which no solution can be found through diplomacy or conciliation, ought to be settled or solved through arbitration, whether by the World Court or by some other tribunal mutually agreed. . . .

We earnestly appeal to the respective authorities of all Christian communions to declare in unmistakable terms that they will not countenance, nor assist in any way in, any war with regard to which the Government of their country has refused a bona fide offer to submit the dispute to arbitration.[2]

This last sentence clearly puts loyalty to the international order above loyalty to national states. Despite its radical character, the resolution was well received in the churches. This was a time of optimism, of hope that through the League of Nations and the churches the world would find the way to peace.

When the League of Nations decided to have a Disarmament Conference in 1932, a number of non-Roman Christian organizations coordinated their supportive efforts in a Christian Disarmament Committee. Participants included the World Alliance for Promoting International Friendship through the Churches, the Universal Christian Council for Life and Work, the YMCA, the YWCA, the World's Student Christian Federation, and the Society of Friends. This committee functioned in two ways. It interpreted Christian opinion to the conference, and through the publications that it circulated it aroused Christian public opinion concerning the conference. Unfortunately, the League of Nations failed to secure the agreement of the participating nations about disarmament.

In 1935 the World Alliance and Life and Work called for arbitration of the dispute between Ethiopia and Italy. Later that year the Ethiopian invasion took place. In the 1936 meeting of Life and Work, Orthodox Archbishop Germanos expressed serious doubts about the League's ability to maintain peace.

Three Views of War

When the Oxford conference met in 1937 the clouds of war were already on the horizon. Considerable attention was given to the subject of war and of international order, and the positions taken provided the basic direction for later ecumenical statements. The conference denounced war in the following language:

> Wars, the occasions of war, and all situations which conceal the facts of conflict under the guise of outward peace, are marks of a world to which the church is charged to proclaim the gospel of redemption. War involves compulsory enmity, diabolical outrage against human personality, and a wanton distortion of the truth. War is a particular demonstration of the power of sin in this world and a defiance of the righteousness of God as revealed in Jesus Christ and him crucified. No justification of war must be allowed to conceal or minimize this fact.[3]

This condemnation of war was not, however, a call to pacifism. The report pointed out three positions that Christians take when, despite efforts to stop it, war actually comes. The first was the pacifist position, which claims that participation in war is totally incompatible with the way of the cross. The second was the "just war" view, which holds that Christians might approve wars with just causes and relatively just methods but might refuse to participate in unjust wars. The third was the "duty to the state" view, which argues that disrespect for the state invites anarchy and that when the state calls men into military service, they should obey. This position did allow for rare exceptions in which a person might disobey the state.

What is very important is that the Oxford conference recognized all three of these as valid positions. Prior to this time, most churches gave no support to conscientious objectors. The peace churches—Quakers, Mennonites, and Brethren—stood quite alone. Most nations gave no support to c.o.'s, though some made exceptions for members of peace churches. In the

United States, for example, peace church members were given some concessions in World War I.

The statement recognizing pacifism as a valid position was not approved without opposition. Some prominent churchmen wanted pacifism to be declared a heresy.

The Just War Theory Is Predominant

It may be helpful to recall that in the history of the Christian Church, pacifism prevailed in the first three centuries, but that after Constantine (313) and especially after Augustine (400) the just war theory was the dominant view for Catholics and, after the Reformation, also for Protestants.

The just war theory as formulated by Augustine came into being after Christianity became a dominant and influential religion in the Roman Empire and after Christians began to feel some responsibility for preserving civilization. Basically, the just war theory affirmed that if the cause is just and the means are just, a war may be justified. It should be conducted by states, not by individuals or unauthorized groups; it should protect justice, for example, by stopping an aggressor; it should be fought in the right spirit; it should accomplish more good than harm; and it should be fought with the right means. For example, the right means would not kill civilians.

Whether the just war theory proved to be much of a check to militant rulers in the Middle Ages or later is open to question. At times the just war degenerated into a crusade in which no attempt was made to maintain any regard for the enemy.

Through most of history, the believers in the just war theory have not been tolerant of pacifist groups. When the Mennonites appeared in Europe they were persecuted by both Catholics and Protestants. Quakers were persecuted in England and in America. By 1937, however, many of the leading Protestants in America were pacifists. The post-World War I form of the social gospel was essentially pacifist.

This new pacifism was, however, different from the original

form. In their beginnings the peace churches called their members to nonparticipation in war on the grounds that war was incompatible with their calling as followers of Christ. Theirs was a vocational pacifism; they felt obligated to nonparticipation as part of their witness. They did not call upon governments to become pacifist and to throw away their weapons. But the new pacifists, reflecting the optimistic view of man of liberal Protestantism, were advocating pacifism and disarmament as a matter of state policy. They believed that the Sermon on the Mount could be applied to problems of international affairs, and they pointed to Gandhi as a model of successful nonviolent resistance. This form of pacifism, which claims that it will work on a national level better than war, is called activist pacifism. It was partly in reaction to the "utopianism" of this doctrine that Reinhold Niebuhr developed his Christian realism, which insisted that Hitler would have to be stopped by military methods.

Since the just war theory was the dominant one in the history of Christendom, it is understandable that it was the most favored of the three positions presented at Oxford. The majority felt that pacifism would not end war; its impact would be to surrender the weak to the aggression of the strong.

The third position, the "duty to the state" theory, is more difficult to account for. It was strong especially in German Lutheranism, with its pessimistic view of man and its great emphasis on obedience to the state. There was an unwillingness to have Christians jeopardize the unity and order of the state by allowing for noncooperation with state policy in time of war. Luther himself had advocated the just war theory, though he opposed crusades. The virtual disappearance of the just war theory in Germany, according to one German scholar, took place during the German resistance to Napoleon's invasion in the nineteenth century. Religion and patriotism became one. Ironically, it was within Germany that a strong Christian opposition against the government developed during World War II.

While the Oxford delegates recognized that Christians

would disagree on positions concerning war, they recognized that they should unite in their efforts to prevent it. This included working for a viable international order (at this point the failure of the League of Nations was apparent to all), working for justice and equal opportunity in the world (thereby eliminating basic causes of war), working for disarmament, and educating for peace.

WORLD ORDER IS NEEDED

While calling for a stronger international order, they avoided utopian expectations. They said, "No international order which can be devised by human effort may be equated with the Kingdom of God." They also pointed out the necessity for a limitation of national sovereignty:

So far as the present evil is political, the heart of it is to be found in the claim of each national state to be the judge in its own cause. The abandonment of that claim, and the abrogation of absolute national sovereignty at least to that extent, is a duty that the Church should urge upon the nations.[4]

Great emphasis was placed on the church itself. Since it is a universal Christian fellowship, the Una Sancta, it unites people of many nations in their loyalty to one Lord. "Here is the first obligation of the church, to be in living fact the church, a society with a unity so deep as to be indestructible by earthly divisions of race or nation or class." [5]

A world order, the conference said, could not succeed without an international ethos, and the church had much to contribute in its development.

All law . . . must be based on a common ethos, that is, a common foundation of moral convictions. To the creation of such a common foundation in moral conviction the Church, as a supra-national society with a profound sense of the historical realities and of the worth of human personality, has a great contribution to make.[6]

Regarding the League of Nations the conference observed:

But the idea on which the league was founded—that of international cooperation—has not been disproved. No alternative conception or method of comparable range has come to light in the intervening period, and the need for an agency of international cooperation is as great as ever, if not greater.[7]

A few years after Oxford the churches had an opportunity to apply their belief that the church is supranational. Nothing could challenge such a belief more than war. Could unity between believers be maintained while nations were at war? There are records that indicate significant efforts were made to keep contact between Christians of both sides. A striking example is the activity of Bishop Bell in England, who tried to keep in touch with leaders of the German Confessing Church such as Dietrich Bonhoeffer, and who made every effort to help the British people avoid condemnation of the German people as a whole while they were fighting the Nazis. Within Germany the Confessing Church carried out a heroic resistance, mindful of the loyalty to the Una Sancta.

In the midst of war, could the rights of pacifists be supported? One example is the action of the Federal Council of Churches in the United States. It was instrumental in persuading the Government to allow alternate service not only for peace church members but for conscientious objectors from other churches as well. Similar developments took place in other countries.

Could the churches keep ideals of justice alive in wartime? One of the just war principles has to do with fighting a war with the right spirit, that is, without hatred. There is evidence that for many participants this war was not so much a vengeful crusade as an unfortunate necessity, and that the churches contributed to this "reluctant warrior" mood more than they had done in World War I. On the other hand, the churches did little to protest the extensive violation of the just war principle that opposes the killing of civilians. Both sides engaged in obliteration bombing. When the world became calloused to it, it was possible for America to drop atomic bombs on Hiroshima and Nagasaki. While the mass bombing of civilians was protested by pacifist groups, few leaders in the "just war" tradition spoke out against it.

Could the churches work toward world order even during a war? In several countries churches were engaged in studies regarding the postwar world. In Great Britain the British Commission on Christian Social Responsibility, headed by Archbishop William Temple, did significant work. In the United States similar activity was carried on by the Commission on a Just and Durable Peace under the leadership of John Foster Dulles, a prominent Christian layman. The American group held several conferences. The International Round Table at Princeton in 1943, bringing together sixty-one Christian leaders from twelve countries, stimulated an international Christian influence on the San Francisco Conference of 1945, at which the charter of the United Nations was drafted.

A New Agency Is Founded

One of the results of the wartime activity was the 1946 conference at Cambridge, England, at which the Commission of the Churches on International Affairs (CCIA) was founded under the joint sponsorship of the International Missionary Council and the World Council of Churches, then in process of formation. Delegates at Cambridge agreed that the church "has a word to say that no one else can say. . . . The Church knows of a forgiveness which includes but also transcends justice and so makes possible a new beginning where international relations have broken down."

The aims of the CCIA as set forth at Cambridge included: the careful preparation of studies on international problems, guidance and help to the churches of the world as they exert their influence on nations in regard to international questions, and contact with international bodies. Point VIII of the aims states the Commission's purpose:

VIII. To represent the parent bodies in relations with international bodies such as the United Nations and related agencies.
In particular, the Commission should maintain such contacts with these bodies as will assist in:
(*a*) the progressive development and codification of international

law and the progressive development of supra-national institutions;

(*b*) the encouragement of respect for and observance of human rights and fundamental freedoms, special attention being given to the problem of religious liberty;

(*c*) the international regulation of armaments;

(*d*) the furtherance of international economic cooperation;

(*e*) acceptance by all nations of the obligation to promote to the utmost the well-being of dependent peoples including their advance toward self-government and the development of their free political institutions;

(*f*) the promotion of international social, cultural, educational and humanitarian enterprises.[8]

Since 1946 the CCIA has played a very significant role as an "international civil service" putting WCC and IMC pronouncements into practice. It is known for its careful study of international problems, its close contacts with the United Nations and other international agencies, and its cooperation with churches in the countries involved in international disputes.

When the World Council of Churches held its first Assembly in Amsterdam in 1948 the note of "messianism" or "utopianism" that had been present in some post-World War I gatherings was gone. A cold war had begun. Atomic annihilation was a possibility. The report on "The Churches and the International Disorder" began with these words:

> The World Council of Churches is met in its first assembly in a time of critical international strain. The hopes of the recent war years and the apparent dawn of peace have been dashed. No adequate system for effecting peaceful change has been established, despite the earnest desire of millions.[9]

Yet the statement went on to affirm "that the world is in God's hands, and that war is not inevitable if men repent and obey God's law."

Even more strongly than the Oxford conference, the Amsterdam Assembly denounced war as a sin. It also noted that there were serious doubts whether, in the light of the new weapons, there could be a just war.

War as a method of settling disputes is incompatible with the teaching and example of our Lord Jesus Christ. The part which war plays in our present international life is a sin against God and a degradation of man. We recognize that the problem of war raises acute issues for Christians today. Warfare has greatly changed. War is now total and every man and woman is called for mobilization in war service. Moreover, the immense use of air forces and the discovery of atomic and new weapons render widespread and indiscriminate destruction inherent in the whole conduct of modern war in a sense never experienced in past conflicts. In these circumstances the tradition of a just war, requiring a just cause and the use of just means, is now challenged. Law may require the sanction of force, but when war breaks out, force is used on a scale which tends to destroy the basis on which law exists.

Therefore the inescapable question arises—can war now be an act of Justice? We cannot answer this question unanimously, but three broad positions are maintained:

(1) There are those who hold that, even though entering a war may be a Christian's duty in particular circumstances, modern warfare, with its mad destruction, can never be an act of justice.

(2) In the absence of impartial supranational institutions, there are those who hold that military action is the ultimate sanction of the rule of law, and that citizens must be distinctly taught that it is their duty to defend the law by force if necessary.

(3) Others, again, refuse military service of all kinds, convinced that an absolute witness against war and for peace is for them the will of God and they desire that the church should speak to the same effect.[10]

Thus, as at Oxford, three stances toward war were given.

THE JUST WAR IS QUESTIONED

The whole concept of a just war was under sharp debate at Amsterdam. George Bell, Bishop of Chichester, asserted that in an age of obliteration bombing and indiscriminate use of atomic force, the distinction between just and unjust wars has disappeared. Modern war is nothing less than barbarism. Frederik van Asbeck of the Netherlands, while agreeing with the bishop that there is no such thing today as a just war, pointed out nevertheless that as long as there is no supranational way of preventing aggression, people feel obliged to oppose violence with violence.

In discussing war, the Amsterdam Assembly was thinking largely of a possible war between the two great powers—the U.S.S.R. and the United States—and how it might be avoided. Not much light was shed on the wars of small countries— guerrilla wars or wars of independence, which were becoming important in the Third World.

As at Oxford, Christians were urged, despite differing views on war, to work together in promoting peaceful change and in pursuing justice. The concern for international law and an international ethos was manifested in the statement:

> The churches have an important part in laying that common foundation of moral conviction without which any system of law will break down. While pressing for more comprehensive and authoritative world organization, they should at present support immediate practical steps for fostering mutual understanding and goodwill among the nations, for promoting respect for international law and the establishment of the international institutions which are now possible. They should also support every effort to deal on a universal basis with the many specific questions of international concern which face mankind today, such as the use of atomic power, the multilateral reduction of armaments, and the provision of health services and food for all men. They should endeavor to secure that the United Nations be further developed to serve such purposes. They should insist that the domestic laws of each country conform to the principles of progressive international law, and they gratefully recognize that recent demands to formulate principles of human rights reflect a new sense of international responsibility for the rights and freedoms of all men.[11]

As a specific contribution to the development of an international ethos, the CCIA worked closely with the United Nations Commission on Human Rights, helped draft the statement on religious liberty that went into the Universal Declaration of Human Rights, and helped make this declaration better known and understood among the churches.

Like Oxford, Amsterdam claimed that the church has an important contribution to make to international relations through its own life and work.

The establishment of the World Council of Churches can be made of great moment for the life of the nations. It is a living expression of this fellowship, transcending race and nation, class and culture, knit together in faith, service and understanding. Its aim will be to hasten international reconciliation through its own members and through the cooperation of all Christian churches and of all men of goodwill. It will strive to see international differences in the light of God's design, remembering that normally there are Christians on both sides of every frontier. It should not weary in the effort to state the Christian understanding of the will of God and to promote its application to national and international policy.[12]

In a sense the Amsterdam Assembly illustrated the above principle, for it was meeting during a cold war, yet drawing Christians from both sides of the Iron Curtain into fellowship with each other and into service in the world.

The Amsterdam Assembly threw its weight on the side of people seeking their independence when it said:

We oppose aggressive imperialism—political, economic or cultural —whereby a nation seeks to use other nations or peoples for its own ends. We therefore protest against the exploitation of non-self-governing people for selfish purposes; the retarding of their progress toward self-government; and discrimination or segregation on the grounds of race or colour.[13]

The Assembly called upon churches to increase their activity in helping to provide homes for refugees and urged the United Nations to broaden the scope of the International Refugee Organization. In subsequent years aid to refugees became one of the most dramatic aspects of church cooperation with government and intergovernmental agencies. Some idea of the scope of its work can be seen by looking at the results of one year's activity. In 1950 the WCC, together with the Lutheran World Federation, helped 85,000 refugees find homes in South America, Australia, Canada, and the United States.

Between assemblies of the WCC, the CCIA was actively engaged in applying the principles enunciated there, responding with realistic proposals to emerging crises. In the late 1940's and the early 1950's it had a staff of two people—Kenneth

Grubb of England, formerly of the Ministry of Information of the United Kingdom, and O. Frederick Nolde, an American theologian who had served as a member of the Commission on a Just and Durable Peace and who had also served as a consultant at the San Francisco Conference on United Nations organization. Later the staff was enlarged.

Church Leaders Are Brought Together

In 1949, during the Netherlands-Indonesia dispute, the CCIA, in addition to supporting the international efforts, made a contribution of its own. It secured memoranda from Christian leaders on both sides and arranged for their exchange. This contributed toward the development of mutual understanding.

The arms race increased in intensity after the 1948 Assembly. The year 1949 saw the formation of NATO, the proclamation of the People's Republic of China, and the end of the United States atomic monopoly. In 1950 the United States exploded its first hydrogen bomb. The Soviet Union did the same within the year.

Shortly after the first hydrogen bomb explosion the WCC Executive Committee said:

The hydrogen bomb is the latest and most terrible step in the crescendo of warfare which has changed war from a fight between men and nations to a mass murder of human life. Man's rebellion against his Creator has reached such a point that, unless stayed, it will bring self-destruction upon him. All this is a perversion; it is against the moral order by which man is bound; it is sin against God.

As representatives of Christian Churches we appeal for a gigantic new effort for peace . . . we urge the governments to enter into negotiations once again, and to do everything in their power to bring the present tragic deadlock to an end.[14]

In its actions the WCC sought to transcend the cold war and not to identify itself with either side. This became very difficult when the Korean war began. The WCC Central Committee was meeting close to the time this war broke out. Advised by the CCIA Executive Committee, the Central Committee gave its support to the UN for this "police measure," stressing that it was an on-the-spot UN commission which had identified North Korea as the aggressor. The Central Committee also emphasized that action be taken for a "just settlement by negotiation and conciliation." This statement produced angry reactions among Christian leaders behind the Iron Curtain.

The CCIA has been involved in many a crisis—Korea, Berlin, Cuba, Nigeria, etc.—seeking to make a contribution to peace on behalf of the churches. One of a number of tangible results was the acceptance in 1950 by the UN of the idea, proposed by the CCIA, of the formation of a UN corps of international peace observers to be sent into areas of tension.

As delegates prepared for the Evanston Assembly of 1954 they were aware of the growing threats to peace—the explosion of the hydrogen bomb, the projection of the cobalt bomb, the escalation of the cold war, the attacks upon human rights, and the revolutionary upsurge of subject peoples.

DISARMAMENT IS URGENT

The dangers presented by the weapons of mass destruction weighed heavily on the minds of the delegates. Concerned to face these challenges, they gave little attention to defining different positions on war as their predecessors had done at Oxford and Amsterdam. In fact, the three positions had been reduced to two—pacifist and nonpacifist. The Assembly said:

> It is not enough for the churches to proclaim that war is evil. They must study afresh the Christian approaches to peace, taking into account both Christian pacifism as a mode of witness and the conviction of Christians that in certain circumstances military action is justifiable. Whatever views Christians hold in respect of these approaches, they must seek out, analyze and help to remove the psychological and social, the political and economic causes of war. Without forsaking their conviction that all weapons of war are evil, the churches should press for restraints on their use. Christians in all lands must plead with their governments to be patient and persistent in their search for means to limit weapons and advance disarmament.[15]

It is not clear what caused the two nonpacifist positions to be reduced to one, namely, that of the just war. It may be that Germany, the land where the "duty to the state" theory was quite strong, was recovering the just war tradition in its Lutheran and Calvinistic heritage in the light of the current situation wherein it might become a battleground for the great powers and might be forced into a fratricidal war between East Germans and West Germans. One of the elements of the just war theory, the idea that civilians must be protected, made a lot of sense in a nuclear age.

It might also be noted that in the 1950's there was increased interest in pacifism. Some of the pacifists called themselves "nuclear pacifists" and asserted that they could not conceive of a just war in a nuclear age.

As has been pointed out, major attention at Evanston was focused on the need to act in regard to controls and disarmament:

An international order of truth and peace would require: (1) under effective international inspection and control and in such a way that no state would have cause to fear that its security was endangered, the elimination and prohibition of atomic, hydrogen and all other weapons of mass destruction, as well as the reduction of all armaments to a minimum, (2) the development and acceptance of methods for peaceful change to rectify existing injustices. . . .

We first of all call upon the nations to pledge that they will refrain from the threat or the use of hydrogen, atomic and all other weapons of mass destruction as well as any other means of force against the territorial integrity or political independence of any state. If this pledge should be broken, the charter of the United Nations provides for collective action and, pending such international action, recognizes the right of national self-defence.[16]

The conference also insisted that "the churches must condemn the deliberate mass destruction of civilians in open cities by whatever means and for whatever purpose."

Test Ban Is Called For

A Japanese delegate brought to the conference a statement signed by 33,000 Christians of his land. The statement protested against the projection and the testing of hydrogen bombs. It is understandable that such a protest should come from Japan, since a number of people there had suffered from the fallout of atomic bomb tests in the Pacific area. The Assembly responded to this statement and to CCIA studies when it said:

We must also see that experimental tests of hydrogen bombs have raised issues of human rights, caused suffering, and imposed an additional strain on human relations between nations. Among safeguards against the aggravation of these international tensions is the insistence that nations carry on these tests only within their respective territories or, if elsewhere, only by international clearance and agreement.[17]

Evanston dealt with other international issues besides disarmament. Conditions for "living together" (a term preferred to "coexistence") in a divided world were outlined. Other topics given considerable attention were technical assistance, nationalism, developing countries, the United Nations, regional organizations, an international ethos, and human rights. In regard to human rights the Assembly selected for special attention the rights of conscientious objectors.

The World Council of Churches' current study and support of the right of conscientious objection, as authorized by the Central Committee in 1951, is a necessary step in the direction of national and international action for its protection. Meanwhile, as far as possible, the churches should plead for just judgment and humane treatment of those who know themselves called to this personal witness for peace.[18]

In the Evanston Assembly and in the subsequent work of the CCIA one can see efforts being made to expand the concept of a "responsible society" to the concept of a "responsible international society." As defined heretofore the term was used largely in connection with the domestic political and economic arrangements, but now some guidelines were being provided for responsible international behavior. In its statement on an international ethos, the Evanston Assembly listed some principles or middle axioms for nations.

Tentatively, we advance the following considerations:

(1) All power carries responsibility and all nations are trustees of power which should be used for the common good.

(2) All nations are subject to moral law, and should strive to abide by the accepted principles of international law, to develop this law and to enforce it through common actions.

(3) All nations should honor their pledged word and international agreements into which they have entered.

(4) No nation in an international dispute has the right to be the sole judge in its own cause or to resort to war to advance its policies, but should seek to settle disputes by direct negotiation or by submitting them to conciliation, arbitration or judicial settlement.

(5) All nations have a moral obligation to insure universal security and to this end should support measures designed to deny victory to a declared aggressor.

(6) All nations should recognize and safeguard the inherent dignity, worth and essential rights of the human person, without distinction as to race, sex, language or religion.

(7) Each nation should recognize the rights of every other nation, which observes such standards, to live by and proclaim its own political and social beliefs, provided that it does not seek by coercion, threat, infiltration or deception to impose these on other nations.

(8) All nations should recognize an obligation to share their scientific and technical skills with peoples in less developed regions, and to help the victims of disaster in other lands.

(9) All nations should strive to develop cordial relations with their neighbors, encourage friendly cultural and commercial dealings, and join in creative international efforts for human welfare.[19]

The Evanston documents gave the CCIA a solid basis for work in the realm of disarmament, and in subsequent years the Commission gave much attention to this area. CCIA did careful research, drawing upon the help of qualified experts, as a basis for its statements. Its positions on disarmament were endorsed in Central Committee meetings in 1957 at New Haven, Connecticut, and in 1958 at Nyborg, Denmark. The 1957 statement on "Atomic Tests and Disarmament" was used all over the world. In many lands churches urged their governments to give it careful consideration. The statements set forth a program on disarmament featuring a ban on atomic tests as a first step, but relating it to a longer-range strategy.

The underlying principles, as summarized in the 1958 statement, were these:

1. The main concern must always be the prevention of war itself, for the evil of war is an offence to the spiritual nature of man.
2. The objectives of a strategy to combat the menace of atomic war are inter-related and inter-dependent, such as ceasing tests, halting production, reducing existing armaments with provision for warning against surprise attacks, the peaceful use of atomic energy, peaceful settlement and peaceful change.
3. If persistent efforts bring no sufficient agreement on any of the inter-related objectives, partial agreements should be seriously explored and, if need be, reasonable risks should be taken to advance the objectives which must continue to stand as inter-dependent.[20]

The 1958 Central Committee meeting added the idea that control through inspection would not be fully accepted and would not really work until better understanding was developed among the nations.

The achievement of these ends requires friendship and confidence between the nations. We need an "open society" where people may meet freely and learn to understand and trust one another. We appeal to the churches to help prepare the way for such an open society.[21]

The East and the West have usually differed in their approaches to arms control. In general, the East has insisted on mutual agreement to disarm before considering any system of control, viewing Western proposals for inspection as a subterfuge for espionage. The West has reiterated its position that effective controls must accompany each and every disarmament step in order to assure actual disarmament. It was within this kind of a conflict of views that the WCC and the CCIA sought to give guidance in the interest of world peace. They did not advocate unilateral disarmament, nor did they identify with one side. They recognized the need for nations to defend themselves and sought to provide policies that would provide adequate security together with gradual disarmament.

THE CHURCH TRANSCENDS POLITICAL DIVISIONS

The studies of the CCIA were reflected in the statement on service adopted by the New Delhi WCC Assembly in 1961:

> Christians must press most urgently upon their governments as a first step towards the elimination of nuclear weapons, never to get themselves into a position in which they contemplate the first use of nuclear weapons. Christians must also maintain that the use of nuclear weapons, or other forms of major violence, against centers of population is in no circumstances reconcilable with the demands of the Christian gospel.[22]

The New Delhi Assembly issued an "Appeal to All Governments and Peoples." It included the following sentences:

> To halt the arms race is imperative. Complete and general disarmament is the accepted goal, and concrete steps must be taken to reach it. Meanwhile, the search for a decisive first step, such as the verified cessation of nuclear tests, should be pressed forward despite all obstacles and setbacks. . . .
> To enhance mutual trust, nations should be willing to run reasonable risks for peace. For example, an equitable basis for disarmament involves, on the one hand, an acceptance of risks in an inspection and control which cannot be fool-proof, and, on the other, the danger that inspection may exceed its stated duties. Those who would break through the vicious circle of suspicion must dare to pioneer.[23]

In many lands church leaders brought this appeal to the attention of heads of governments.

One of the specific recommendations made at New Delhi was that the WCC bring together churchmen of East and West to a conference in which disarmament experts from both sides would explain their stand. Such a consultation on Peace and Disarmament took place in 1962 in Geneva under the auspices of the CCIA. It proved to be of great help to all involved; its long-range effect is hard to measure. In bringing Christians from both sides of a dispute together, it followed a long-established pattern of the CCIA.

One step forward in the direction advocated by the WCC was taken in 1963 when the U.S.S.R., the United Kingdom, and the United States signed the Test Ban Treaty agreeing to ban tests in outer space, in the atmosphere, and under water. Still another step was taken in 1966 when the UN General Assembly approved a treaty outlawing nuclear weapons in space and prohibiting military use of the moon and other celestial bodies. A third step was taken in 1967 when the Nonproliferation Treaty was agreed upon. But these were just beginning steps in the long, hard road to disarmament.

The Churches Confront the Vietnam War

The CCIA has been actively involved in clarifying and helping to resolve many conflicts in the world. Its involvement in the Vietnam conflict began in 1954 through consultations with delegates at the Geneva conference on Indochina. In the following years, it viewed with particular concern the buildup of military activity. Its offices maintained contact with a number of national and regional commissions of the churches. At times the views of the commission were communicated to governments and to the United Nations.

An important consultation on the subject took place in 1965 in Bangkok. It brought together representatives of the East Asia Christian Conference and of the National Council of the Churches of Christ in the U.S.A. A visit of Japanese churchmen to America in the same year manifested the concern of many Asian Christians over U.S. policy in Vietnam and the responsibility of American churches in this matter.

World Council thinking was influenced by these consultations as well as by CCIA studies. The Central Committee of the WCC, meeting in Geneva in 1966, proclaimed:

The primary objective must be to stop the fighting as the most effective step to starting discussion and negotiation. This is not an easy task and we are not unaware of the deep rooted obstacles which have thus far prevented progress from the battlefield to the conference table. This is all the more urgent because by continuing the conflict both sides face acute problems—on the one side the United States of America and its allies face increase of bitter racial and other resentments against the USA and the West, and on the other hand the Vietnamese face the vast destruction of their people and resources. The prospect of victory at the end of the conflict does not justify the inevitable cost.[24]

Then the Central Committee listed ten measures which it believed must be undertaken as promptly as possible. These measures indicate the general direction of WCC thought at that time and later:

In order to keep human suffering to a minimum and to contribute to a climate more conducive to negotiation, we set forth the following measures which we believe should be undertaken as promptly as possible:

1. that the United States and South Vietnam stop bombing of the North, and North Vietnam stop military infiltration of the South;

2. that the United States now announce its commitment to a withdrawal of its troops phased in accordance with provisions for peacekeeping machinery under international auspices and deemed adequate in the judgement of an international authority;

3. that all parties recognize the necessity of according a place in negotiations both to the government of South Vietnam and to the National Liberation Front (Viet-Cong), in proportions to be determined, and that arrangements be encouraged for negotiation between the government of South Vietnam and the National Liberation Front in the hope that there may be found a negotiating authority representative of all South Vietnam;

4. that North and South Vietnam develop greater flexibility in the initiation of and response to negotiation proposals;

5. that all parties give every possible protection to non-combatants and relieve the plight of those suffering from the fighting;

6. that all parties recognize the extent to which what is happening in Vietnam is part of a social revolution and that, freed from foreign intervention, Vietnam, both North and South, ought to be in a position to determine its own future, with due consideration of the demands of peace and security in South East Asia;

7. that all parties recognize the futility of military action for the solution of the underlying political, social and economic problems of Vietnam and the necessity of massive and generous development programmes;

8. that in order to relieve present international tension, the United States review and modify its policy of "containment" of communism and communist countries supporting "wars of liberation" review and modify their policy;

9. that every effort be made to bring the 700 million people of

China through the government in power, the People's Republic of China, into the world community of nations in order that they may assume their reasonable responsibility and avail themselves of legitimate opportunity to provide an essential ingredient for peace and security not only in South East Asia but throughout the entire world;

10. that another cease-fire be mutually and promptly agreed upon of sufficient duration to serve as a cooling-off period and as an opportunity for testing possibilities of negotiation, with a considerably enlarged unit of the International Control Commission (India, Canada, and Poland) to ensure that cease-fire commitments are honoured.[25]

The 1966 Geneva conference on Church and Society gave major attention to economic and social development, but it also dealt with disarmament and world order. This was not an official WCC Assembly but rather a study conference which made recommendations to the next Assembly. Besides dealing with problems of nonproliferation, nuclear-free zones, and other aspects of the nuclear arms race, it dealt also with conventional wars, pointing out that they carry the seeds of nuclear war. Furthermore, "even conventional war becomes genocide if its objective is not a just peace but the enemy's total destruction." Its statements on Vietnam were similar to those taken in the same year by the Central Committee. It also advocated the seating of the People's Republic of China in the United Nations. "Her isolation is a growing danger to world peace, and disarmament negotiations cannot be satisfactory without her participation." [26]

After the Geneva conference Paul Ramsey, an American theologian, wrote a critique of the meeting entitled *Who Speaks for the Church?* In it he argued that WCC meetings were departing from the pattern set at Oxford of providing middle axioms or general principles and theological perspectives and instead were advocating particular policies, thereby intervening in the area belonging to the magistrates. A church meeting is not competent in such a short meeting to develop sound policies on many subjects. Even though the conference leaders claimed that it was a study conference speaking to the churches and not for them, Ramsey felt that in practice it functioned as if it were speaking for the churches. He was particularly critical of the policies advocated in regard to the Vietnam war by the conference as well as by the earlier Central Committee meeting. Government policies such as bombing North Vietnam were often denounced, he said, without careful consideration of the alternatives.

Several writers responded to Ramsey's book, all welcoming the challenge he presented and agreeing with much of what he said. Their responses, however, suggested that Ramsey did not fully appreciate the difference between a study conference and an official conference; that he did not sufficiently recognize that there are times when the church needs to be specific, as, for example, when a Nazi state is destroying Jews; and that he erred in the opposite direction of the Geneva conference in that he was not being critical enough of U.S. policy in Southeast Asia.

The Middle East Demands Attention

The tensions in the Middle East were consistently a subject of concern for the CCIA. When the Six-Day War took place in 1967 with Israel emerging victorious over its neighbors, the ecumenical bodies threw their support behind the efforts for a peace settlement. The Central Committee of the WCC, meeting in August 1967 in Heraklion, Greece, issued a statement which said in part:

We do not consider it our task to enter into all the details of a political settlement. We do hold, however, that the following elements are essential to any peace founded upon justice and recognition of the equality of all peoples in the region.

(1) No nation should be allowed to keep or annex the territory of another by armed force. National boundaries should rest upon international agreements freely reached between or accepted by the people directly concerned.

(2) Effective international guarantees should be given for the political independence and territorial integrity of all nations in the area, including both Israel and the Arab nations.

(3) There can be neither reconciliation nor significant development in the area unless, in the general settlement, a proper and permanent solution is found to the problem of the Arab refugees, both old and new. We therefore urge:

That all persons who have been displaced in recent months should be permittted to exercise their right to return to their former places of residence. . . .[27]

The Uppsala Assembly of 1968 reaffirmed the statement made at Heraklion, adding several observations:

a) The independence and territorial integrity and security of all nations in the area must be guaranteed. Annexation by force must not be condoned.

b) The World Council of Churches must continue to join with all who search for a solution of the refugee and displaced person problems.

c) Full religious freedom and access to holy places must continue to be guaranteed to the communities of all three historic religions preferably by international agreement.

d) National armaments should be limited to the lowest level consistent with national security.

e) The great world powers must refrain from pursuing their own exclusive interests in the area.[28]

The 1968 Uppsala Assembly welcomed the nonproliferation treaty and urged all nations including China and France to sign it. Furthermore, it advocated the extension of the 1963 nuclear test ban treaty to include underground tests, and an agreement between the United States and the U.S.S.R. concerning the prevention of establishment of antiballistic missile systems. It also said: "The avoidance of atomic, biological or chemical war has become a condition of human survival. Such warfare is absolutely unjustifiable." Regarding nuclear warfare it stated further:

The churches must insist that it is the first duty of governments to prevent such a war: to halt the present arms race, agree never to initiate the use of nuclear weapons, stop experiments concerned with, and the production of weapons of mass human destruction by chemical and biological means and move away from the balance of terror towards disarmament.[29]

It also urged limitations in conventional wars:

Such limitation involves the attempt to preserve the social fabric of the enemy, to spare non-combatants, to lessen human suffering and to recognize that military force alone never ensures the emergence of a new order and may even prevent it. . . .

A special danger today is the encouragement of wars by proxy through the competitive delivery of armaments, so aggravating the dangers in many explosive situations.[30]

In the context of the deliberations on human rights the issue of selective conscientious objection was discussed, and the Assembly approved the idea of recognizing the right of a person to hold this position. This was a live issue in the United States, where many young men, while objecting to the Vietnam war, did not object to all wars and thus could not be classified as conscientious objectors. Advocates of selective conscientious objection in effect extended to individuals the right to use the just war theory as a guide for their personal decisions. Historically, it has been used primarily as a guide to nations. A precedent for this position had been set in a statement of the Oxford conference of 1937:

But if the state requires its citizens to participate in wars which cannot be thus justified, the advocates of the just war theory believe that Christians should refuse, for the state has no right to force its citizens to take part in sinful actions.[31]

The Assembly said:

Protection of conscience demands that the churches should give spiritual care and support not only to those serving in the armed forces but also those who, especially in the light of the nature of modern warfare, object to participation in particular wars they feel bound in conscience to oppose, or who find themselves unable to bear arms or to enter the military service of their nations for reasons of conscience. Such support should include pressure to have the law changed where this is required, and be extended to all in moral perplexity about scientific work on weapons of mass human destruction.[32]

The last sentence adds a significant new dimension. It voices objection not only to war but to work on war matériel.

Strong as the total statement is, the youth delegates at Uppsala found that it did not go far enough. They wanted the churches to commit themselves to calling on Christians personally to opt out of direct involvement in the process of manufacturing weapons of mass destruction and the system that threatens to use them.

The chairman of the meeting inquired whether this would mean that churches would excommunicate all members of the armed forces of the great powers. A sharp discussion ensued. The unrevised proposal as stated above won out over the youth proposal by a small majority, leaving many youth quite angry.

THE CHURCHES SUPPORT THE UNITED NATIONS

The Uppsala Assembly gave strong support to the United Nations, pointing out that

its future effectiveness in peace-keeping depends on the moral authority it can secure through unrelenting support of all men of goodwill in the implementation of its decisions, the financial resources provided by the member governments and also on the inclusion of all nations in its membership.[33]

It also endorsed the Geneva conference proposal for admittance of the People's Republic of China and adopted a resolution on Vietnam which reads in part:

A political solution, so urgently needed in Vietnam, cannot be achieved by military victory, but must in the final analysis be dependent upon the choice of the Vietnamese people themselves. The appalling situation of the Vietnamese people today offers an example of the tragedy to which unilateral intervention of a great power can lead. Moreover, such intervention creates rather than solves political, social and economic problems. The achievement and guarantee of peace should be the responsibility of international organizations. We therefore ask all governments to heed the bitter lessons of South-East Asia and to strengthen the United Nations both in its political authority and in its material strength.[34]

The Uppsala Assembly was as troubled about the Nigerian conflict as it was about the Vietnam war. Already more than 100,000 people had starved and the WCC was deeply involved in providing relief supplies. After considerable debate the

Assembly adopted a statement on the Nigerian conflict calling for an end to hostilities and resumption of negotiation.

At the Uppsala Assembly some changes were made in the Commission of the Churches on International Affairs and a new constitution for it was adopted. The changes were made partly as a result of criticism that had been made of the CCIA over the years, the major one being that it was too Western in its staff and orientation and that it did not give adequate attention to the Third World. The staff consisted of British, Swiss, and Americans. Thus the new constitution called for a more representative body. There had been other criticisms, too. There was the claim that the nonpacifist CCIA staff was not open to the pacifist witness. There was the charge that the staff tended to dominate and control the section on international affairs at Assembly meetings. While seeking to correct these and other limitations, the Assembly expressed deep appreciation for the work done by the CCIA over the years. Eugene Carson Blake, general secretary of the WCC, strongly supported the idea of increased Third World involvement in leadership. Subsequently, Leopoldo J. Niilus, a Lutheran lawyer from Argentina, was appointed as the new director.

Shortly after the Uppsala Assembly, Czechoslovakia was invaded by armies from the Soviet Union, East Germany, Poland, Hungary, and Bulgaria. The movement toward "socialism with a human face," carried out under the leadership of Alexander Dubcek, was ruthlessly crushed. The officers of the World Council of Churches immediately issued an appeal to the Soviet government to remove all its troops from Czechoslovakia and to renounce the use of force on its allies. The WCC officers also expressed their sympathy with the churches and people of Czechoslovakia and their support of the "peaceful resistance to the reimposition of spiritual, intellectual and social controls."

A very significant development in the late 1960's was the establishment of a joint working committee of the World Council of Churches and the Pontifical Commission on Justice and Peace. It was called the Committee on Society, Development, and Peace and came to be known by an acronym—SODEPAX. Since its formation in 1968 the new agency has held one conference on development and one on peace. The latter was held at Baden, Austria, in 1970. Eighty participants from thirty-nine countries explored many problems such as the question of violence and the responsible use of power, conscientious objection to military service, the morality of nuclear deterrence, disarmament, international agencies for peace, liberation movements among oppressed people.

In reading the report of this conference one can see that the participants were drawing upon two traditions of social teachings—that of the World Council of Churches and that of the papal encyclicals and the Second Vatican Council. Perhaps more important than what the group said was the fact that it was meeting and thereby opening up a new era of worldwide Christian cooperation in the pursuit of peace.

The part of the report dealing with world peace concludes with a section called "Vision of Peace," which begins:

> In trying to live their responsibility for peace, Christians respond to their concrete situations. Their concerns and their responses differ in emphasis. Yet within the world-wide Christian faith-community their different perspectives and experiences find mutual correction and enrichment. As Christians we are united in one vision of peace as it was given to men in Christ Jesus and united in the one prayer for the coming of His Kingdom of peace, justice and joy.[35]

SUMMARY

In looking back over the period from 1925 to the present, one finds that certain themes are constantly being expressed. War is consistently condemned as being contrary to God's will, and there is particularly strong condemnation of nuclear war, a type of war which could not possibly be a just war. At the same time it has been recognized that Christians may take different positions when a war does come and these positions merit respect. From 1937 onward the pacifist position has been recognized by nonpacifist Christians as a valid position. By

1968 the idea of selective conscientious objection was also recognized.

The dominant view of the churches, however, was along the lines of the traditional "just war" theory, and one can see its application in the positions taken by the WCC. For example, the denunciation of the bombing of centers of population was an application of the just war principle of regard for civilians. The condemnation of nuclear war applies the doctrine of proportionality, i.e., the idea that more good than harm should result if a war is to be justified. This is inconceivable in a nuclear war. The doctrine of proportionality was applied to the Vietnam war, with the conclusion that "the prospect of victory at the end of the conflict does not justify the inevitable cost."

Throughout the period ecumenical leaders have been concerned to eliminate the causes of war, also to develop preventive measures through the establishment of world order and international law. The churches supported both the League of Nations and the United Nations. The approach toward the second was more realistic and less utopian than the initial approach toward the first. Recognizing the limits of the United Nations, the WCC supported it, sought to improve it, interpreted its workings to the churches, and cooperated closely with it.

In the area of international relations, more than in other realms, the WCC was equipped to implement its pronouncements. The CCIA was an active agency implementing WCC teachings in its work with the United Nations, with governments, and with churches. Some of its most effective work was that of bringing together churchmen from the different countries that were involved in a conflict and equipping them to be informed reconcilers. The WCC has assumed that a world body of Christians has a distinctive contribution to make to world peace.

It has recognized that before the UN can become a truly effective international order there needs to be developed an international ethos. The WCC attempted to contribute toward the development of this ethos in several ways—through helping develop, interpret and implement the Universal Declaration of Human Rights, by providing through its own life and work a model of international cooperation, and by developing middle axioms regarding responsible behavior of nations in a responsible international society.

The WCC has been particularly active in the field of disarmament. It called for multilateral rather than unilateral disarmament. The rights of nations to protect themselves was recognized. Programs proposed allowed for protection while reducing the burden and the danger of armaments. Nevertheless, it should be said that nations were constantly being prodded to take risks for peace.

CORRELATION WITH ROMAN CATHOLIC SOCIAL THOUGHT

The Roman Catholic Church has held to the just war theory more consistently than most other churches. Rather than allowing for the three positions enunciated at Oxford, the Roman Catholic Church has, until recently, allowed for only one. Not until the close of the Second Vatican Council (1965) was conscientious objection recognized as a valid position. In general, countries with Catholic majorities do not yet allow for conscientious objection. Selective conscientious objection was approved by the National Conference of Catholic Bishops in the United States.

In the preparation of the encyclical *Pacem in Terris* issued by Pope John XXIII in 1963, Vatican leaders had at their disposal full documentation on the positions taken by the WCC and the CCIA. The views expressed by Pope John were very similar to those taken by the WCC in the previous decade. As the WCC documents had done earlier, *Pacem in Terris* called for steps for multilateral disarmament, for cessation of testing, for a ban on nuclear weapons, for support of the United Nations, for support of human rights, for colonial independence, for economic assistance, and for peaceful adjustment. For example, *Pacem in Terris* said:

Justice, then, right reason and humanity urgently demand that the arms race should cease. That the stockpiles which exist in various countries should be reduced equally and simultaneously by the parties concerned. That nuclear weapons should be banned. And that a general agreement should eventually be reached about progressive disarmament and an effective method of control.[36]

The Second Vatican Council in its Pastoral Constitution on the Church in the Modern World also expressed peace aims similar to those of the WCC. It said: "Any act of war aimed indiscriminately at the destruction of entire cities or of extensive areas along with their population is a crime against God and man himself. It merits unequivocal and unhesitating condemnation." [37]

So similar were the approaches of the WCC and the Vatican on issues of war and peace that it was possible in the late 1960's to form a joint agency, SODEPAX (Committee on Society, Development, and Peace), whereby Catholics, Protestants, and Orthodox could pursue peace together.

V

Communism

One of the greatest challenges Christianity has faced in modern history has been the confrontation with Communism. By the 1950's one third of the world's people lived under Communist rule. In one way or another the whole of mankind was affected by this dynamic ideological, economic, and political movement.

Naturally such a phenomenon had great implications for the ecumenical movement. It was getting started at about the same time that the Russian revolution brought Communism into power in a national state for the first time.

The Life and Work movement in the time of preparation for Stockholm (1925) did not dig very deeply into the issues raised by Russian Communism. It was not equipped at that time for a very thorough study. A deep concern of the ecumenical movement in the early 1920's was religious liberty, and there were a number of protests by churches in the West against the persecution of Christians by the Bolsheviks. Refugees from Russia brought to western Europe grim accounts of their experiences.

Discussions and addresses at Stockholm did deal to some extent with Communism. Since many were critical of capitalism at that time, they were hesitant to make total condemnations of the Russian system. Rather, they distinguished the humanitarian elements from the revolutionary, atheistic, and materialistic elements and, in the then-current spirit of optimism, expressed hope that the negative elements could be overcome. Some felt that the churches themselves were partly responsible for the coming into being of the negative elements. An American leader at Stockholm, Worth M. Tippy, asserted that if the churches had identified with and supported the poor rather than the rich, then such a specter as atheistic Communism would not have arisen. Had Communism arisen, it would have been Christian rather than atheistic.[1]

This view was, no doubt, based on historical observation. Karl Marx lived in Europe, and his view that religion was an opiate of the people and that it was being used by the privileged in their exploitation of the workers was based on observation of what was happening in France, Germany, and England. The working classes had been largely alienated from the church because of its conservative social stand, and it was among them that Communism was making inroads.

While the early Life and Work leaders tended to take a fairly optimistic view of Communism, the International Missionary Council was expressing a more pessimistic view, bearing some resemblance to the views of Russian emigrants. In the IMC's Jerusalem meeting of 1928, secularism was pictured as the real enemy of Christianity, and Communism was listed as one of the forms of secularism that was serving as a substitute for Christianity.

In none of the ecumenical statements did the churches declare a crusade against Communism. There were protests against religious persecution in Russia, but there were no official pronouncements in the 1920's on the social order in Russia. There was no felt need for an intensive study of it. It was widely held that the European forms of socialism were wiser corrections and developments of Marxism than the Leninist form, and that there was value in working with democratic socialist movements.

While the ecumenical movement did not engage in intensive studies of Marxism in the 1920's, it was spurred to do so in the 1930's. One factor was the worldwide economic crisis and the other was the rise of national socialism. The economic crisis sharpened the critique of capitalism and encouraged many to look at the positive social elements of Communism. The conflict with national socialism, which was the central problem for the ecumenical movement in the 1930's, stirred ecumenical leaders into a deeper examination of totalitarianism, not only of the fascist kind but of the Communist kind as well.

In the early 1930's, with new outbreaks of religious persecution in Russia, churches in the West again raised their protests. The World Alliance for Promoting International Friendship Through the Churches gave particular attention to the problem of religious liberty in Russia. In the late 1930's a group jointly sponsored by the World Alliance and the Universal Christian Council for Life and Work sought to travel to Russia to discuss the problem of religious liberty with government leaders, but all efforts along this line were rejected by the Soviet leaders.

In the period between Stockholm (1925) and Oxford (1937), the Universal Christian Council for Life and Work did have an opportunity to do deeper studies of Marxism. Among the contributors to the discussion were Russian Orthodox intellectual emigrants such as Berdyaev, Bulgakov, and Alexeiev, who had set up the St. Sergius Institute in Paris. In France there were now a million Russian Orthodox exiles. Some of the findings of these scholars appeared in the pre-Oxford-conference studies.

Nikolai N. Alexeiev, whose education was in the field of law, was a professor in the Sorbonne in Paris. His writings on Marxism explored particularly Marxist anthropology. He saw Marxist thought as a secular expression of the doctrine of the Kingdom of God. In the Marxist view salvation comes through a this-worldly social revolution. Man has no value in himself, only through a future order. Thus there is freedom to use any means on the way to that order. Marxist humanism seeks to deify man through man. Marxism has its roots in Western Christian humanism, whose activism was lost within Christianity but was now appearing in the titanic spirit of Marxism. The earlier teachings of Marx are not so much in conflict with Christian views as are the later dogmatic developments of Marxism. On this point one can see a similarity between Alexeiev's efforts to distinguish positive and negative elements in Marxism and the parallel efforts of a number of ecumenical leaders. Alexeiev was critical of the "complete absorption of the individual personality by the community." [2] Here is a point where the thought of ecumenical leaders at this time was particularly close to his.

Churchmen Oppose Totalitarianism

J. H. Oldham of England, a leader in the preparation for the Oxford conference and also for years a leader in the International Missionary Council, began in 1934 to use the term "totalitarianism," and from that time onward it was used extensively in the ecumenical movement to describe both fascist and Communist states. Actually the term was being used primarily against Hitler's national socialism and secondarily against the Bolsheviks. In the 1930's national socialism seemed to be a more immediate threat than Communism, which at that time seemed to be restricted to current boundaries.

Drawing upon the studies being done in preparation for Oxford, J. H. Oldham wrote the following in 1935:

The totalitarian state is a state which lays claim to man in the totality of his being; which declares its own authority to be the source of all authority; which refuses to recognize the independence in their own sphere of religion, culture, education and the family; which seeks to impose on all its citizens a particular philosophy of life; and which sets out to create by means of all the agencies of public information and education a particular type of man in accordance with its own understanding of the meaning and end of man's existence. A state which advances such claims declares itself to be not only a state but also a Church. . . .

In the Soviet Union the totalitarian claim is pushed to the extreme limit. The aim of Communism is to establish an integral culture on the basis of an integral philosophy of life. No quarter must be given to religion. . . .

The deeper meaning of totalitarian claims will be missed if they fail to open our eyes to a state of things which is found in every country. The life and death struggle of the Christian Church is not with the state as such but with modern paganism. When the state adopts a pagan philosophy of life and seeks to impose its principles and standards on the whole community, the struggle becomes acute. But the conflict is none the less real when the general mind of the community becomes paganized, even though the state may remain politically neutral. What is common to the whole world is a far-reaching secularization of thought and life.[3]

Here is clearly a continuing influence of the Jerusalem meeting, which saw secularism as a basic problem of modern man. Communism is one form of secularism, but there are many others. However, this becomes vicious in that it is being imposed by a powerful state.

The Oxford conference, as was noted in an earlier chapter, had much to say about capitalism, its strengths and its weaknesses—with considerable emphasis on the current weaknesses —and it saw the rise of socialism and Communism as a direct result of the failure of capitalism. It pointed out that the hostility against religion can be directly traced to the church's failure to care about the plight of the poor.

Facing this situation, the Christian churches must first of all acknowledge and repent for their blindness to the actual situation; for this blindness is partly responsible for such hostility as exists between themselves and the radical movements which aim at social justice. The churches must not regard an attack directed against themselves as an attack directed against God. They must acknowledge that God has spoken to their conscience through these movements, by revealing through them the real situation of millions of their members. On the other hand, the churches must continue resolutely to reject those elements in the actual development of Communism which conflict with the Christian truth: the *utopianism* which looks for the fulfillment of human existence through the natural process of history, and which presupposes that the improvement of social institutions will automatically produce improvement in human personalities; the *materialism* which derives all moral and spiritual values from economic needs and economic conditions, and deprives the personal and cultural life of its creative freedom; and finally, the *disregard for the dignity of the individual* in which communism may differ theoretically, but does not differ practically, from other contemporary totalitarian movements.[4]

THE SPIRIT OF PENITENCE

Here are themes that were often heard in subsequent ecumenical statements—the need to confront the challenge of Communism with a spirit of penitence, inasmuch as the failures of the church helped bring it about, and the need to separate the negative from the positive elements in Communism and to oppose the negative elements.

Among the Americans who helped formulate this statement at Oxford were Reinhold Niebuhr and John C. Bennett. Niebuhr had been criticizing capitalism for its basic errors, such as the idea of the harmony of interests, inequality, etc., but had become very critical of the social gospel for its sentimental or utopian approach to the problem. His realism was influenced by Marxism, which assumed that economic privileges would not be willingly given up by those who had them. They would have to be taken away through coercion. But he was, nevertheless, critical of Marxist failings in assuming that the proletariat would use their power responsibly after the revolution, that is, for assuming that evil could be removed by removing a capitalist environment. Later he referred to the social gospelers as "soft utopians" and to Communists as "hard utopians." At the time of the Oxford conference Reinhold Niebuhr was a Christian socialist.

The International Missionary Council meeting held in December 1938 in Tambaram (near Madras, India) pursued further some of the themes of the 1928 meeting in Jerusalem. Speaking on Communism, it said:

Communism is also a powerful force in many parts of the world. It appeals to youth because it challenges existing evils, offers a clear-cut programme of action, and attempts to provide a scientific analysis of economic and political situations.

Communism as an economic program should be distinguished from Communism as a philosophy. In its concern for the under-privileged, in its demand for a more equitable distribution of wealth and opportunity, in its insistence upon racial equality, it has points of contact with the social message of Christianity. Its capacity for eliciting sacrifice calls Christians to penitence for their lethargy, and its emergence is a rebuke to the church for entanglement in the evils of an unjust society and acquiescence in the status quo.[5]

The statement then listed the same negative elements which had been given at Oxford.

During World War II, church groups in several lands were engaged in studies of peace aims. W. A. Visser 't Hooft of the Netherlands, general secretary of the World Council of Churches in Process of Formation, kept these groups informed about each other's work. The American conference in Delaware, Ohio, dealing with "A Just and Durable Peace," sponsored by the Federal Council of Churches and headed by John Foster Dulles, envisioned a world federation with executive, legislative, and judicial branches, and with a world police force. It presupposed that the world would be dominated by democracies. This world federation seemed quite unrealistic to the Europeans. As Dr. Visser 't Hooft pointed out, it could not work without the foundation of an international ethos that did not then exist.

PROBLEMS OF POSTWAR COOPERATION

Constantly the issue was raised concerning the possibility of democratic countries working together with Communist Russia. It wasn't clear whether the existing Russian politics was the traditional Russian imperialism in a Communist form or if it was the promotion of world revolution with Russia at the center.

One of the most realistic observers was Visser 't Hooft. He observed that the war with Finland and the pressure on the Baltic states made it clear that Russia had not given up world revolution. Other observers, particularly in England and America, considered the expansion into Europe to be motivated by concern for security rather than by desire for world revolution. In 1944 Visser 't Hooft told an English peace-aims group that he anticipated a divided Europe with Russia controlling the eastern countries, which would be satellites—half independent and half slaves. The decisive danger of the Soviet Union, he said, was that its national policy consisted of a mixture of nationalism and Communism. He foresaw a divided Europe, not a European federation. He also foresaw great dangers for countries then under Nazi totalitarianism. Once conquered they would be easy prey for a new form of totalitarianism.[6]

Some ecumenical leaders considered the possibility that Communism might change and that the humanitarian elements might come to the fore. They saw a difference between national socialism and Communism in that the former did not contain humanitarian elements while the latter did. Reinhold Niebuhr called Communism a Christian heresy in contrast with national socialism, which he called an anti-Christian heathenism. Communism did not believe in racial superiority, and, theoretically at least, did not believe in political power as such but expected the state to wither away. Therefore, despite its brutality, it did not fall into complete cynicism.

Some were optimistic about the decline of religious persecution in Russia and hoped that the church would be free to be the church in the full sense in the postwar period. But again there was a negative side to this. Perhaps the church was now being persecuted less because it was perceived as a useful instrument of the government. The church had helped to inspire the resistance of Russians against the Nazis. Thus it was potentially useful to the state. This also raised the question of what would happen if a politically controlled church would join the World Council of Churches.

The end of World War II found the churches facing a different international situation. The fascist totalitarian powers had been defeated by a joint effort of the Western democracies and the Communist totalitarian powers. During the war there had been movements for friendship between Russia and the Western nations.

After the war Communism was no longer the official philosophy of one state. It was now forcibly brought into control in several eastern European countries including the eastern half of Germany, the part in which Protestantism was the strongest. Now the cities in which Luther lived and taught were in Communist hands. Berlin, an island in the east zone, occupied by four powers, was a constant source of conflict.

The East-West alliance rapidly faded. In 1946 Winston Churchill gave a famous speech using for the first time the term "iron curtain." A cold war had begun.

THEOLOGIANS DIFFER ON COMMUNISM

Between 1946 and 1948 the preparatory studies for Amsterdam took place, and one of the issues was the problem of Communism. Theologians differed in their approaches. For example, in Switzerland Emil Brunner took a very strong stand against Communism because of its violation of basic human rights. Karl Barth, who had been influential in the Confessing Church's resistance to Hitler, took a neutral stand. He viewed the East-West conflict as a conflict of great powers for influence in the world and one which the church should transcend. He was concerned about helping the churches under Communism find a basis for action. It meant repentance for failures that had led to the present situation, and it meant working within Communist societies to bring the redemptive power of Christianity to bear upon that culture. In working for social justice, the churches, he felt, should not be tools of Communist governments and they should not be tools of Western anti-Communist crusades.

Before the Amsterdam Assembly the International Missionary Council held its meeting in Whitby, Ontario, Canada. It linked its protest against Communism with a protest against religious totalitarian systems. In effect, it was saying that some Catholic countries and some Moslem countries belonged in the same category as Communist countries in that they all denied religious liberty.[7]

One half year before the 1948 Amsterdam Assembly, Czechoslovakia was taken over by the Communists. In the same year

Berlin was blockaded by the Russians, and the Allies responded with an airlift. The Russian Orthodox Church, rejecting the WCC invitation to join, accused the WCC of being allied to Western imperialism, and some of the Orthodox churches of eastern Europe followed suit.

THE CHURCH TRANSCENDS THE IRON CURTAIN

The World Council of Churches sought to be a universal body transcending political divisions without compromising in any way its prophetic message. This was a difficult task. To dramatize the desire for universality, one Christian leader from the West, and one from the East, was selected for the part of the program dealing with international affairs. The leaders selected were John Foster Dulles, prominent Presbyterian layman and statesman from the United States, and Josef Hromádka, prominent theologian from Prague, Czechoslovakia. Hromádka was a refugee from Nazism who had taught at Princeton Theological Seminary, Princeton, New Jersey, during World War II but who had returned to his homeland after the war. When his country became Communist in February 1948 he chose to stay and bring Christian influence on the nation from within. His outlook bore some similarity to that of Karl Barth, but he was much more positive toward the new order in the East. Both Dulles and Hromádka had also written papers for the preparatory material for Amsterdam.

In his paper, Dulles stressed the idea of a God-given moral law that taught the value of a free society and respect for persons. Communism, he said, is a materialistic philosophy that rejects the universal moral law, using any means to achieve its ends. Western nations must not accept the inevitability of war but must work instead through peaceful competition in extending the free society.

Dr. Hromádka commented on the crisis of Western civilization. Western nations won World War I but lost the peace. They do not live by their ideals but seek to perpetuate their privileges. Now a world revolution is taking place. A sterile anti-Communism is of no avail. The West needs to recover its own ideals and to contribute from its heritage to the world revolution for social justice. Hromádka distinguished between Communism and the Soviet system, claiming that the second could exist without the first. He did not deny the authoritarianism of the Soviet system; he tried to explain it in the light of Russian history. He also expressed the hope that the system might change as Russians draw on their own great literary and Christian heritage.

The assembly addresses of Dulles and Hromádka followed essentially the same themes as their preparatory papers. Something like a middle position between the two was taken by Reinhold Niebuhr of Union Theological Seminary in New York. Unlike Dulles, Niebuhr admitted the validity of much of Hromádka's indictment of Western civilization. But he insisted that the Communist alternative to the "liberal world" is unacceptable because it promises personal and social redemption through the destruction of the capitalist social institutions instead of through "the perpetual dying to self of the Christian gospel."

In the section dealing with social questions, an attempt was made to transcend the world conflict by denouncing both laissez-faire capitalism and Communism. The responsible society would have the marks of neither. The report stated:

The Christian churches should reject the ideologies of both communism and laissez-faire capitalism, and should seek to draw men away from the false assumption that these extremes are the only alternatives. Each has made promises which it could not redeem. Communist ideology puts the emphasis upon economic justice, and promises that freedom will come automatically after the completion of the revolution. Capitalism puts the emphasis on freedom, and promises that justice will follow as a by-product of free enterprise; that, too, is an ideology which has been proved false. It is the responsibility of Christians to seek new, creative solutions which never allow either justice or freedom to destroy the other.[8]

The statement aroused a great deal of objection both in the West and in the East. In the West, many churchmen were angry to see capitalism denounced in the same sentence with Communism. They pointed out that the limitations of capitalism came nowhere close to the brutalities of a police state. In the East the statement attacking Communism was used to substantiate the view that the World Council was under the control of the imperialistic West.

POINTS OF CHRISTIAN-COMMUNIST CONFLICT

The section on social questions at Amsterdam in 1948 recognized, as had the conference at Oxford in 1937, that the rise of Communism was related to failures in the industrial society.

Christians who are beneficiaries of capitalism should try to see the world as it appears to many who know themselves excluded from its privileges and who see in communism a means of deliverance from poverty and insecurity. All should understand that the proclamation of racial equality by communists and their support of the cause of colonial peoples makes a strong appeal to the populations of Asia and Africa and to racial minorities elsewhere. . . .

Christians should recognize with contrition that many churches are involved in the forms of economic injustice and racial discrimination which have created the conditions favourable to the growth of communism, and that the atheism and anti-religious teaching of communism are in part a reaction to the chequered record of a professedly Christian society. It is one of the most fateful facts in modern history that often the working classes, including tenant farmers, came to believe that the churches were against them or indifferent to their plight. Christians should realize that the Church has often failed to offer to its youth the appeal that can evoke a disciplined, purposeful and sacrificial response, and that in this respect communism has for many filled a moral and psychological vacuum.

Much like Oxford, Amsterdam listed the points of conflict between Christianity and Communism, except that now there were five points instead of three:

The points of conflict between Christianity and the atheistic Marxism-Communism of our day are as follows: (1) the communist promise of what amounts to a complete redemption of man in history; (2) the belief that a particular class by virtue of its role as the bearer of a new order is free from the sins and ambiguities that

Christians believe to be characteristic of all human existence; (3) the materialistic and deterministic teachings, however they may be qualified, that are incompatible with belief in God and with the Christian view of man as a person made in God's image and responsible to him; (4) the ruthless methods of communists in dealing with their opponents; (5) the demand of the party on its members for an exclusive and unqualified loyalty which belongs only to God, and the coercive policies of communist dictatorship in controlling every aspect of life.[9]

The pronouncements of Amsterdam did not deal with the possibility of Communism's blending with national traditions in order to provide a new social order for Asian or African countries, nor did it deal with Hromádka's idea of the possibility of positive changes within the Soviet system.

The section on International Affairs also had something to say about the East-West conflict. The following paragraph is indicative of its approach:

The greatest threat to peace today comes from the division of the world into mutually suspicious and antagonistic blocs. This threat is all the greater because national tensions are confused by the clash of economic and political systems. Christianity cannot be equated with any of these. There are elements in all systems which we must condemn when they contravene the First Commandment, infringe basic human rights, and contain a potential threat to peace. We denounce all forms of tyranny, economic, political or religious, which deny liberty to men. We utterly oppose totalitarianism, whenever found, in which a state arrogates to itself the right of determining men's thoughts and actions instead of recognizing the right of each individual to do God's will according to his conscience. In the same way we oppose any church which seeks to use the power of the state to enforce religious conformity. We resist all endeavors to spread a system of thought or of economics by unscrupulous intolerance, suppression or persecution. . . .

A positive attempt must be made to ensure that competing economic systems such as communism, socialism or free enterprise may co-exist without leading to war.[10]

At the time of the Amsterdam conference the churches of eastern Europe were seeking an appropriate stance toward a Communist society, and leaders like Hromádka were instrumental in finding it. Essentially it included these elements: cooperating in the social progress of the nation, avoiding any synthesis between Marxist ideology and Christian theology, and rejecting atheistic materialism. This detached cooperation was given in the hope that the system would change in the future and allow a fuller Christian activity.

The presence of Christians from Communist countries in the World Council of Churches provided fuel for the fire of those who made attacks upon the Council. One of the most vocal critics was Carl McIntire, a minister of the Bible Presbyterian Church in Collingswood, New Jersey. Removed from the ministry of the Presbyterian Church in the U.S.A., McIntire in 1941 organized the American Council of Christian Churches, which devoted much time to attacking the Federal (and later, the National) Council of Churches. Though representing not more than a million members, McIntire was given a hearing on hundreds of radio stations.

When the Amsterdam Assembly met, McIntire organized the International Council of Christian Churches with the express purpose of fighting the WCC. The "International Call" that he issued pictured the harm the ecumenical movement would do "in misleading the nations, in opposing the pure gospel, in closing doors to faithful missions, and in advancing socialism and political intrigue with the state." Although the Call went to many people in many lands, only fifty persons participated in the organizing meeting in Amsterdam, which was planned to coincide with the WCC assembly. Nevertheless, McIntire was given much attention by the press. In subsequent ecumenical conferences, he was frequently present, holding press conferences and attacking the radicalism of the WCC. Essentially, he identified Christianity with the American Way of Life, and concluded that any body which criticized any American policy was unchristian.

Conflict Over Religious Liberty

At Amsterdam an important resolution on religious liberty was adopted. Its essence was incorporated later in the same year in the Universal Declaration of Human Rights. Not long after Amsterdam the WCC came into conflict with Communist countries over the issue of religious liberty. Both the WCC and the Lutheran World Federation protested the arrest of some eastern European churchmen, notably the arrest of Lutheran Bishop Lajos Ordass in Hungary.

The Central Committee of the WCC, meeting in 1949, issued a strong attack on totalitarianism, which included these words:

> The totalitarian doctrine is a false doctrine. It teaches that in order to gain a social or political end everything is permitted. It maintains the complete self-sufficiency of man. It sets political power in the place of God. It moulds the minds of the young in a pattern opposed to the message of the Gospel. It sanctions the use of all means to overthrow all other views and ways of life.
>
> We call statesmen and all men who in every nation seek social justice to consider this truth: a peaceful and stable order can only be built upon foundations of righteousness, of right relations between man and God and between man and man. Only the recognition that man has ends and loyalties beyond the State will ensure true justice to the human person. Religious freedom is the condition and guardian of all true freedom.[11]

There was real anxiety among ecumenical leaders in regard to religious freedom in Communist countries. They felt that the church was being used by Communist governments for its own ends, and that religion was being forced to function as a spiritual aroma rather than as the salt of the earth. Only one person from eastern Europe was present at this Central Committee meeting—Josef Hromádka. He expressed the view that the committee was missing the key issue by concentrating on religious liberty and by comparing eastern European countries with western democracies on this one issue. He insisted that there was still some degree of religious freedom in eastern Europe. The real problem for the Christians in eastern Europe was that they were too bound to traditional ways and systems to proclaim the Word of God in the new social situation.

It should be added that despite such strong protests against violations of human rights the WCC, unlike the Vatican, did not give support to political opposition in eastern European churches. It did not join the Vatican in protesting Cardinal Mindszenty's arrest, nor did it protest the arrest of some Bulgarian ministers whose political activity was supported by American funds. Visser 't Hooft saw Mindszenty as a monarchist, and the Bulgarian ministers obviously did have some political connections with the West. The WCC did not wish to be an arm of Western political systems.

China Becomes Communist

In 1949 a conference jointly sponsored by the WCC and the IMC met in Bangkok to consider the social witness in Asia. The challenge of Communism was very real in the light of the Communist victory in China. The conference recognized the revolutionary ferments in Asia and challenged the Christians to work for righteousness.

In considering Communism, the Christian must distinguish between the social revolution which seeks justice and the totalitarian ideology which interprets and perverts it. . . .

Regarding the situation in China, the conference said:

The political situation vis-à-vis Communism varies widely in different countries. The revolution in China, though led by Communists, may not yet have manifested fully the evil consequences of the moral relativism integral to Communism; and the churches' witness in China may be specifically to provide a moral and religious foundation for the new sense of social freedom and economic justice among the people.[12]

The World Council tried to transcend the East-West conflict, but the task was rendered almost impossible by several problems, especially the problem of the Korean war. As was pointed out in the preceding chapter, the WCC Central Committee endorsed the United Nations' action in that war. The reverberations of this action were very great in China and in eastern Europe. T. C. Chao, who had represented Chinese Christians in the ecumenical movement since 1928, resigned as one of the World Council presidents. Strong protests came from Hungary and Czechoslovakia. Bishop Albert Bereczky of the Reformed Church in Hungary resigned as a member of the Commission of the Churches on International Affairs and asked to be counted as just an observer, no longer as a member of the Central Committee.

The representatives from the Communist nations charged that the World Council of Churches had given up its position of transcending all political systems and was identifying with one side. Visser 't Hooft answered the charges by pointing out that the freedom of the churches to judge all systems does not impose on them the obligation to remain neutral, but rather the obligation to condemn injustice wherever it is found. By supporting the United Nations, the WCC was supporting the only instrument capable of bringing about international order. Hromádka responded that the UN is also an instrument of power politics, and, in this case, of the West.

Another difficulty appeared in the early 1950's when the WCC was asked to participate in the World Peace Conference, and to join in the Stockholm Appeal for Peace to all nations. The WCC discerned that the conference was Communist-controlled and did not participate. The Eastern European churches did, and so did the Russian Orthodox Church, which at that time was not yet a member of the WCC. Some resentment was expressed in the East about the nonparticipation of the WCC. Tension over this point may have been a factor in the further postponement of Russian Orthodox participation in the WCC. It was at about this time that some efforts were being made to involve the Russian Orthodox Church in the ecumenical movement. Martin Niemöller of Germany, a member of the WCC Executive Committee, visited Patriarch Alexei in Moscow in the winter of 1951–52. Upon his return he observed that the Russian Orthodox Church was not a free church but a tool used for propaganda purposes, especially for the peace movement, but that it was nevertheless a Christian community with a rich spiritual life and a secret desire to come to an understanding with the ecumenical movement. Thus the WCC continued its efforts to keep in touch with the Orthodox Church in Russia.

In the 1950's the younger nations came increasingly to the fore. The Lucknow conference in 1952 was an Asian preparation for the Evanston Assembly. The conference was enriched by the presence of a number of members of the Central Committee of the WCC, whose meeting followed the study conference. It met at a time when the United States was in the throes of "McCarthyism," and the government's policies were characterized by anti-Communism rather than by positive approaches to world problems. This was a hysterical reaction to the loss of China to Communism, the frustrations of the Korean war, and the presumed evidence of Communist infiltration of the U.S. Government. The world situation was reflected in the Lucknow statement:

The present world struggle with its hot and cold wars militates against progress in social reconstruction. We cite the following as evidences of this in East Asia:

(1) When American foreign policy is determined by the criterion of anti-Communism it generally strengthens conservative and reactionary political groups in the East Asia scene and tends to weaken the forces of healthy social reform. This line is bound to be self-defeating because in the final analysis social and spiritual health is the best answer to Communism.

(2) Large scale rearmament reduces the capacity of the more developed countries to help the underdeveloped economies of East Asia. At the same time world tension forces the countries of East Asia to spend a disproportionate amount of their budget for defense and thus reduces the sources available for social development.

(3) The relatively large emphasis upon military power to defeat Communism, which is one of the important results of increasing international tension, involves in itself a threat to movements of national freedom and social justice. Military power has value mainly as a means of giving nations time to achieve positive democratic and responsible social change. This, however, tends to be overlooked in the increasing tensions of the world situation.[13]

COMMUNISM RELATES TO NATIONAL LIBERATION

The report noted the failure of the colonial powers to recognize that legitimate unmet aspirations of a nation can drive it into the Communist fold. Regarding developments in Malaya and Indochina, the Lucknow conference had something to say which had an important bearing on current and later wars fought in that part of the world.

The peril of the present military situations in Malaya and Indochina is that on the one hand defense against Communism might become a means of suppressing the movement of national liberation and social justice in the country, and on the other hand the national liberation movements are in danger of being exploited by world Communism and abusive tyrannies. However, in any final appraisal it is necessary to make an assessment as to how far this peril has been overcome in these situations by a conscious attempt to meet legitimate national and social aspirations and thus secure the cooperation of progressive-minded people in the military action.[14]

At Evanston in 1954 the Chinese churches were not represented. There were delegations from East Germany, Czechoslovakia, Yugoslavia, and Hungary. Some American groups, including the American Legion, objected to the entry of churchmen from Communist countries into the United States. Suspicions were cast by the press concerning one Hungarian delegate, Bishop Janos Peter, who was rumored to be a member of the secret police. There may have been cause for suspicion in this one case. Several years later, after the suppression of the 1956 Hungarian revolution, Peter left his church post to become the Hungarian foreign minister. At Evanston, Josef Hromádka of Czechoslovakia made an important contribution, as he had done at Amsterdam.

Among the speakers were two German churchmen who had had direct experience with Communism. One was Bishop Otto Dibelius, a president-elect of the WCC. As bishop of the Evangelical Union Church of Berlin-Brandenburg, he had a jurisdiction over territory three fourths of which lay in East Germany. He had been active in the Confessing Church in its resistance to Hitler, and now actively opposed the police state methods in East Germany. Yet he sought to guide the church in such a way that it would transcend political lines and avoid identification with the ideology of East or West.

H. G. Jacobs, an East German church leader, spoke on the possibilities for Christian witness in East Germany. He gave a vivid picture of the governmental pressures to bring into line with Communist dogma all of society—schools, youth activities, professional life, etc. Yet, he said, there are times when the state postpones a goal for tactical reasons, and the church then has an increased opportunity.

The section dealing with "The Responsible Society in a World Perspective" devoted part of its report to "The Church in Relation to Communist–non-Communist Tensions." It reaffirmed those statements of Oxford and Amsterdam that outlined points of conflict between Christianity and Communism, also the assessment that the rise of Communism is a judgment on modern societies for their social failures. It reflected the concerns expressed at Bangkok about the dangers of ignoring the existing social revolution on the one hand, and of allowing the Communists to pervert it on the other. It warned against the completely negative approach to Communism that was present in some democratic societies to the extent that civil liberties were endangered. It also warned against too great a dependence on the military defense against Communism. It recognized the difficulty of realizing a responsible society in a Communist land, but pointed out that the churches nevertheless bear responsibility for speaking the Word of God and witnessing to his power.

In view of the differences in the societies in East and West it seemed appropriate to address one set of questions to Christians in Communist lands and another set to Christians in non-Communist lands.

Here are two of the seven sets of questions that Christians in Communist countries were asked to consider:

What are the ways and what is the content of Christian witness in the face of atheistic ideologies?

At what points can the church and Christians cooperate with government in their plans for social reconstruction? What are the limits of this cooperation? How does Christian social responsibility avoid both surrender to Communism and the temptations of a negative resistance?

Here are two of the questions addressed to Christians in non-Communist lands:

Does secularism in the noncommunist world differ from the materialism in the communist world?

How far are the churches in noncommunist lands genuinely prophetic in their relation to society and the state? [15]

The international affairs section at Evanston also dealt with the East-West conflict as it discussed "Living Together in a Divided World." It avoided the use of the term "coexistence," since this was a political term with particular connotations. It laid down some of the conditions of "living together," such as seeking social justice, avoiding war, respecting the pledged word, pursuing disarmament, submitting disputes to international bodies. As was noted in an earlier chapter, the Evanston Assembly took a strong stand on nuclear weapons, calling upon nations to pledge to refrain from their use. It also opposed mass destruction of civilians and advocated step by step progress toward disarmament, with controls, that would ultimately eliminate nuclear weapons. This statement of Evanston had its effect upon the Russian Orthodox Church and facilitated its entry into the World Council of Churches seven years later.

THE WCC MEETS IN HUNGARY

In 1956 the World Council of Churches held its first meeting in a Communist country. It was a meeting of the Central Committee. Visser 't Hooft explained the attitude of the committee in coming to Hungary:

By accepting the invitation, the World Council showed once again that it lives its own life in complete independence from any particular political or economic system or ideology, and desires to render its witness in all parts of the world, wherever it can get a chance to do so.[16]

Delegates from Rumania who had not been permitted by their government to attend the assemblies in Amsterdam and Evanston were allowed to come to this meeting. But there was also great joy because of the presence of Bishop K. H. Ting of China. The absence of the Chinese delegates from the World Council of Churches ever since the Korean war had been a source of regret for ecumenical leaders. At the Tambaram conference of 1938 the Chinese delegation had been one of the strongest. Ever since the Chinese walk-out, there were constant efforts to renew contacts. Things looked hopeful in the mid-1950's when Rajah B. Manikam, a WCC representative in Asia, was allowed to visit China, and now Bishop Ting was present at the Central Committee meeting. He was invited to speak to the committee.

It was no secret, he said, that the Chinese churches had been dissatisfied with certain positions taken by the World Council in the last few years, and that this fact accounted for the tension existing between the Chinese churches and the World Council of Churches. He expressed hope for a normalization in the relationship. Christians in China, he said, did not pretend to agree with the Communist views on matters of faith, but appreciated the many important reforms that the People's Government was bringing about. The experience of liberation was, in his view, a turning point in Chinese history. He set the numerical strength of non-Roman Christians in China at somewhere between 700,000 and one million.

The Central Committee expressed hope that a WCC delegation would be able to visit China in the near future. The Committee minutes read: "The Central Committee expresses the additional hope that such a deepened fellowship will aid in the building of a peaceful world of freedom, truth and justice for all people." Yet no opportunities for official contacts emerged, despite the fact that the Commission of the Churches on International Affairs was engaged in exploring the possibilities of Red China's acceptance into the United Nations.

The official statement of the Central Committee contained a rather strong paragraph about freedom:

People must be free to travel, to meet and to know their neighbors, through personal encounter to seek understanding and create friendship, and thus to achieve mutual confidence and respect. They must also be free to choose by whom and in what way they wish to be governed. They must be free to obey the dictates of their consciences. They must be free to worship God, to witness to their faith and to have their children educated in it in church, school, or youth meeting.[17]

Only two months after the conclusion of the conference, the Hungarian revolution took place. For a short time some of the freedoms which had been lost were restored. Most church leaders were removed from office and replaced by others not tainted by collaboration with the Communists. The Russian occupation which followed the revolution returned things to their previous status. Again the church leaders were changed, and again only men favored by the government were put in leadership positions.

Some Communists accused the World Council of Churches of fostering this revolution, a charge which was hard to substantiate. The revolution had its own initiative and momentum.

The response of the WCC officers to the crushing of the revolution was as follows:

Christians throughout the world are profoundly shocked and sorrowstricken at the tragic reversal suffered by the Hungarian people, who had clearly asserted their desire for freedom and independence in national and church life. . . . Fear and suspicion cannot be replaced by respect and trust unless powerful nations remove the yoke which now prevents other nations and peoples from freely determining their own government and form of society.[18]

After the repression of the Hungarian revolution, the WCC became involved, as it had many times before, in helping refugees from Communism to find new homes in other parts of the world.

CHRISTIAN PEACE CONFERENCE FORMS

In the late 1950's an organization known as the Christian Peace Conference came into being in eastern Europe. Centered in Prague, it brought together churchmen from eastern Europe and other parts of the world for the purpose of discussing theological and social issues. Approved by eastern European governments, it gave churchmen an opportunity to have fellowship with each other under the banner of peace. One of the reasons for its establishment was the conviction of some eastern Europeans that the WCC was dominated by Westerners and Western views, and that an Eastern-oriented Christian peace movement was needed. There was no official connection between this organization and the WCC, though there were some individuals, such as Dr. Hromádka, who were active in both. The very existence of such a group suggests the difficulty that the Christian world faced in transcending the barrier of the Iron Curtain and the ideological conflict between East and West.

The New Delhi Assembly of 1961 called for flexibility in seeking the kind of state that would meet the needs of a particular nation. But it also had warnings about states that violate human rights.

In keeping with the Evanston emphasis on "living together," the New Delhi Assembly urged churches to contribute to the deflation of suspicion. Viewing the divided world, it said:

Do official ideologies really determine national policies? Does any action really live by its textbooks? The Marxist-Leninist view of basic conflict with capitalism does not necessarily mean that global nuclear warfare will inevitably take place. On the other hand the goals of Western society do not necessarily imply an armed crusade. There still remains a suspicion that the other side is out to win completely. The fact cannot be minimized that the USSR has developed a firm confidence that its way of life is superior to the West and must prevail. The West has a similar conviction about its institutions. Yet responsible leaders in both power blocs do appear to entertain the hope that the two great systems can co-exist and even peacefully compete. It has even to be asked whether the two systems are as different in every respect as both sides suppose.

Another cause of distrust is the isolation of large parts of mankind from the community of nations. It develops in the absence of the disciplined intercourse of nations a vicious circle of misinformation, suspicion, fear, distortion and further withdrawal. Reconciliation is impossible in the absence of one of the parties.[19]

The last paragraph referred to the absence of the Republic of China from the United Nations. In the previous year the Commission of the Churches on International Affairs was asked by the Central Committee "to continue the study and to help in the creation of conditions which will permit the 650,000,000 people of China to share in the benefits and accept the responsibilities common to all members of the international community."

Regret was also felt at New Delhi over the absence of the East German churchmen whose government did not allow them to attend the Assembly, and a special message was sent to them from the Assembly.

The Russian Orthodox Church Joins the WCC

An important development at New Delhi was the Russian Orthodox Church's entry into the WCC. The event produced mixed reactions. On the one hand, it meant that a large section of Christendom from behind the Iron Curtain was now represented in the Council and that most of the Orthodox churches were in the ecumenical movement. On the other hand, there was the question of the actual freedom of the Russian church to act independently of its government. Would it be a tool of the government in the discussion of social issues within the World Council of Churches?

In his message to the Assembly, Alexei, Patriarch of Moscow and All Russia, rejoiced in the occasion and expressed the church's deep concern for Christian unity. In a part of his message he dealt with social issues and said:

Today the atmosphere in the world is full of tension. In performance of their duty of peacemaking, churches, religions, congregations and all Christians must resolutely call upon and induce the leaders of states to start negotiations, with the aim of achieving at least agreement on universal and complete disarmament, with effective international control, and also on other problems that are a source of concern to mankind.[20]

It is interesting to note that the patriarch advocated "effective international control"; this sounded more like a Western proposal than a Soviet one.

During the Cuban missile crisis in 1962 the World Council of Churches got itself into an awkward situation by sending two different messages to the UN Security Council. The one, sent by the officers criticizing American unilateral action, was severely criticized by member churches. It had been sent before the full facts were known regarding the degree of danger posed by the Russian missiles placed in Cuba. The other was a more balanced statement appealing for international settlement. Later these statements were reconciled. Apparently the officers were seeking to apply the Evanston pronouncement urging nations not to act as the sole judge in their own cause and not to resort to war to advance their own policies, but rather to seek to settle disputes by direct negotiation or by submitting them to conciliation or arbitration.

North-South Conflict Replaces East-West Conflict

When the Geneva Conference on Church and Society met in 1966, the world situation was far different from what it had been at the time of Amsterdam or even Evanston. The emphasis was placed now not so much on the conflict between East and West as on the conflict between North and South, i.e., between the industrialized nations and the developing nations.

In the eyes of the Third World, the Soviet Union was no longer the leader of the world revolution, but rather one of the white, dominant, industrial nations that were increasing their lordship over the world through technical assistance. Neither the Soviet Union nor the Western nations were looked upon as models or sources of inspiration. Both were primarily places from which the developing nations could get technical assistance.

At the Geneva conference some admiration was expressed for the Chinese system. Bola Ige of Nigeria stated openly that whereas India had been a model in the 1950's, China was a model now. In general, the delegates from Asia and Africa showed little interest in the theory of Communism. They were looking for a practical and convincing revolutionary concept of social development. The key word of the conference was "revolution." Insofar as Marxist categories were helpful in diagnosing the problems of capitalism and in providing an idea of the good society, many were willing to use them.

The situation in Latin America was succinctly described in one of the preparatory study volumes for the Geneva conference. Gonzalo Castillo Cardenas of Colombia wrote that Roman Catholicism was losing its cultural monopoly. Protestantism, he wrote, is a small minority remaining on the fringe of the great problems. Now secular systems of values provide the basis for the masses in their struggle for human dignity and social transformation. Communists, socialists, and other groups of the political left have been preaching a new system of values aimed at social justice. It is little wonder, he continued, that a number of Catholic and Protestant leaders in Latin America see value in Marxism as a source of historical interpretation and revolutionary stimulus, though none of them accept Marxism as a consistent scheme and none of them seek support from Chinese or Soviet Communism. They simply advocate that Christians should work with Marxists for social justice.

None of the Geneva conference participants attempted to combine Marxism and Christianity. For example, J. M. Lochman of Prague pointed out that while churches in Czechoslovakia are ready to serve in a socialist society, they neither wish to mix Marxism and Christianity nor do they wish to have a theology of anti-Communism, which would prevent them from proclaiming the gospel to the atheists.

The effect of the cold war upon development was strongly denounced.

Though the developed nations have made political development possible in Africa, Asia and Latin America, the fact remains that they have also contributed heavily to political conflict, injustice, and corruption. The attempt to use "third world" nations as instruments of Cold War politics, for example, has resulted in several international wars of major proportions, such as those in Korea and Vietnam, as well as many lesser conflicts. In areas where there have been tensions, the big powers have added to the risk of these situations escalating into war by their gifts and sales of military equipment. Furthermore, the economic and ideological interests of developed nations, particularly some of those in the North Atlantic area, have often led them to support—economically, diplomatically, and militarily—ruling elites in the developing nations whose rule is oppressive and whose policies are clearly indifferent to the aspirations of the majority of those whom they govern. In this connection we note the serious debate and struggle over socialism, democracy and communism in their various forms. But the usually indiscriminate use of an ideology of "anti-communism" to resist change of any sort has had a divisive and destructive effect among many of the people of Africa, Asia and Latin America.

Nevertheless, certain conflicts which have broken out, both between and within some of the sovereign nations of the "third world," have been primarily the responsibility of the belligerents themselves. . . .[21]

CHRISTIAN-MARXIST DIALOGUE BEGINS

In the 1960's the churches, both Catholic and Protestant, were taking a more positive attitude toward the secular world than in the previous decades. They recognized more and more that secularization had taken place all over the world, that the era of Christendom (i.e., of society dominated by the church) was over, and that the church's task was to work with unbelievers as well as with non-Christian religious groups to bring about justice in a secularized society. Related to this development was the emergence of some rather significant Christian-Marxist dialogues in several parts of Europe, in which both Catholics and Protestants became involved. The Marxist theoreticians who were present at these dialogues were recognizing that contemporary Christians have been contributing to the social transformation of the world, and that twentieth-century religion was very different from the "opiate of the people" opposed by Marx a century ago. Christians, on the other hand, were finding that Marxists do have something to contribute to humanization and social justice.

The Sociological Institute of the Czechoslovakian Academy of Science joined the Paulus Gesellschaft, a Roman Catholic organization in Germany, in sponsoring a conference in April 1967 which was attended by over two hundred Marxists, Christians, and scientists. In April 1968 a similar consultation of Christians and Marxists was sponsored by the Department on Church and Society of the WCC.

In some ways this development was a vindication of what Josef Hromádka had been saying in the late 1940's namely, that Marxism was incomplete in its understanding of man, and that some day Marxists would be ready to learn from Christians, provided that Christians had meanwhile demonstrated concern to improve the world.

In 1968 a new opportunity opened in Czechoslovakia. Under Alexander Dubcek's leadership, the "Prague Spring" blossomed out, advocating "socialism with a human face." The socialist economic system was maintained, but democratic freedoms—of speech, press, and religion—were added. It was a new experiment in "democratic communism," and the church leadership was enthusiastically involved. But for a number of reasons, including military security, the Russians marched in and crushed it. Hromádka wrote a letter of protest to the Soviet government expressing his bitter disillusionment with Russian policy. The Christian-Marxist dialogue came to an end in Czechoslovakia and declined in other parts of Europe as well, and its leadership seems to have shifted to Latin America.

In the spring of 1968 the Russian Orthodox Church was the host for a WCC conference held in the theological academy at Zagorsk. The conference explored the theological foundations of world development and of revolutionary social change more thoroughly than the Geneva conference of 1966 was able to do. According to Paul Abrecht, this was the first study conference on social questions ever to be held in Russia in modern times under church auspices.

SUMMARY

In responding to the challenge of Communism, the ecumenical movement has frequently stressed the need for penitence. It viewed the rise of Communism as a consequence of the failure of the Christian world to bring about social justice. An attitude of penitence, it believed, would help people avoid a self-righteous crusade against Communism.

Ecumenical social thought has separated positive and negative elements within Communism and has focused its condemnations largely on the negative elements. While appreciating the concern for social justice, it has condemned the violation of human rights, the utopianism, the materialism, the ruthless methods, and the inadequate understanding of human nature. It centered much of its criticism upon Communism as a form of totalitarianism, and made frequent attacks upon the infringement of religious liberty in Communist countries. The WCC insisted that "only the recognition that man has ends and loyalties beyond the state will ensure true justice to the human person."

As the WCC developed a set of criteria for evaluation of society in its concept of "the responsible society," it found Communism lacking particularly in the realm of freedom of expression. Though it recognized the incompatibility of the existing social systems of East and West, it had a number of recommendations for "living together," and steadfastly recommended that conflicts be solved through peaceful methods rather than through war.

The WCC did not carry on a consistent theoretical study of Marxism as such. It responded to Marxism in its political forms (Stalinism, Maoism, etc.) and to crises (the cold war, the Hungarian revolution, the persecution of churches, etc.).

The Council was concerned with Communism as it affected people and as it bore upon the life and mission of the church.

As a supranational Christian body, the WCC sought to maintain the fellowship of churches on both sides of the Iron Curtain, to enable them to learn from each other, and to strengthen the prophetic witness of churches on both sides. It recognized the problems involved in dealing with church delegates from countries in which there was much state control over the church, but it believed that it was worth the risk to bring about the Christian fellowship and to incarnate the words of the hymn, "in Christ there is no East or West." The headquarters of the WCC (Geneva) and most of its member churches were in the non-Communist world. There was no real danger of its coming under the control of the Iron Curtain churches or their governments.

As a supranational body, the Council also wanted to avoid identification with either side in the cold war and to avoid becoming a tool of either power or ideology. At the same time it wished to speak out against the violation of human rights. These interests came into conflict on several occasions, most notably in the Korean war. The stand taken by the WCC in support of the United Nations' action was viewed by Eastern church leaders as identification with the West, and it resulted in the departure of Chinese Christian leaders from the fellowship of the Council.

While many of the pronouncements dealt with Communism in its Soviet form, in time they addressed themselves to other forms as well. Statements in the 1950's recognized the rather common blend of nationalism and Communism, the folly of policy-making that took a monolithic approach to Communism, and the possibilities of change within the system.

In the 1960's the Council gave its encouragement to the Christian-Marxist dialogue fostered by European Catholics and Protestants. The dialogue received a great setback at the time of the Russian occupation of Czechoslovakia, but it continued, particularly in Latin America.

CORRELATION WITH ROMAN CATHOLIC SOCIAL THOUGHT

Prior to the 1960's Roman Catholic social thought generally condemned both socialism and Communism, whereas World Council thought distinguished between them from the beginning, leveling strong attacks against Communism but making relatively mild criticism of socialism, especially in its democratic form. In its attack on Communism, Catholic thought prior to the 1960's condemned Communism as a whole, particularly because of its atheism, whereas World Council thought distinguished the positive and negative elements within it and aimed its attacks against the negative side.

In 1937 Pope Pius XI issued the encyclical *Divini Redemptoris* ("On Atheistic Communism"). It attacked Communism for its atheism, messianism, materialism, denial of basic liberties, undermining of the sacredness of marriage and the family, denial of parents' rights regarding education, and persecution of the church. It contained these blunt words:

> The enslavement of man despoiled of his rights, the denial of the transcendental origin of the State and its authority, the horrible abuse of public power in the service of a collectivistic terrorism, are the very contrary of all that corresponds with natural ethics and the will of the Creator. . . . Communism is intrinsically wrong, and no one who would save Christian civilization may collaborate with it in any undertaking whatsoever.[22]

The situation changed in the 1960's. In the encyclicals of Pope John XXIII and in the statements of the Second Vatican Council there is a change of tone in the attitude toward atheists and Communists. The atheists are viewed as fellow humans rather than as adversaries to be opposed. Distinctions are made between positive and negative elements in Communism. Cooperation with Marxists in work toward social justice is recognized as valid in some cases.

In *Pacem in Terris* Pope John said:

Moreover, one must never confuse error and the person who errs, not even when there is a question of error or inadequate knowledge of truth in the moral or religious field. The person who errs is always and above all a human being, and he retains in every case his dignity as a human person; and he must always be regarded and treated in accordance with that lofty dignity. . . .

It is therefore especially to the point to make a clear distinction between false philosophical teachings regarding the nature, origin and destiny of the universe and of man, and movements which have a direct bearing either on economic and social questions, or cultural matters, or on the organization of the state, even if these movements owe their origin and inspiration to these false tenets. While the teachings, once they have been clearly set forth, are no longer subject to change, the movements, precisely because they take place in the midst of changing conditions, are readily susceptible even to profound change. Besides, who can deny that those movements, in so far as they conform to the dictates of right reason and are interpreters of the lawful aspirations of the human person, contain elements that are positive and deserving of approval? [23]

Pope John went on to say that cooperative action must be "in accordance with the principles of natural law, with the social doctrine of the church and with the directives of ecclesiastical authorities." Thus, while providing for greater collaboration, he still maintained the authority of the church. Furthermore, the encyclical devotes much attention to basic human rights. It is evident, then, that collaboration will not take place at the price of compromising the basic rights of man.

Likewise, Vatican II went on record as saying:

While rejecting atheism, root and branch, the Church sincerely professes that all men, believers and unbelievers alike ought to work for the rightful betterment of this world in which all alike live. Such an ideal cannot be realized, however, apart from sincere and prudent dialogue.[24]

In addition, there is the humble recognition in the Vatican Council statement that believers may have forced the birth of atheism by their neglect, errors, or deficiency in teachings and actions.

The recognized necessity of cooperation between believers and nonbelievers for the solution of human problems and in the construction of the world in which both will live is bound to two elements which appeared at the Vatican Council: (1) the acceptance of the complete secularity of the state, and (2) the recognition of the legitimate autonomy of earthly realities in which "created things and societies themselves enjoy their own laws and values which must be gradually deciphered, put to use and regulated by men. . . ."

These assumptions parallel those of the WCC. Both bodies saw the necessity for Christians everywhere in the world to accept secular societies and to work within them, and these secular societies would also include Communist societies. Especially in the 1960's one finds a convergence of WCC and Roman Catholic thought on secularism and on the Christian approach to Communism.

VI

Racial and Ethnic Relations

The titanic problems of racial justice faced by the Christian church in the twentieth century are the inheritance of previous centuries of European expansion and world domination. As white European nations extended their empires they spread a way of life deemed by them to be superior to other forms of civilization because of its advanced technology. Meanwhile missionaries carried to the four corners of the earth the faith they held to be the only true one, motivated not by desire for territorial aggrandizement, but by the vision of saving souls, of conquering paganism by Christianity.

Daisuke Kitagawa, former World Council of Churches Secretary for Racial and Ethnic Relations, summarized in this way what had happened in human attitudes as a result of the European expansion:

The inadvertent coupling of the western missionary movement with the economic, industrial and political expansion of modern Europe into all parts of the world helped to produce a feeling of superiority in the West. The collective experience of western people, religiously Christian and racially Caucasian, with people outside of Europe over four centuries, led them to conclude that non-Caucasians who were also pagans were without question inferior to them. The various pseudo-scientific theories of European racial superiority evolved about a hundred years ago represented attempts to rationalize this feeling.[1]

Only a conviction that some people are less human than others can account for the fact that for centuries the "Christian" nations were subjugating other people or even selling large numbers of them into slavery. On the other hand, it is worth noting that while some "Christians" were selling and buying slaves, much of the protest against slavery was coming from other Christians, sensitive men such as Woolman, Wilberforce, and Livingstone.

Thus the twentieth century faced the wounds and injustices that had been inflicted by the racism of the past. It faced the racism that continued to exist despite the fact that slavery had been abolished and that some social and educational advances had been made.

The missionary movement discovered that racism was a great obstacle to its activity. The brotherhood preached by the missionaries was obviously ignored by the very nations that sent them into the mission field.

An ecumenical leader who was instrumental in stirring interest in this problem was J. H. Oldham of England, for many years a leader in the International Missionary Council. His book *Christianity and the Race Problem,* written in 1924, presented a challenge to the churches and influenced both the Stockholm conference of 1925 and the Jerusalem conference of 1928, particularly the latter. Surveying the world scene, Oldham wrote:

And apart from iron-handed repression the new forces that are stirring in Asia and Africa cannot be held in check. . . .
The Negro race in the U.S. is seeking larger opportunities and a fuller recognition of its claims. . . .
Everywhere we are confronted with a challenge to the position at present held by the white race.[2]

The problem of race relations was discussed in several commissions at the Life and Work conference in Stockholm in 1925, but it did not receive adequate attention, partly because non-Western nations were not well represented. One of the commission reports affirmed that people were equal before God, that in God's plan there is a place for different races and peoples, and that all should have equal opportunity. But it also indicated that there are inequalities of capacity among individuals and among races.

The first thorough treatment of race in an ecumenical context took place in 1928 at the International Missionary Council meeting in Jerusalem. There were more nonwhite representatives present there than at Stockholm. Preliminary papers on race relations, giving particular attention to South Africa and the United States, were distributed in advance. These were realistic reports, pointing both to the intolerable existing conditions and to the signs of hope. The reports on the United States dealt with the discrimination against the Japanese on the West Coast as well as with the general discrimination against Negroes.

THE MISSIONARY MOVEMENT TAKES A STAND

The Jerusalem conference was the first meeting in which the missionary-sending churches of Europe, North America, and Australia were represented by approximately the same number of delegates as the receiving churches of Asia, Africa, and Latin America. Delegates expressed anger about discrimination in all parts of the world.

The report of the conference began by pointing out that

the Fatherhood of God and the sacredness of personality are vital truths revealed in Christ, which all Christian communities are bound to press into action in all the relationships of life. . . .

Our Lord's thought and action, the teachings of His apostles, and the fact that the Church, as the Body of Christ, is a community transcending race, show that the different people are created by God to bring each its peculiar gift to His City, so that all may enhance its glory by the rich diversity of their contributions. . . . Any discrimination against human beings on the grounds of race or color, any selfish exploitation and any oppression of man by man is, therefore, a denial of the teachings of Jesus.[3]

The discussion of the topic produced sharp disagreements. A European argued that "the sacredness of personality" is not taught in the gospel but is based on a law of nature in the spirit of the American constitution and the American liberal social gospel. Other delegates criticized the idea of equality arguing that God had made people different and that by His will the better endowed were to rule over the lesser endowed. This was an interpretation of Reformation teaching that had been used by Puritans in America and by Dutch Reformed in South Africa. Some Lutherans objected that the teaching of equality violated the doctrine of the two realms: there is equality in the Christian community, the community of grace, but not in the sinful world where law and coercion reign— there inequality is inevitable.

Besides seeking to provide a Christian foundation for racial justice, the conference also advocated a constructive program. It presented a number of goals for situations where two or more races are living side by side in the same country, such as equality of opportunity in society and increased religious interracial fellowship. It provided some suggestions for the treatment of subject peoples, such as the developing of the resources of the land in the interest of the indigenous people, and it expressed some ideas on migration and colonization, including the assertion that race should not be a factor in immigration restrictions. The conference concluded that "the missionary enterprise itself, as an instrument of God for bringing into being among all races the Church of Christ, has in its power to be the most creative force for world-wide inter-racial unity."

The Oxford conference of 1937 gave the clearest and strongest statement to date of the church's responsibility in race relations. It acknowledged that the problem of suppressed races the world over was severe and it recognized a particular threat in Nazism, which was making racism a foundation stone of its philosophy. It was the issue of racism that produced a conflict in Germany between the Confessing Church and the "German Christians." In 1935 the Confessing Church declared that the new Nazi religion had made idols out of blood and race, and that it therefore was in direct opposition to the first of the Ten Commandments.

OXFORD PROBES THEOLOGICAL FOUNDATIONS

The Oxford conference clearly grounded its views on race
in the creative and redemptive work of God:

The existence of black races, white races, yellow races, is to be accepted gladly and reverently as full of possibilities under God's purpose for the enrichment of human life. And there is no room for any
differentiation between the races as to their intrinsic value. . . .
The sin of man asserts itself in racial pride, racial hatreds and
persecutions and in the exploitation of other races. . . .
For Christians, the starting-point in this, as in every problem of
the relations of men, is the affirmation that all men are by birthright
children of God created in His image; and, therefore, brothers and
sisters to one another. They are, moreover, "brothers for whom
Christ died," and intended by God to be brought within the fellowship of his one true Church.
Each of the races of mankind has been blessed by God with distinctive and unique gifts. Each has made, and seems destined to continue to make, distinctive and unique contributions to the enrichment
of mankind. . . .[4]

Responding to the current racism, Oxford declared:

The assumption by any race or nation of supreme blood or destiny
must be emphatically denied by Christians as without foundation in
fact and wholly alien to the heart of the Gospel.[5]

In diagnosing racism as a worldwide problem, the conference called attention to the types of situations that caused
great tension:

It is to be noted that the problem within nations is most acute
where, as in North America, the minority were first introduced into
a country by violence and at the instance and solely for the benefit
of the people which now denies them social equality; or, as in many
parts of Africa, Asia, and Australasia, where the dominant people
themselves are an alien minority in a land originally belonging to
those whom they now dominate; or, as in the case of the Jewish nation, of a people forcibly exiled from their homeland who were
originally welcomed for what they could contribute to the dominant
nation's welfare. In the first two instances especially the dominant
motive was economic exploitation and aggrandizement. In brief, the

most acute situations today are largely due to movements of population initiated by white and so-called "Christian" nations for their own advantage. Individual Christians and their churches bear a heavy guilt.[6]

Then the statement went on to point out principles for which Christians ought to work, such as the right of every person "to the conditions essential for life as a person, to education, to opportunity in his vocation, recreation and social intercourse," and emphasized "the necessity of such economic and social change as shall open the way to full opportunity for persons of all races."

In keeping with the conference theme "Let the Church Be the Church," the Oxford delegates put special stress on the church's obligation to be a truly interracial body within its own life. How could the church ask society to cease segregation if the church itself was segregated?

But it is a first responsibility of the Christian Church to demonstrate within its own fellowship the reality of community as God intends it. It is commissioned to call all men into the church, into a divine society that transcends all national and racial limitations and divisions. In its services of public worship, in its more informal fellowship, and in its organization, there can be no place or any pretext whatever for exclusion or compulsory segregation because of race or color. "In Christ there is neither Greek nor Jew, barbarian nor Scythian, bond nor free." The congregation or communion which allows its line of action to be determined by such racial discrimination denies the Gospel whose proclamation is its task and commission.[7]

T. Z. Koo of China, one of the speakers at the conference, exposed the church's failure to hold up its spiritual standards to society. Rather than shaping society's patterns, he said, the church allows society to determine its patterns in such matters as the treatment of the colored people. But a church that tolerates racial discrimination in its own fellowship becomes an object of contempt. The church becomes secular whenever, through its divisions, it denies the universality of Christianity.

In later years several writers viewed the Oxford conference as a springboard for advance in race relations. A foreign observer of the United States wrote that there seems to have been no widespread stirring of conscience in regard to segregated worship before 1930. In his opinion it was the Oxford conference of 1937 and its resolutions on race that provided the stimulus needed to lift the American churches into a crusading movement.

A year after the Oxford conference the International Missionary Council held a meeting in Tambaram, near Madras, India. In discussing race, the delegates did not achieve complete unanimity, but the dissenters helped solidify the agreement of the vast majority. A German delegate expressed disagreement with the findings concerning the relationship of the church and the changing social and economic order. He argued that for the present period of history the orders of sex, family, nation, and race are divinely established, and therefore the Christian church is not allowed to dissolve them.

"MANKIND IS ONE"

Working with the tools of ethical insight and social knowledge, the Christian church, according to Tambaram, should respond in repentance and rededication to the inbreaking of the new order, by treating man as man and by working for his complete development.

We would, therefore, make the unit of cooperation the human race. We cannot stop within the unit of class or state or race or ecclesiasticism and say, Thus far and no further will our cooperation extend. We stop at one place, evil. Apart from that we go to man as man. Mankind is one. There are undeveloped races and classes, but none permanently superior or inferior, for every man has within him infinite possibilities.[8]

The statements of Oxford and Tambaram were helpful to Germany's Confessing Church in its resistance to Nazi racism. The World Council of Churches (in process of formation) gave its support to the Confessing Church as it battled the German Christians, that is, the group within the church which collaborated with the Nazis. For Christians the problem of anti-Semitism was primarily a religious issue, but since the Nazis persecuted the Jews on racial grounds the churches dealt with the racial issue also.

During the war the WCC Refugee Department helped save Jews and cooperated with the World Jewish Congress to that end. As we look back upon this activity now, it becomes evident that the churches of the world did not respond adequately to the warnings that were being given in the early 1940's concerning the impending genocide of the Jews.

In other areas, however, the influence of Oxford and Tambaram was more noticeably felt during World War II and immediately afterward. During the war the churches in several nations engaged in studies about postwar reconstruction. Concern about racial justice and about human rights in general emerged as one of the issues. The war itself contributed to the urgency, for many soldiers of minority groups sent abroad to fight for human rights were determined to insist upon them at home also.

It is generally accepted now that the influence of the churches helped bring about the United Nations Commission on Human Rights, and it is understandable that the churches would maintain an ongoing interest in this commission. When in 1946 the WCC and IMC jointly formed the Commission of the Churches on International Affairs, they made the pursuit of human rights one of its mandates. Two of the CCIA's earliest actions were to help the UN produce the best possible bill of human rights and to educate the churches to support it.

Following World War II, there were rising expectations all over the world. Asian and African peoples were breaking away from European colonialism. Minorities in the United States were demanding equality.

The 1947 meeting of the International Missionary Council in Whitby, Ontario, Canada, called attention to the complicated mixture of racial feelings in the current struggle.

In many parts of the world there is manifest an increase of racial tensions and hatreds. In part this is due to the resurgence of pride of nation, race and culture among peoples kept long in subjection. In part it is due to economic motives, the desire of some to maintain a superiority which they feel to be threatened, or the fear of exploitation. Anti-Semitism, though checked in its most violent forms, is still a factor to be reckoned with in many countries.[9]

When the World Council of Churches held its first Assembly in Amsterdam in 1948, it reflected in its report, as did Oxford, a deep sense of penitance for the way in which the church was conforming to the world more than it was transforming it.

Within our divided churches, there is much which we confess with penitence before the Lord of the Church, for it is in our estrangement from Him that all our sin has its origin. It is because of this that the evils of the world have so deeply penetrated our churches, so that amongst us too there are worldly standards of success, class division, economic rivalry, a secular mind. Even where there are no differences of theology, language or liturgy, there exist churches segregated by race and colour, a scandal within the Body of Christ. We are in danger of being salt that has lost its savour and is fit for nothing.[10]

The church was called upon to eliminate segregation within itself and also to "call society away from prejudice based upon race or colour and from the practices of discrimination and segregation as denials of justice and human dignity."

Amsterdam Attacks Anti-Semitism

The Amsterdam Assembly also called upon the churches to combat anti-Semitism:

We call upon all the churches we represent to denounce antisemitism, no matter what its origin, as absolutely irreconcilable with the profession and practice of the Christian faith. Anti-semitism is sin against God and man. Only as we give convincing evidence to our Jewish neighbors that we seek for them the common rights and dignities which God wills for his children, can we come to such a meeting with them as would make it possible to share with them the best which God has given us in Christ.[11]

One can see in the Oxford and Amsterdam statements the background for the later efforts of the American churches to bring about a "non-segregated church in a non-segregated society." In all fairness it has to be admitted, however, that in the United States civil rights groups, political forces, and other secular agencies were often moving much more rapidly in the realm of desegregation than the churches. In 1954 the Supreme Court declared segregation in the public schools to be unconstitutional. Sports groups, restaurants, and places of entertainment were making significant progress in integration.

World Council statements and activities gave their support to these progressive religious and secular movements in the United States just as they undergirded the Confessing Church in Germany in the struggle against Nazism.

A part of the world which received a great deal of attention in the 1950's and 1960's was the southern part of Africa, and especially the Union of South Africa, where "apartheid" (separation of the races) was the national policy. Here a non-white majority was dominated by a white, primarily Dutch, secondarily English, minority. The churches of English origin tended to be critical of the apartheid policy whereas the dominant Dutch churches generally supported it. The problem of South Africa was vividly pictured by an Anglican layman, Alan Paton, in his novel *Cry, the Beloved Country*. In South Africa, contact with Western civilization has had a more devastating and disintegrating effect on the old collectivistic rural tribal society than it has had in areas where Europeans are not present in such large numbers.

In 1950 the Federal Missions Council of the Dutch Reformed Church of South Africa held a conference in which it sought to formulate a constructive racial policy. It favored a more thoroughgoing apartheid than the existing one, and it called for conversion of certain areas into true homelands of the Bantu, thus giving them a better opportunity for their full development and self-government. The conference defined apartheid as a "process of development which seeks to lead each section of people in the clearest and quickest way to its destination under the gracious providence of God." This would have involved great sacrifice for the whites. The government was definitely not ready to accept this proposal. Thus the Dutch Reformed Church had to consider some alternate policy.

Most of the other South African churches rejected the apartheid principle, believing that the franchise should be accorded to all capable of exercising it, and that it should take place in a multiracial society.

Central Committee meetings of the WCC from 1949 onward gave considerable attention to the problem of South Africa. In 1952 Visser 't Hooft, general secretary of the World Council, accepted an invitation from the South African churches. One of the results of his visit was a more direct involvement of South Africans in the preparatory studies on race for the 1954 Evanston Assembly.

The Preparatory Commission for the Evanston Assembly submitted a comprehensive world survey on race relations. The report on the United States pointed out the almost complete segregation of American churches at the level of the local congregations. It said that less than one half of one percent of American Negro Christians worship customarily with white Christians.

The Evanston Assembly provided opportunities for discussion and debate on the subject. One of the participants was Ben Marais, a sensitive and open-minded leader in the Dutch Reformed Church of South Africa, who in 1952 produced a book entitled *Colour: Unsolved Problem of the West*. As he reflected on the difference between the situation in the United States and that in his country, he commented:

> When I notice the extremely deep-rooted fear and suspicion that exists even to-day in the minds of the white community in the U.S.A., where numerical superiority is on the side of the whites in a ratio of ten to one, I realize that our situation is well-nigh hopeless.[12]

Some indication of the differences that can exist within the ecumenical movement is seen in the fact that at Evanston two quite different churches from South Africa were admitted to the WCC. One was the Bantu Presbyterian Church of South Africa, which is entirely African, and the other was the Dutch

Reformed Church of South Africa in Cape Province, which has separate congregations for the members of different races.

EVANSTON DENOUNCES SEGREGATION

In his address to the plenary session, Benjamin Mays, president of Morehouse College in Atlanta, said:

> Even if we laid no claim to a belief in democracy, if the whole world were at peace internationally, if atheistic communism had never developed, if fascism had never been born, if nazism were wholly unknown, a non-segregated church and social and economic justice for all men are urgent, because we preach a universal gospel that demands that our deeds reflect our theory.[13]

The conference itself took the strongest stand thus far for racial integration. It stated that the church's calling is to witness within itself to the Kingship of Christ and to the unity of all people, and to witness to his kingship through striving for peace, freedom, and justice for all members of society "as a foretaste of that kingdom into which all the faithful will be gathered." Segregation was strongly denounced,

> for such segregation denies to those who are segregated their just and equal rights and results in deep injuries to the human spirit, suffered by offender and victim alike.[14]

The statement denounced attempts to justify segregation on the basis of cultural differences or residential patterns.

> The church is called upon, therefore, to set aside such excuses and to declare God's will both in words and deeds.[15]

In calling Christians to repentance and obedience, the statement claimed that separation from one's fellowman is related to separation from God.

> We need to repent of our separation from God, from which these spring, and of our feeble grasp of the truth of the gospel. To us is given power to become the sons of God and to be every one members one of another. . . .
>
> When we are given Christian insight the whole pattern of racial discrimination is seen as an unutterable offence against God, to be endured no longer, so that the very stones cry out.[16]

The church was called to repent, to challenge the conscience of society, to create and keep open lines of communication between peoples, to support those individuals who take risks in standing alone against society, and to alert all of its members to their responsibilities. The church was urged to seek to change unjust laws, and to be understanding of those engaged in civil disobedience.

As part of its task of challenging the conscience of society, it is the duty of the church to protest against any law or arrangement that is unjust to any human being or which would make Christian fellowship impossible, or would prevent the Christian from practicing his vocation.

Some of its members may feel bound to disobey such law. The church does not contemplate lightly any breaking of the law, but it recognizes the duty of a Christian to do so when he feels he has reached that point where the honour and glory of God command him to obey God rather than man. In so doing, the church must point out the possible consequences of such action and the consequent necessity for spiritual discipline according to the gospel.[17]

Regarding interracial marriage the Evanston Assembly said:

While it can find in the Bible no clear justification or condemnation of intermarriage but only a discussion of the duties of the faithful in marriage with partners of other religions, it cannot approve any law against racial or ethnic intermarriage, for Christian marriage involves primarily a union of two individuals before God which goes beyond the jurisdiction of the State or of culture.

A minister of the Church should advise young people, when preparing them for the grave responsibilities of intermarriage, both of the potential richness of such marriages and of the painful consequences in some situations, which consequences are often caused by the hardness of men's hearts and by cultural differences. There is no evidence that the children of such marriages are inherently inferior, and any treatment of them as such should be condemned.[18]

As part of its statement on Intergroup Relations, the Evanston Assembly adopted four resolutions. The first called for action against segregation, the second for action in favor of civil rights. The third condemned anti-Semitism and urged the Central Committee to conduct a special study on this subject. The fourth called for a Secretariat on Racial and

Ethnic Relations to be jointly sponsored by the WCC and the IMC.

The first resolution, dealing with segregation, contains the essence of the Assembly pronouncements, and has often been quoted since:

The Second Assembly of the World Council of Churches declares its conviction that any form of segregation based on race, colour or ethnic origin is contrary to the gospel, and is incompatible with the Christian doctrine of man and with the nature of the Church of Christ. The assembly urges the churches within its membership to renounce all forms of segregation or discrimination and to work for their abolition within their own life and within society.[19]

The resolution also observed that some churches in the WCC membership would find this very difficult and it offered them the strength and encouragement that can be given through ecumenical fellowship.

While the delegates of the three Reformed churches of South Africa did not agree with the resolution on integration, they did not try to amend it. But they did feel constrained to make a statement to the Assembly. C. B. Brink, speaking for them, said:

We appreciate the argument that no resolution of this assembly has mandatory power over member churches and that certain recommendations, and especially Resolution No. 1, are intended to stimulate the independent thought and action of certain churches in specific situations. But we feel constrained to say that, at this stage of our ecumenical discussions in this matter, it may have the opposite effect by so prejudicing the issue at stake for some churches that fruitful action for them will be gravely jeopardized. . . . However, we are not offering an amendment, nor do we intend to record our votes against what is being prepared. At this stage we dare not commit our churches either way, but wish to keep the door open for further conversation. We wish to place on record that we have experienced at Evanston much evidence of what we truly believe to be real Christian goodwill and an attempt to understand the peculiar difficulties we have to face.[20]

A Secretariat Is Established

The World Council was slow in implementing its resolution to add a staff member to deal with race relations. Perhaps it was relying too much on the prophetic word. Meanwhile, a significant service was rendered to the WCC by Oscar Lee of the National Council of Churches in the U.S.A. He visited many countries of Asia and Africa to carry out some follow-up activity on Evanston's work in intergroup relations. In 1959 the Central Committee established a Secretariat on Racial and Ethnic Relations within the Department on Church and Society and called Daisuke Kitagawa of the United States to take charge.

In the 1950's and the early 1960's the WCC focused its attention on South Africa's apartheid policy. Almost every meeting of the Central Committee dealt with it. In 1960 an emergency situation arose in South Africa. During a demonstration in Sharpeville, police shot into a crowd, killing 69 black people and wounding 180 others. The incident was followed by a four-month state of emergency. A WCC representative went on a mission of fellowship to the churches of South Africa. His visit produced an agreement to hold a consultation. Six leaders of the WCC, a multiracial team, met with ten representatives from each of the eight churches in South Africa in December 1960 in Cottesloe, near Johannesburg. They considered the ways of Christian witness for racial justice in a land practicing apartheid. Eighty percent of the participants approved the statement of the consultation, which repudiated exclusion from the church on the grounds of race, and pointed out the suffering of the Africans caused by communal separation and by restrictions on their participation in economic and political life. It appeared as though the South African churches were about to reconsider their stand on the apartheid doctrine. In the presence of the WCC officials they indicated their willingness to stand together against racial discrimination.

Delegates of two of the Reformed churches issued separate statements. One asserted "that a policy of differentiation can be defended from the Christian point of view, that it provides the only realistic solution to the problems of race relations and is therefore in the best interests of the various population groups." The other stated that "separate development is the only just solution of our racial problems," and proclaimed the necessity to "reject integration in any form, as a solution of the problem." [21]

Later the Cottesloe Report was repudiated by all three Dutch Reformed churches of South Africa. Furthermore, all three withdrew their membership in the World Council of Churches, partly because of the political pressures placed upon them by their government. They have remained outside of the World Council ever since. Thus, in effect, the effort at reconciliation produced only a painful parting of the ways.

In early 1961 the Commission of the Churches on International Affairs called attention to the ruthless methods used by the Portuguese to suppress freedom movements in Angola. Soon thereafter the Executive Committee of the WCC issued a statement saying that

It deplores the mounting evidence of a rapidly deteriorating situation as a result of which large numbers of Angolans are being deprived of life and liberty;

It appeals to the government of Portugal in the name of humanity and of the Christian principles so long professed in Portugal, to refrain from deliberate action involving the death and maiming of thousands of Africans, including women and children, and the attack on those with education and gifts of leadership, as well as the widespread destruction of property.[22]

Later in 1961 the New Delhi Assembly reaffirmed the stand taken at Evanston opposing segregation in church or society and gave its encouragement and support to those involved in the struggle. It noted that the problem of race had become even more acute.

As peoples have achieved nationhood and as depressed racial groups have achieved new status and dignity, new tensions have been created. The struggle between the old privileged groups and the new aspiring ones is intensified and extended. The Christian Church is deeply involved and is called to proclaim its principles with clarity and act upon them resolutely.

The difficulty is that principles which are clear in the abstract are not always seen to be involved in actual situations. On the race issue the church usually reflects the pattern dominant in the community. Most church members are apathetic and too many are easily intimidated or manipulated by a vociferous minority of racialists inside and outside the church. We are encouraged by the fact that there are individuals and groups in every society who at great cost have given themselves to the cause of racial justice.[23]

As to methods of action, New Delhi said:

Christians should not be tied to any one way of action but should make creative use of various means—conciliation, litigation, legislation, mediation, protest, economic sanctions and nonviolent action— including cooperation with secular groups working toward the same ends. . . .

Where oppression, discrimination and segregation exist, the churches should identify with the oppressed race in its struggle to achieve justice. Christians should be ready to lead in the struggle. The revolution is taking place whether we recognize it or not, and without Christian leadership it may be tragically perverted. The churches also have a duty to the oppressor in a ministry of education and reconciliation.[24]

The statement went on to stress the importance of nonviolent methods.

The Assembly rejoiced in the fact that eleven of the twenty-three churches which joined the WCC at New Delhi were from Africa. It said, "We pray that as the people of Africa move into their new day the Church of Christ will play an ever increasing creative role in promoting understanding, justice, faith, hope, and love." It also saw fit to issue a special message to Christians in South Africa.

The New Delhi Assembly reaffirmed the Amsterdam stand on anti-Semitism and added its own statement:

The Assembly renews this plea in view of the fact that situations continue to exist in which Jews are subject to discrimination and even persecution. The Assembly urges its member churches to do all in their power to resist every form of anti-semitism. In Christian teaching the historic events which led to the Crucifixion should not be so presented as to fasten upon the Jewish people of today responsibilities which belong to our corporate humanity and not to one race or community. Jews were the first to accept Jesus and Jews are not the only ones who do not yet recognize him.[25]

Part of the debate was on the extent to which anti-Semitism was a social or racial phenomenon rather than a religious phenomenon. John C. Bennett of the United States said:

There is a mid-way position between the view of anti-Semitism as merely a racial issue and that which regards it as being based on theological factors. . . . Anti-Semitism is in part a result of the misuse of Christian teaching and Christian symbols. Religious feeling is an essential factor in its development. . . . We are dealing with the deposit of centuries of religious hostility, a kind of cultural memory of the West. It is an indication of the problem that Pope John XXIII has deleted some words from the Good Friday Liturgy because they help to perpetuate religious hostility towards the Jews. Similarly, in the United States there has been a review of Christian educational curricula with the same intention.[26]

In the 1950's much emphasis in the civil rights struggle had been placed on the changing of the attitude of whites and on leadership exerted by whites. In the 1960's the blacks provided more and more of their own leadership and set their own directions. In the United States, Martin Luther King was one of several leaders who solidified and inspired black people in the struggle to break down barriers to equality. Chanting "we shall overcome" they moved from one difficult task to another—desegregating buses, theaters, restaurants, etc. But on each step their efforts were met by bitter resistance.

The Civil Rights Movement Influences WCC

In August 1963 the Central Committee of the WCC met in Rochester, New York. In the same month the march on Washington organized by several civil rights groups set an important milestone in American race relations. The Central Committee was cognizant of the struggle of vast numbers of people seeking dignity and self-respect. It said:

We give thanks to God that he has called many Christians to share in the leadership of this struggle for racial equality. We ask all Christians and the churches as such to join them and support them.

We acknowledge with deep shame that many Christians through hesitation and inaction are not engaged in this struggle, or are on the wrong side of it.[27]

The Central Committee denounced the increasingly repressive and restrictive measures of the South African government, increasing insecurity and fear. It urged the African Christians to consider once again the Cottesloe Report, which outlined the measures necessary for reversing the trend toward increasing conflict.

We call on Christians to remember in their prayers those of all races in South Africa who take great risks and incur severe penalties in the cause of justice and human solidarity. Christians outside the Republic must work to inform world opinion and to impress upon other countries and governments their responsibility in respect to this great crisis. The pursuit by governments of selfish national interests, particularly in the economic spheres, in their relations with South Africa can do much to defer the realization of racial justice for all her peoples. All Christians must do everything in their power to show their care for the victims of discrimination, and to relieve the needs of refugees from the Republic. . . .[28]

CONSULTATION IN ZAMBIA

Between 1960 and 1963, Kitagawa directed the World Council Secretariat on Racial and Ethnic Relations. During this time he made many visits and organized several consultations in different parts of the world. One of the most important consultations was held in Kitwe, Zambia, in 1964 under the joint auspices of the Mindolo Ecumenical Foundation, the South African Institute of Race Relations, and the World Council of Churches. Sixty church leaders and laymen from seven countries in southern Africa were in attendance. The participants gathered as individuals, not as official representatives of churches or organizations. Though Kitagawa was no longer on the WCC staff, he accepted the invitation to chair the conference. Included in the consultation were Christians from Zambia (formerly Northern Rhodesia), Southern Rhodesia, Malawi (formerly Nyasaland), South Africa, High Commission Territories, Tanganyika, and the Congo. They were members of Lutheran, Anglican, Methodist, Congregationalist, Baptist, Presbyterian, Dutch Reformed, and Pentecostal churches.

The conference report called attention to the deterioration of race relations and to the growing belief that nonviolence cannot solve the racial problem.

In reaction to white prejudice, many non-whites are developing a revolutionary attitude born of the realization that the white group which sets the patterns of society is oblivious to the deepest human aspirations of its underprivileged partners. . . .

The urgency of the situation in South Africa is further increased by the conviction of leading Africans that, as all peaceful measures tried by African political organizations over a period of many years to bring about an ordered change have proved abortive, only one avenue remains open—that of violence. On the other hand, it is precisely this conviction and possible resultant action which consolidates the white electorate, hardens its general attitude, and leads to ever-increasing measures which eventually precipitate the danger they wish to avoid. . . .

The Consultation feared that if the urgency of the situation is not recognized, negotiation established, and further effective measures taken, violence will increase.[29]

The report called upon Christians to take leadership in working for justice. It said:

The victims of these economic injustices are looking to the church largely in vain, to secure relief for their grievances. There is already much disillusionment with Christianity and many are looking elsewhere for relief. Churches have to prepare themselves to speak out against specific injustices in economic life; they must set an example in their institutional life and by their sacrificial witness and action for man in society; and they must support every movement leading to the improvement of economic conditions for the African.[30]

The WCC Executive Committee, meeting in Tutzing, West Germany, in 1964, urged the churches to study the report of the conference in Zambia and to take it seriously. It also commended the National Council of Churches in the United States for the part it played in securing passage of the civil rights bill.

The Central Committee, meeting in Enugu, Eastern Nigeria, in 1965 urged contributions for the legal defense of victims of unjust accusations and discriminatory laws in South Africa, Rhodesia, and elsewhere. It also appealed to the Dutch Reformed churches in South Africa to work for human and racial rights.

Like the Kitwe conference of 1964, the Geneva conference on Church and Society of 1966 stressed the fact that racial justice is dependent upon great changes in political and economic structures. It observed that the wealth of the world was essentially in the hands of whites, and that investment policies often help those groups which sanction discrimination. It deplored the failure of some major powers to use full economic sanctions against South Africa and Rhodesia. It called upon Christians everywhere to urge their governments to ratify and enforce the various United Nations Covenants on Human Rights.

The Central Committee meeting in 1967 gave its support to several sections of the Geneva statement including the part which said,

We urge Christians and Churches everywhere
—to oppose, openly and actively, the perpetuation of the myth of racial superiority as it finds expression in social conditions and human behavior as well as in laws and social structures. . . .
—to use the powers inherent in its administrative structure, such as those that come from the investment of its resources or from the influence of its means of communication, to correct racial malpractice in society as well as within the church itself.[31]

On the basis of studies made by the CCIA and the Lutheran World Federation, the WCC Executive Committee asserted in February 1968 that the trials and sentences in Pretoria, South Africa, violate the fundamental provisions of the United Nations Declaration of Human Rights.

Uppsala Attacks Racism

At the Uppsala Assembly in 1968 racism was an important topic and there were strong pressures for the WCC to become more directly involved in the attempts to solve this problem. The pressures were particularly strong from churchmen in Africa and in the United States.

It needs to be recognized that in the 1960's, particularly in the second half of that decade, a strong movement of black consciousness or black power emerged in America, and it appeared also in the churches. The movement stressed the furtherance of self-respect or black pride through studies of black history, furthering of Afro-American relationships, taking over the leadership of racial justice movements by blacks, and practicing separatism to find black identity. In 1969 a Black Manifesto was issued demanding that the churches pay reparations to the black people for the damage done to them through slavery. The money was to be used for education and economic development to help blacks catch up with whites. This manifesto produced a considerable storm in the American churches.

One of the speakers at the Uppsala Assembly was James Baldwin, a well-known black writer from the United States. Speaking on "White Racism or World Community," he introduced himself as one who had always been outside the church, even when he had tried to work in it. He said: "I address you as one of God's creatures whom the Christian Church has most betrayed. . . . I wonder if there is left in the Christian civilization the moral energy, the spiritual daring, to atone, to repent, to be born again?"

The Uppsala Assembly spoke in strong language about racism. It said:

Contemporary racism robs all human rights of their meaning, and is an imminent danger to world peace. The crucial nature of the present situation is emphasized by the official policies of certain governments, racial violence in many countries, and the racial component in the gap between rich and poor nations. Only immediate action directed to root causes can avoid widespread violence or war.

Racism is a blatant denial of the Christian faith. (1) It denies the effectiveness of the reconciling work of Jesus Christ, through whose love all human diversities lose their divisive significance; (2) it denies our common humanity in creation and our belief that all men are made in God's image; (3) it falsely asserts that we find our significance in terms of racial identity rather than in Jesus Christ.

Racism is linked with economic, and political exploitation. The churches must be actively concerned for the economic and political well-being of exploited groups so that their statements and actions may be relevant. In order that victims of racism may regain a sense of their own worth and be enabled to determine their own future, the churches must make economic and educational resources available to underprivileged groups for their development to full participation in the social and economic life of their communities. They should also withdraw investments from institutions that perpetuate racism. They must also urge that similar assistance be given from both the public and private sectors. Such economic help is an essential compensatory measure to counteract and overcome the present systematic exclusion of victims of racism from the main stream of economic life. The churches must also work for the change of those political processes which prevent the victims of racism from participating fully in the civic and governmental structures of their countries. . . .

The Secretariat of Race Relations of the World Council of Churches needs to be strengthened to help the churches embark on a vigorous campaign against racism.[32]

The Uppsala Assembly had given the WCC a mandate to act. Thus in May 1969 it sponsored a consultation on racism in Notting Hill (London), involving qualified people from various parts of the world. Chairing the consultation was George McGovern, a U.S. senator, who had served as a delegate of the Methodist Church at the Uppsala Assembly.

The consultation itself reflected the tensions in the world. There were disruptions and abusive utterances from National Front and Black Power representatives. The participants divided into three working groups which dealt with these topics: Spiritual and Moral Issues for Christians in Opposing Racism, Realities of Racism Today, and Priorities and Methods in Eradicating Racism.

Unlike some earlier ecumenical conferences, this one dealt with racism in many parts of the world. There was a consensus of opinion that the elimination of racism will require more than the private commitment of individual Christians, that indeed, it will require the entire church's commitment to an action program on a broad social, economic, and political front. The conference made a series of recommendations to the WCC and its member churches in the areas of education, economic sanctions, political action, and support of resistance movements, thereby demonstrating church support to groups struggling for racial justice.

Addressing the conference, Visser 't Hooft, former general secretary of the WCC, summarized the defects of past WCC work in race relations as follows:

(a) We have believed too much in persuasion by declarations and not been sufficiently aware of the irrational factors in the situation.

(b) We have not given adequate attention to the economic factors making for racial injustice.

(c) We have insisted too little on the very considerable sacrifices which have to be made if racial justice is to prevail.

(d) We have not yet found common answers to the problem of violence and non-violence as methods of transforming present patterns and present structures.

(e) We have not yet done our home-work concerning the basic cultural problem. . . . Our problem is how to combine a cultural pluralism with a sufficient amount of consensus or common culture to allow pluri-racial societies to function.[33]

Anti-Racism Program Is Begun

The Central Committee, meeting in Canterbury in 1969, took up the report of Notting Hill and endorsed several of its recommendations. It committed the WCC to a five-year program of study, assistance to member churches in developing strategies to combat racism, and the establishment of a special fund to which the WCC would contribute $200,000. The Central Committee decided to appeal to the member churches to raise an additional $300,000. It agreed that this special fund be distributed to organizations of oppressed racial groups or organizations supporting victims of racial injustice whose purposes are not inconsonant with the general purposes of the World Council and . . . to be used in their struggle for economic, social and political justice.[34]

The Central Committee did not decide, however, which groups fit the above criteria. It delegated this task to the Executive Committee.

First steps to carry out the Central Committee's decision were taken in February 1970 when the Executive Committee appointed staff and an international advisory committee. Baldwin Sjollema, a sociologist from the Netherlands, was appointed executive secretary of the Ecumenical Program to Combat Racism. Later appointments included Naway Dawood, a lawyer from Ceylon, and Charles Spivey, formerly executive director of the Department of Social Justice, National Council of Churches (United States).

The critical decision regarding which groups to support was made by the Executive Committee, which met in Arnoldshain, Germany, in September, 1970. That decision stirred the world. It decided upon nineteen freedom movements—two in Australia, two in the Caribbean, one in Japan, one in Colombia, and fourteen in Africa. Four of the latter had used violence in their resistance activity in Mozambique, Angola, and Guinea. But all four were also engaged in education, social work, health services, and economic aid. The Executive Committee made it clear that money would be given to these groups with the understanding that it be used for social and not for military purposes. This was a courageous and risky step which the Executive Committee took, but it was a step consistent with the ecumenical thinking of the previous years.

After the decision to support the four African movements became known, reactions were expressed around the world. Strongest opposition came from Switzerland, Germany, and the white churches of Africa. Several German church leaders opposed the use of church funds for groups that use violence, finding this incompatible with the church's task of proclaiming the gospel of reconciliation. One of the objections of churches in southern Africa was that they had not been consulted during the decision-making process. Nevertheless, they resisted government pressures upon them to withdraw from the WCC.

But there was support, too. Strongest endorsement came from Holland, Sweden, England, Japan, Indonesia, East Germany, and particularly from the black churches of Africa to whom the WCC action brought great encouragement. The All Africa Church Congress called it "A Revolution in the Thought of the Givers."

In several countries there was a polarization of views within the churches, comparable to the earlier American reaction to the Black Manifesto. In West Germany, the synod of Hesse-Nassau strongly supported the program from the beginning, although the national leadership of the Evangelical Church of Germany was at first opposed to it, or, at best, very critical. Many German individuals, youth groups, theologians, expressed their disagreement with the initial stand of the national leaders by sending their contributions directly to Geneva.

The response in the United States was divided but, unlike in West Germany, the leadership was predominantly behind the Executive Committee action. The largest single contribution in the first year was a $50,000 grant from The United Methodist Church (United States).

The Program to Combat Racism was engaged in more activity than the support of liberation movements. Among its first projects were: a symposium on the Indian problem in Latin America, a fact-finding research project on the aboriginal problem in Australia, a fact-finding project on the proposed Kumene Dam in southern Angola, and a Land Rights symposium involving people from many countries.

But the center of world attention was on the freedom movements and on the question of violence. In the late 1960's the question of violence and nonviolence was frequently discussed in the ecumenical movement. The 1966 Geneva conference discussed it in regard to social revolution. The Uppsala Assembly, in its resolution honoring Martin Luther King, called upon the Central Committee to initiate a study on nonviolent methods of social change. At Kitwe, Notting Hill, and Canterbury, it was discussed in regard to racism.

In the debate over means used by liberation movements, ecumenical leaders often pointed out that the real question is —who decides? One aspect of white racism is its paternalism, as manifested in the habit that whites have of deciding things for blacks. They emphasized the idea that the ecumenical movement was to identify with oppressed people but not make their decisions for them. Thus the Program to Combat Racism made no decision about the compatibility of violence with the Christian ethic. That question is still open for worldwide deliberation. A decision was made to use this fund as a symbol of solidarity with the oppressed.

In January of 1971 the antiracism program was thoroughly discussed in the Central Committee meeting in Addis Ababa, Ethiopia. The WCC had received requests to change the program. The committee chose to clarify the program but not to change it. It stated clearly that the WCC does not identify itself with any political movements and that the Central Committee made it possible for churches to elect particular programs for direct support. In some respects these actions pacified the European churches having the greatest objections. But the tension in southern Africa remained unabated. The Central Committee ratified the program again in later meetings.

Clearly the World Council of Churches' social thought was put to a real test—the test of the pocketbook. By supporting or withholding support, the churches took a stand on a principle that they had earlier supported by many prophetic-sounding words.

Besides reaffirming the anti-racism program, the Central Committee meeting in Addis Ababa in 1971 inaugurated a two-year study on the problems and potentialities of violence and nonviolence in the struggle for social justice. This was a response to the Martin Luther King resolution at Uppsala as well as to the controversy aroused by the racism program.

David Gill of Australia, a staff member of the Department on Church and Society, was placed in charge. In 1973 the Central Committee meeting in Geneva approved a statement resulting from this study entitled "Violence, Nonviolence and the Struggle for Social Justice." It appeared in print in the October 1973 issue of *The Ecumenical Review*. Surveying the world scene, the statement recognized that Christians are involved in both violent and nonviolent struggles and it posed questions for consideration to both groups, thereby enabling them to see more clearly the ethical issues involved in their views and in their methods.

In the early 1970's member churches of the WCC were urged to use their influence upon corporations asking them to withdraw investments from southern Africa in view of the fact that many corporations are in effect giving economic, political and moral support to apartheid and colonialism. Furthermore, the Central Committee decided that the WCC should withdraw its investments from corporations which are directly involved in investments or trade with southern Africa. This symbolic action, it was felt, exhibited the kind of moral leadership that the worldwide church should be providing.

SUMMARY

Ecumenical statements on racial and ethnic relations tended to move from the more general and idealistic to the more specific and realistic, reaching the height of specificity in the Program to Combat Racism initiated in 1970. In the early period it was believed that by preaching the brotherhood of man and by education race prejudice would be eliminated. Too little attention was given to economic factors and to the nonrational character of race prejudice.

The missionary movement uncovered some of the evils of racism as it faced the great contradiction between the alleged belief and the actual practice of colonizing nations. In the twenties the Jerusalem conference of the International Missionary Council made the most significant early statements on Christianity and race.

In the 1930's and the early 1940's the main battle was fought against such racist doctrines as the anti-Semitism of Nazi Germany. The experience of the Confessing Church had a considerable impact on the ecumenical movement, as seen in the statements of the Oxford conference.

The Oxford conference provided theological foundations for the social teachings on race. It pointed to the doctrine of Creation, affirming that God had made many races, all of which were equally valuable in his sight, to the doctrine of sin, of which racial pride is a power manifestation, and to the doctrine of redemption. Since Christ came to reconcile man to God and man to man, the church as the body of Christ is a reconciling agency. American church slogans about a "non-segregated church in a non-segregated society" have their roots in the Oxford and Amsterdam statements. One of the most frequently quoted statements is the 1954 resolution from Evanston denouncing segregation and discrimination in church and society.

Implementation of the pronouncements during most of this period depended largely upon the member churches. In the latter part of the period the WCC added staff to aid in the implementation.

The geographical areas that received the most attention were the United States and the countries of southern Africa, especially the Union of South Africa. The WCC made available its services for several consultations in southern Africa which at times showed signs of progress, but at others did not. The strong stand of the WCC caused three Dutch Reformed churches in the Union of South Africa to withdraw their membership from the world organization.

As more nations in Africa became independent and as American Negroes became more aggressive in their demands for rights, pressures were brought to bear upon the WCC to take more drastic action. The Geneva conference (1966) and the

Uppsala Assembly (1968) took strong stands against racism, and called for more direct implementation in economic, political, and educational areas. In 1970 the Central Committee voted to support a many-faceted program to combat racism, including support of selected liberation movements, and called upon the churches to support it. This produced one of the most widespread controversies in the ecumenical movement but also gave the nonwhite churches greater assurance that the ecumenical movement understood their situation and identified with them.

CORRELATION WITH ROMAN CATHOLIC STATEMENTS

A parallel to the Oxford attack on racism, especially as manifested in Nazism, can be found in Pope Pius XI's encyclical *Mit brennender Sorge* ("On the Present Position of the Catholic Church in the German Empire"). Issued in 1937, it said,

> Whoever exalts race, or the people, or the State, or a particular form of State, or the depositaries of power, or any fundamental value of the human community—however necessary and honorable be their function in worldly things—whoever raises these notions above their standard value and divinizes them to an idolatrous level, distorts and perverts an order of the world planned and created by God: he is far from the true faith in God and from the concept of life which that faith upholds.[35]

In the mid-1950's, at the same time that Visser 't Hooft wrote a pamphlet for UNESCO on "The Ecumenical Movement and the Race Problem," Yves Congar wrote for the same agency a pamphlet entitled "The Catholic Church and Race."

Pope John XXIII's encyclical *Pacem in Terris,* issued in 1963, contains statements on segregation similar to those of the WCC in the previous decade. It says in part:

> Nor can one overlook the fact that, even though human beings differ from one another by virtue of their ethnic peculiarities, they all possess certain essential common elements and are inclined by nature to meet each other in the world of spiritual values, whose progressive assimilation opens to them the possibility of perfection without limits.[36]

In the Second Vatican Council the relationship of Christians to Jews was widely discussed. Like the New Delhi statement of the WCC (1961), Vatican II's "Declaration on the Relationship of the Church to Non-Christian Religions" called for cessation of blame upon Jews because some of their ancestors helped bring about the crucifixion of Jesus, and for a deeper bond with these people to whom Christians owe so much in regard to their spiritual heritage. Vatican II put it this way:

True, authorities of the Jews and those who followed their lead pressed for the death of Christ (cf. Jn. 19:6); still, what happened in His passion cannot be blamed upon all the Jews then living, without distinction, nor upon the Jews of today. . . .

The Church repudiates all persecutions against any man. Moreover, mindful of her common patrimony with the Jews, and motivated by the gospel's spiritual love and by no political considerations, she deplores the hatred, persecutions, and displays of anti-Semitism directed against the Jews at any time and from any source.[37]

In the late 1960's WCC and Roman Catholic leaders were cooperating through an agency called SODEPAX (Committee on Society, Development, and Peace). In a consultation on Christian Concern for Peace held in Austria in 1970, the participants commended Christians in Africa for their united stand on racial discrimination.

We of this consultation express our admiration for, and solidarity with, the Roman Catholic bishops of Rhodesia for their unequivocal determination not to obey laws which clash with the Christian conscience, and with efforts made by other churches through the National Christian Councils of Rhodesia and of South Africa to resist policies of segregation and apartheid. It was, after all, the greatest African Christian of all time, St. Augustine of Hippo, who affirmed that an unjust law is no law at all. This conviction flows from the heart of the Gospel, the Christian religion. This, too, is the conviction of this consultation.[38]

Thus Augustine, spiritual father of both Catholics and Protestants, is quoted in support of a common stand taken on racial justice.

VII

Economic and Social Development

In Chapter III attention was given to social systems within a country. The question under consideration was, What kind of political and economic orders would a Christian seek to realize? In this chapter attention is being focused on the international economic order, on the questions of colonialism and neocolonialism, on rapid social change, on the responsibilities of Christians in a world in which there are rich and poor countries. It has to do with a fair distribution of the world's resources, with the possibilities of economic and political independence for peoples, with just trade policies, and with the use of technology for the benefit of all mankind.

The roots of Christian concern for international development go back to the beginnings of the missionary movement. While spreading the gospel, missionaries also sought to improve education, agriculture, medicine, etc. It can be said that churches were pioneers in the work of technical assistance and economic aid. Sometimes missionaries taught new skills, helped set up small-scale industries, helped start cooperatives for making and selling new products, helped conduct experiments which led to the introduction of new foods and plants. The preaching of the gospel has given people a new sense of their dignity and rights as human beings and has stimulated revolutionary movements for independence and equality.

While missionaries did aid in economic development, they were usually lacking in any general theory of economic development. They usually assumed that this was the responsibility

of the Western colonial regimes, and often their social thinking was the same as that of the colonial masters. The missionary history shows a mixture of reactions to colonialism. On the
one hand, there is evidence that missionaries directly supported and directly benefited from colonialism. On the other
hand, there is evidence that some missionaries were among the
sharpest critics of its evils.

On the negative side, there is ample evidence of teaching
natives to accept obediently the rule of their white masters, of
relying upon the economic and political power of the colonial
nation to help advance the missionary cause, and of completely
ignoring social issues. One reason for this neglect was that
many missionaries were imbued with pietism which stressed
individual conversion and social service but opposed social action. On the positive side, it can be shown that missionaries
fought against slavery, forced labor, land alienation schemes,
opium traffic, and other commercial activities which clearly
violated human rights.

In 1925 the Stockholm conference on Life and Work, a predominantly Western conference, gave some attention, but not
a great deal, to the issue of injustice caused by colonialism. It
came up particularly in the section dealing with Christianity
and International Relations. Reports in that section called
attention to the ruthless, competitive process of economic imperialism whereby the great powers of the West exploited the
undeveloped resources of Africa and other regions of the earth,
leaving the exploited countries of the earth out of the decision-
making process.

A high point of ecumenical concern for international economic development was the 1928 Jerusalem meeting of the
International Missionary Council, a body that grew out of the
1910 World Missionary Conference at Edinburgh. At the earlier meeting social issues were not given major attention and
representatives of the churches in mission lands were few in
number. The Jerusalem meeting, involving for the first time
Christians from the younger churches in a significant way, had
things to say which still sound pertinent in the second devel-

opment decade of the United Nations, that is, the 1970's. In several countries in Asia, Christians took very seriously the responsibility of preparing themselves for the conference. In China, for example, there was an interdenominational conference in 1927 on "Christianizing Economic Relations." Among its recommendations to the Jerusalem meeting were the following:

3. That missionaries and Christian people they represent should exert their influence individually and collectively upon international trade, in order that trade which is harmful to the people of the buying countries may be restricted or abolished, while it is recognized that trade in useful commodities should be developed to the benefit of all concerned.

4. That the missionary movement should use its influence to see that any foreign investments of capital in borrowing countries be made only on equitable terms of mutual benefit without any motive or possibility of political aggression.

5. That when foreign and industrial enterprises are established in countries where industrial conditions are less satisfactory, foreign employees should be encouraged to set a standard consistent with the best practices in their own countries and to use their influence toward the general application of such a standard. . . .

9. That Christians of all nations sympathize with and support movements of the people of weaker nations in their struggle for emancipation.[1]

A similar report came from Japan.

PRESSURE FROM ASIAN CHRISTIANS

Evidently many of the Christians of Asia were not content to receive the Christian message purely as personal salvation. They wanted to see the ethical expression in society, and they expected their missionaries to be active in bringing about a more Christian society. To do this the missionaries would need to try to influence the policies of the countries from which they came. Asian Christian leaders wondered what guidance Christianity could give to people beginning to experience industrialization, a phenomenon which had come from the "Christian"

West. If no Christian answer could be given, perhaps they would turn elsewhere for guidance.

Among the speakers at Jerusalem was R. H. Tawney of the London School of Economics, author of *The Acquisitive Society* and *Religion and the Rise of Capitalism*. He pointed out that medieval Christianity regarded the sphere of economic and social life as unquestionably within the orbit of the Christian ethic, and deplored the modern tendency to separate the spheres. Another speaker was Bishop Francis J. McConnell of the Methodist Episcopal Church of the United States, who was widely known for his leadership in the social gospel movement. His address included this statement:

I know that missionaries often dare not speak out because they will be deported from the mission fields by government authorities if they do. If the time should ever come when missionaries feel that they must take risks in speaking on economic situations, particularly in their fields, there is an obligation on the church and the mission boards to stand by them, sharing their peril and finding new fields for them.[2]

Latin America was represented by an articulate spokesman, Samuel Guy Inman, secretary of the Committee on Cooperation in Latin America. He was particularly caustic as he pointed out how U.S. policy undermined missionary efforts:

Have churches and Christian leaders really stopped to consider how difficult the message of the American missionary has been in Mexico while the Association for the Protection of American Rights was filling the United States with libels on Mexico; in Santo Domingo and Haiti while the United States Marines ruthlessly established martial law in those lands; in Nicaragua while American bombing planes are destroying hundreds of Nicaraguan lives; in Colombia while its citizens read our boast of how we took Panama? . . . Certainly it is clear that the task of Christian churches in the countries that are sending their economic forces to those lands is not only to send messengers of the Gospel to the people, but to help to work out a way for the Gospel to be applied in the solution of the great economic and social questions brought about by the new situation. It also seems clear that the Christian Church within Latin America must prepare its citizens to face these overwhelming problems intelligently and with a Christ-like spirit of honesty, justice and brotherliness. If the Christian Church cannot find the solution for the new industrial problem in Latin America, industrialism will soon eliminate the church from any effective influence in those lands.[3]

The Jerusalem meeting divided into groups to discuss the subjects of Industrialism, Race Relationships and Rural Problems. All have bearing on the subject of development. It was the report, however, of the Section on Industrialism which became most specific. One of the contributors to the thought of this group was Harold Grimshaw of the International Labor Organization. Among the recommendations were these:

1. Investment of Capital in Undeveloped Areas.

   a. Public loans made for the development of industrially undeveloped areas are so fraught with the possibility of international misunderstandings and of dangerous combinations between exploiting groups in lending and borrowing countries that such loans should be made only with the knowledge and approval of the League of Nations and subject to such conditions as it may prescribe. . . .

   b. Private investments should in no case carry with them rights of political control over the country in which the investment is made, and in no case should the political power of the government of the investing country be used to secure the right of making loans and of obtaining concessions and other special privileges for its nationals.

   c. The development of the economic resources of backward countries should as far as possible be entrusted to undertakings of a public-utility character which have regard not merely to economic profit but to social considerations, on the government of which the people of the country concerned should be adequately represented. . . .

3. Protection Against Economic and Social Injustice

   It is essential that governments concerned with undeveloped areas should apply to them the knowledge gained by a century of experience of the measures needed to prevent economic and social injustice, and in particular that they should:

   a. stop at once the practice of employing forced labor by companies or private individuals, and also, except in cases of immediate and unforeseen national emergency, by public authorities.

   b. ensure that contracts of labour entered upon by workers of primitive races should be fully understood by them, should be voluntarily entered upon, and should be subject to the approval of the administrative authorities, particularly in regard to their stipulations concerning the following points . . .[4]

Then a list of conditions was given, essentially those adopted earlier by the ILO.

JERUSALEM EXPLORES THE SOCIAL GOSPEL

The IMC at Jerusalem was obviously taking the social gospel, previously applied primarily within nations, and seeking to apply it to the world scene. The dominant philosophy had some of the optimism and crusading spirit manifested in the Stockholm conference, and opposition at Jerusalem came again from continental theologians who saw these efforts to bring about social change as incompatible with the gospel, which they viewed as purely for individuals. The IMC said plainly in its message that "the Gospel of Christ contains a message, not only for the individual soul, but for the world of social organization and economic relations in which individuals live."

The Jerusalem meeting worked with a theme which became important a decade later at Oxford, namely, secularism. Addresses dealt not only with the Christian confrontation of Hinduism, Buddhism, Confucianism, and Islam, but also with the Christian confrontation of secularism. In his address Rufus Jones defined "secular" as "a way of life and an interpretation of life that include only the natural order of things and that do not find God, or a realm of spiritual reality, essential for life and thought." In its statement the conference made it clear that it appreciated the world but deplored a self-sufficient secular world.

We appreciate also the noble elements that are found in nationalist movements and in patriotism, the loyalty, the self-devotion, the idealism, which love of country can inspire. But even these may lead to strife and bitterness and narrowness of outlook if they are not dedicated to Christ; in His universal Kingdom of Love all nations by right are provinces, and fulfill their true destiny only in his service. When patriotism and science are not consecrated they are often debased into self-assertion, exploitation, and the service of greed.[5]

To implement its findings, the International Missionary Council established a Bureau of Social and Economic Research. This was set up in Geneva, where it cooperated with a similar bureau of Life and Work, with the YMCA, and with the International Labor Office. J. Merle Davis was appointed to head the work. In the course of the next twenty years he conducted important studies on Africa and Latin America, and on the problem of providing an adequate economic base for the support of the younger churches. However, the Bureau did not explore all the areas suggested by the Jerusalem meeting, partly because of the opposition of a number of European churchmen.

Although the Oxford conference of 1937 is justly labeled as a landmark in Christian social ethics, it had relatively little to say about the problems of colonialism and development. This was a predominantly Western conference facing enormous problems of the Western world—impending war, economic crises, and, above all, totalitarianism.

Yet there are sections of the report that do indicate an awareness of the problem of development. The introduction to the section on the economic order includes this statement:

> This brief survey would be incomplete without calling attention to the effect of capitalistic development upon countries, such as China and India, which had not been active participants in the process. Their observation of the process in other nations and their reaction to economic exploitation by capitalistic powers have prompted a widespread demand for radical social change through which the benefits of industrialization might be secured and the evils from which the industrialized nations of the West are suffering might be avoided.[6]

In the report on "the Universal Church and the World of Nations," attention is called to the dangers involved when one nation dominates another:

> In lands where states, either as a result of conquest or treaty or through mandates, govern subject peoples it is incumbent upon the Christian churches to bear insistent witness to the spiritual dangers inherent in their relationship and to insist that the welfare of those peoples is a sacred trust to be exercised under the judgment of God.

Public administration in such countries should be directed toward preparing the people for a progressive share in the affairs of government.[7]

Oxford took the theme of secularism introduced at Jerusalem and developed it much further:

> Since the Renaissance the secular order has gradually established its independence of ecclesiastical control. The Church is no longer authoritative and dominant, it is only one among the many influences and movements of the modern world. Today convinced Christians are everywhere in a minority in a predominantly un-Christian world. For the relation of the Church to the community the mission field is now normative.[8]

Forms of secularism seen as particularly dangerous were nationalism and Communism, which had come to be pseudo religions. The discussion of nationalism did not group all kinds together and condemn them all, but distinguished among the different types.

In the year following the 1937 Oxford conference the IMC held a meeting in Tambaram, near Madras, India. Just as Jerusalem gave the younger churches a chance to come to grips with the issues raised at Stockholm, so the Tambaram meeting gave them an opportunity to consider the problems discussed at Oxford.

SOCIAL ACTION IS RESISTED

As one reads the Tambaram report, it is evident that the battle was still being waged in the IMC as to whether the Christian mission also involves Christian social action. In the previous years there had been attacks on the Bureau of Social and Economic Research, thereby narrowing and limiting its work. Tambaram asserted, "As to whether we should center upon individual conversion or upon social change to realize this Kingdom, we reply that we must do both."

While some of the earlier conferences stressed greater equality within a country, Tambaram called for a greater equality on a world scale.

Since economic means can purchase opportunity there can be no equality of opportunity without a re-distribution of the world's economic goods. We therefore stand for a just distribution of those goods among the nations, and within each nation, so that every man may have enough to promote his full growth as a child of God and not too much to stifle it.

Among the causes of war we recognize the present inequality of economic opportunity open to various nations which gives to some a privileged position in access to the world's raw materials, financial assistance and open areas which is denied to others.[9]

The report called attention to the cultural changes that took place in industrializing societies and to the moral perils involved. It noted the move to the cities, the breakup of village life, the rebellion against accepted moral sanctions.

The confusion is seen in the economic life by the introduction of an individualistic economy as over against the communal system; by the commercialization of agriculture, with its increasing dependence on an outer world economy; by the decay of arts and crafts and traditional occupations; and by a social development depending upon a competitive rather than co-operative industrialization controlled by a minority and often involving imperialistic domination.[10]

World War II followed shortly after Tambaram, and this war proved to be a landmark in missionary strategy. Before the war most churches in the colonies were mission churches, very much dependent on parent churches. Thus the pronouncements tended to appeal to the goodwill of the nations that controlled their destiny. After the war, churches as well as nations gradually became independent and churchmen of newly independent lands increasingly provided the leadership themselves for bringing about social change.

Paul Abrecht, director of the WCC Department on Church and Society, summarized concisely the prewar mission church strategy for social change, observing that it was based on

(1) opposition to the materialistic spirit and the socially disruptive effects of the rapid spread of the Western competitive industrial system,

(2) efforts to better economic conditions by such methods as vocational training, rural development, self-help co-operatives and small-

scale industry, where these would not disturb local social structures and customs, and

(3) proposals for the redistribution of world economic resources, through co-operative efforts to overcome poverty.[11]

During World War II, churches in various countries engaged in studies concerning the postwar world. Included in these reports were some recommendations concerning economic development. For example, the Federal Council of Churches conference in Delaware, Ohio (1942), made recommendations on elimination of restrictions on world trade, preparation of colonies for independence, and the establishment of an international bank to make development capital available without control.

Also during the war, churches carried on a remarkable program of international mutual aid as they provided for "orphaned missions" through the coordinating efforts of the International Missionary Council. Kenneth Scott Latourette and William Richey Hogg provided a vivid description of this unique development:

The outbreak of the war obviously severed German missions from their base at home. Shortly, too, French, Danish, Norwegian, Finnish and Dutch missions were similarly "orphaned." Prompt action averted what otherwise would have been a tragedy. A new and thrilling chapter was written in the history of the church. From China, from Mexico and Argentina, from the Congo, from the Straits Settlements, from Syria, from Great Britain and the United States—yes even from Japan—money was contributed by many denominations for the support of missions that had been cut off from their home source of income. Since November, 1938, well over five and a half million dollars have been contributed to the Orphaned Missions Fund. And so far as is known, as a result of the Fund not a single Protestant missionary anywhere in the world has had to leave his post during the war years because of lack of funds.[12]

In 1947 the IMC held a meeting at Whitby, Ontario, Canada, to deal with the problems of missions in a postwar world. One of its concerns was the elimination of ecclesiastical "colonialism" and the fostering of independence of the younger churches. These were to be hereafter under local leadership with missionaries serving as partners in obedience rather than as directors.

The studies preliminary to the Amsterdam conference included some articles on the situation in Asia, but none on Africa or Latin America. One of the articles on Asia was written by M. M. Thomas, an Indian Christian scholar and a leader in the World Student Christian Federation who in subsequent years played a leading role in helping to shape ecumenical social thought in the area of development. He began his article by calling attention to two events which had deeply stirred Christians in the East. One was Tambaram, the IMC meeting in 1938, which brought together Christians from sixty nations in a manifestation of unity in Christ. The other was Hiroshima 1945. The annihilation of two Japanese cities had made another kind of impact. This symbolized the harsher political relations, which include the story of Western imperialist exploitation and the rise of Asian nationalism in resistance. Both the missionary and the political contacts are made possible, he said, by science, the machine, and technological progress.

Thomas proceeded to point out that the machine age did not have the same benefits for Asia that it did for Europe. It shattered the traditional society, but did not provide real economic growth. Instead, it made Asia into a raw materials source for the countries which had the machines. In the Indian culture he saw the church as the one "community of persons." To carry out its mission of working for justice, the church would need to draw upon the noblest European and American traditions of freedom and equality while opposing the imperialist policies of the governments of those nations. He wrote:

Under such circumstances it is only natural that the Asiatic Christians should view the political forms of western Europe and North American countries as being capable of being maintained only at the cost of keeping over half the population of the globe in the position of a mechanical impersonal mass, and he will ask his Christian brethren in those countries to examine whether there is not a fundamental contradiction within the system of their corporate life which necessitates the imperialist domination of nations, and the segregation and suppression of races other than their own.[13]

At Amsterdam the discussion on social questions was influenced by the cold war situation. The responsible society, as defined, was identified with neither East nor West. Concern to preserve peace and to extend human rights was uppermost. Some attention was paid to the particular problems of underdeveloped countries, but not a great deal. Section III, dealing with "The Church and the Disorder of Society," had this to say:

The second factor is that society, as a whole dominated as it is by technics, is likewise more controlled by a momentum of its own than in previous periods. While it enables men the better to use nature, it has the possibilities of destruction, both through war and through the undermining of the natural foundations of society in family, neighborhood and craft. It has collected men into great industrial cities and has deprived many societies of those forms of association in which men can grow most fully as persons. It has accentuated the tendency in man to waste God's gift to them in the soil and in other natural resources.

On the other hand, technical developments have relieved men and women of much drudgery and poverty, and are still capable of doing more. There is a limit to what they can do in this direction. Large parts of the world, however, are far from that limit. Justice demands that the inhabitants of Asia and Africa, for instance, should have the benefits of more machine production. They may learn to avoid the mechanization of life and the other dangers of an unbalanced economy which impair the social health of the older industrial peoples. Technical progress also provides channels of communication and interdependence which can be aids to fellowship, though closer contact may also produce friction.[14]

Section IV, dealing with "The Church and the International Disorder," also had some pertinent words:

No nation has the moral right to determine its own economic policy without consideration for the economic needs of other nations and without recourse to international consultation.[15]

Asian Christians Confer

According to several Asians, the few references in the statements to the problems of the younger churches were overshadowed by the many statements reflecting Western concerns. Paul D. Devanandan of India commented, "Some of us from the so-called younger churches left Amsterdam with a heavy heart, because we could not help but feel that somehow we did not belong."

Between the Amsterdam Assembly (1948) and the Evanston Assembly (1954), two conferences took place in Asia that made contributions to the ecumenical social thought of subsequent assemblies. The East Asia Christian Conference, held in Bangkok in December 1949, was jointly sponsored by the WCC and the IMC. Conference discussion was greatly affected by recent developments in Asia, the most striking of which was the victory of Communist leadership in China. Also of great significance was the independence movement. Indonesia was on the verge of independence and in the previous two years India, Ceylon, Pakistan, and Burma had become free. Bangkok suggested that a true social democracy would be the answer to Communism.

The second conference was held in Lucknow in 1952 under the sponsorship of the Study Department of the WCC. Its report included statements on land reform, planning for production and raising the standard of living, the effects of the world situation on social and economic reconstruction, and the role of the church in political and social action. In regard to production, the conference stressed the need for industrialization and for a development balanced between agriculture and industry. To achieve this end economic aid from the industrialized nations was seen as a necessity and as a matter of social justice. Such aid, the report said, should be given without political strings attached and with sensitivity to the economic and social goals of Asian peoples. The conference recognized the importance of the problem of overpopulation, but did not have time to go into the many complex aspects of the issue.

THE CHURCHES SUPPORT TECHNICAL ASSISTANCE

In the early 1950's the WCC, the IMC, and several national councils of churches put much stress on support for technical assistance. At this time new programs were being developed by the British Commonwealth, the United States, and the United Nations.

At the enlarged meeting of the Committee of the International Missionary Council held in 1952 in Willingen, Germany, a statement was adopted pertaining to international technical assistance. It said in part:

> Believing that the extreme inequalities of wealth between different areas constitute a challenge to the Christian conscience, we consider that it is the duty of Christians everywhere to encourage and assist the governments concerned in programmes for raising the standard of living of the hungry and underprivileged areas of the world.[16]

Then it proceeded to give recommendations to governments and other agencies offering technical assistance. It urged that high-quality personnel be selected, that the persons providing technical assistance respect the rights and cultural heritage of the people served, that emphasis be placed on helping people help themselves, and that technical assistance be dissociated from military aid.

It also had recommendations to churches and missions suggesting that they cooperate with the work, help in the recruitment of qualified personnel, and encourage in people a desire for self-development. At the same time the conference said that churches should avoid being diverted from their primary tasks.

The preparatory study material for the Evanston Assembly drew upon the results of Asia study conferences, the work of the CCIA and the IMC, and the actions of the WCC Central and Executive committees. It called attention to the need for a new approach to social justice on a world scale, and to the need for pursuing clear-cut goals in the rapid social change of the developing nations. It noted that the churches themselves, through their missionaries, had put in men's minds a divine discontent with things as they are. Since missions had provided most of the educational opportunities in developing countries, they had developed the revolutionary leaders.

The report noted that technical assistance had become a major concern of the CCIA, which maintained consultative relations with the Food and Agriculture Organization, UNESCO, and the technical assistance agencies of the United Nations.

At the Evanston Assembly in 1954, the impact of the earlier study conferences at Bangkok and Lucknow was plainly seen. The section report on "The Responsible Society in a World Perspective" had a section dealing with "The Problems of the Economically Underdeveloped Regions." The section began:

> Society in Asia, Africa and some parts of Latin America today is characterized by the urge to national self-determination in political and economic matters. There is a growing shift of social, economic and political authority from those persons and institutions who by inheritance or tradition possessed it, to those who exercise it because of the function they perform. The peoples of these countries have awakened to a new sense of fundamental human rights and justice and they are in revolt against enslaving political, economic, religious and social conditions. There is also the pressure to achieve changes rapidly. All of the processes of social development—increasing productivity, raising standards of living, democratization and the rest— which have taken centuries in the West, demand in these areas to be completed together and within decades. The temptation is to use irresponsible means of collectivism, whether of the right or of the left, in the desire for rapid results. In such circumstances the church has the duty to point the way to responsible society and herself to follow it.[17]

Then the statement called attention to the specific recommendations of the Lucknow conference.

The section on international affairs also devoted some attention to economic and social development in the context of a statement entitled "What Nations Owe to One Another":

In the new context of our age, relations between peoples hitherto "subject" and "ruling" should be one of partnership and cooperation. Countries enjoying new political freedom urgently need economic and technical help.

The response of more developed countries through expanded international programs of technical assistance is one of the brightest pages of recent history; but the effort thus far has been small in comparison with the needs of the less developed countries and the resources of those more developed. A progressively sustained effort will for a long time be required and involves mutual responsibilities and benefits which challenge all who cooperate in such endeavors.

Many of the politically new nations are old nations with centuries of culture and civilization behind them. In this partnership of sharing they have their own distinctive contribution to make. But for the partnership to be fruitful there is required in nations "young" or "old" a readiness to learn from one another.[18]

STUDY ON RAPID SOCIAL CHANGE

By way of implementing the actions of the Evanston Assembly, the WCC Central Committee, meeting in Davos, Switzerland, in 1955, gave its approval to a study program entitled "The Common Christian Responsibility Toward Areas of Rapid Social Change." Chairman of the working committee was Egbert de Vries, a sociologist from the Netherlands. Staff persons included Paul Abrecht and Daisuke Kitagawa in Geneva. Staff consultants were M. M. Thomas in Asia and John Karefa Smart in Africa. Between 1955 and 1960 extensive work was done in Asia, Africa, Latin America, and the Middle East in close cooperation with mission leaders, laymen, and theologians. Nearly $250,000 was contributed toward the project.

While the study on rapid social change was going on, there were other ecumenical endeavors in similar directions. A study conference in Arnoldshain, Germany, made up of representatives of Europe and North America, considered the world dimensions of the responsible society. Considering the responsibilities of the industrialized nations to the Third World it urged the citizens of wealthy nations to accept higher taxes so that their governments could do more for world development, and also to support those economic policies of their own countries which would bring about closer international cooperation and a balanced development of other countries. It also urged ecumenical action in regard to the population problem.

Responding to this challenge in the same year, the CCIA Executive Committee said:

> The CCIA Executive Committee wishes to emphasize the urgency of the population problem for the international order. It emphasizes the need to study the theological and ethical issues involved in family planning and to review the data which will assist in the formulation of policy.[19]

Plans were then made to hold a study conference on this subject. The CCIA also called for a more responsible overall strategy of development, urging the United Nations to take the lead.

When the Central Committee met in Galyatetö, Hungary, in 1956, it reflected upon the problems of development in relation to the concept of the responsible society. A responsible international society, it said, is one "where all men can act in freedom with consideration for all the needs and rights of others; and where the several members have regard for the well-being of one another and that of the whole family of men." It then pointed out the responsibilities of the stronger nations to help the weaker nations, but not by dominating them. "When one nation dominates another politically or economically, the dependent or subject people is deprived of the possibility of developing a fully responsible society." The Central Committee also expressed the need for study and action on the population problem.

As one considers the church's concern about government activity in development, it is necessary to recognize the church's own deep involvement in such programs. About five million dollars are channeled annually through the WCC for development-type projects. This is only a small percentage of the amount spent by Protestant Churches for this kind of work; most of the money is sent through mission boards. In 1967

Church World Service in the United States dispersed in the developing world thirty-four million dollars worth of material plus about twelve million in cash programs.

RESPONSIBLE PARENTHOOD IS STUDIED

In April 1959 the study group on "Responsible Parenthood and the Population Problem" met at Mansfield College, Oxford, England. The twenty-one participants included theologians, doctors, economists, and students of international affairs who came from five European countries, the United States, Nigeria, India, and the Philippines. Richard M. Fagley, executive secretary of the CCIA, served as secretary of the group. It produced a report which the WCC Executive Committee authorized as a study document but not as an official WCC pronouncement. Since Eastern Orthodox thinking on contraception is closer to the Roman Catholic position than to the Protestant one, it was not likely that an ecumenical consensus could be achieved on this question. The report included several quotations from a document produced the previous year by a committee of the Lambeth Conference of the bishops of the Anglican communion.

Calling attention to the population crisis, the Mansfield Report stressed the importance of programs to limit population growth, while at the same time pointing out that these are not in themselves a solution. "The application of science and technical progress in agriculture and industry and the maintenance of peace and international cooperation will have to play a major role."

In its discussion of the Christian understanding of marriage the report spoke of the "one flesh" union and the covenant relationship between husband and wife. Unlike traditional Roman Catholic thought, it did not talk about procreation as the primary purpose of marriage and other purposes as secondary.

Companionship and parenthood are therefore established together as the purposes of marriage from the beginning, with sexual union

as the ordained servant of both. Marriage has its fulness where both
are attained. (Gen. 2:18–25; Matt. 19:4 ff., 13 ff.)[20]

The report suggested matters that responsible couples would
consider in planning the size of their families: (*a*) the integrity
of the marriage—each decision should be a joint one, (*b*) the
claims of children as persons in their own right, (*c*) the witness of the Christian family in society, (*d*) the needs of the
social order in which the family forms part, and (*e*) church
tradition.

Regarding means of birth control, it said that there was
no inherent distinction among them. "It remains that the
means employed be acceptable to both husband and wife in
Christian conscience, and that, on the best evidence available,
they do neither physical nor emotional harm." Abortion, however, was disapproved.

The Christian conscience cannot approve of abortion, involving as
it does the destruction of human life—unless, of course, the termina-
tion of a pregnancy is necessary to save the life of the mother.[21]

In subsequent years this report received wide attention. A
direct by-product of the conference was the publication in
1960 of a book by Richard Fagley entitled *The Population
Explosion and Christian Responsibility.*

The climactic event in the study on rapid social change
was a conference held in Thessalonica, Greece, in 1959. The
theme of the conference, "Christian Action in Rapid Social
Change: Dilemmas and Opportunities," was considered under
three sub-headings: (1) Man in Rapid Social-Cultural Change;
(2) Christian Responsibility in Political Action; and (3) Christian Responsibility for Economic Development.

In considering man it called attention to the great changes
brought about in personal and family life by technology.
Christians have a great responsibility to help persons find
themselves in a time when old values are breaking down. The
extended family is reduced to the nuclear family, bringing
both new freedom and new insecurity. Family planning is a
great challenge of the new age for which church guidance is

needed. Education is an area where the church has much to contribute. The report said,

Christians and churches are called to be with God in His work in rapid social change. To be with God means to be able to discern where He is at work, and where developments in society are demonic. It means to be used by Him in the midst of rapid social change, so that there may be clear and convincing signs of His Kingdom for men to see and follow.[22]

In discussing Christian responsibility in political action, the report dealt with, among other things, the question of the neutral or secular state. It urged Christians to support such a state, one that allowed religious liberty and did not establish any particular religion. A distinction was made between a "secular state" and one that promotes "secularism," that is, one based upon dogmatically secularist assumptions. Here was foreshadowed a discussion on secularity and secularism which became prominent in ecumenical thought in the 1960's.

In discussing politics the delegates noted the real conflict in the minds of Third World churchmen in choosing between a democratic system, which stresses the rights of the individual, and an authoritarian system, which diminishes the individual's rights in order to move the nation forward. It was believed that a democratic system was best but that it would have to be an indigenous democracy.

In its section on economic development the report observed that developed countries should think not only of technical assistance and financial help as their responsibility but about the effects on poorer nations of their national policies in regard to immigration, tariffs and subsidies in foreign trade, stabilization of commodity prices, defense, the use of surpluses, and the whole trend of industrial development toward more or less self-sufficiency. "Above all, the rich countries need to be aware of the impact of what they do on others." The report explored problems of capital development, management and labor, and the role of the church in economic development. Finally, a special section was devoted to Community Development in Rural and Urban Areas. The Thessalonica conference provided much food for thought for subsequent ecumenical meetings and for local churches.

In the years just prior to the New Delhi Assembly, considerable discussion took place in regard to the relationship between the IMC and the WCC. In view of the vast increase of autonomous churches in "mission lands" and the general movement toward partnership, it seemed desirable to merge the two organizations. Some were concerned, however, that the missionary emphasis might not be adequately carried out by the WCC. The IMC, meeting in Accra, Ghana, in 1958, voted in favor of the union with the understanding that the concerns of the IMC would be carried on in a newly formed Commission on Mission and Evangelism of the WCC. In a statement of the Ghana meeting it was asserted that the distinction between older and younger churches was no longer valid, because the distinction obscured the fact that every church, because it is a church, is called to the missionary task.

IMC AND WCC MERGE

In the New Delhi Assembly of 1961 the integration of the two organizations took place. Implicit in the establishment of the new Commission was the understanding of mission as pertaining to the whole world, not just to a movement from West to East, or North to South. The New Delhi statement said, "We are concerned not with three continents but six." Eighteen of the twenty-three new churches that joined the WCC at New Delhi were from the Third World.

Several of the addresses at New Delhi had an important bearing on development. Masao Takenaka of Japan, in presenting the theme, "Called to Service," described the ministry of Christian service to the world as an essential sharing in Christ's ministry. He pointed to the danger of limiting Christian service to personal charity, important as that is, and of neglecting the search for social justice. He placed significance upon the layman's service to Christ through the ordinary secular life.

Egbert de Vries of the Netherlands, a leader in the study on rapid social change, urged churches to help people everywhere understand that their nations "can only live and prosper in the context of a world economy and a world community."

A key ethical concept in the Assembly report is "solidarity with all men." The absolute Lordship of Jesus Christ over history is the main theological concept. It is confidence in the Lordship of Christ that enables a Christian to work with confidence in changing systems and to work for increased human dignity.

The Christian is not afraid of change, for he knows how heavy are the burdens of poverty and privation carried today by the majority of mankind. He is ready to initiate changes and forward reforms that serve the ends of freedom and justice, that break the chains of poverty; and is willing to cooperate with all who share his concern for the welfare of mankind. He knows that the gifts of God can be perverted and directed to evil ends, but he knows also that this is God's world. In his time his purpose will prevail, and it will be manifest that he is indeed in control.

Hence, the attitude of the Christian should be one of positive but discriminating participation, based on compassion for his fellow-men and on unshakeable confidence in the loving wisdom of God. To those whose sense of security is today so drastically threatened we can speak a word of courage and hope. . . .

In the specific field of economic development, we welcome the vigorous effort to increase production and raise living standards. In much of the world the basic needs of man for food, clothing, shelter and health remain unmet or are constantly endangered. There are areas of particular frustration remaining static in the midst of surrounding progress. There are countries where economic progress has been slow or erratic, because they depend on the fluctuations of a market outside their control and—to remind us that man does not live by bread alone—there are wealthy societies plagued by anxiety and frustration because the demands of people seem to be endless.

Thus a world strategy of development is overdue. . . .[23]

THE UN DECADE OF DEVELOPMENT

The United Nations gave high priority to development when it launched its Decade of Development, scheduled to run from 1960 to 1970. United Nations agencies provided technical assistance and financial aid and also encouraged nations to do the same. In 1960 the UN General Assembly adopted a resolution endorsing the idea that the WCC Central Committee had proposed in 1958, namely, that developed countries divert at least one percent of the national income to development loans and grants. Unfortunately, the percentage granted in most countries did not increase, but instead declined. Later in the decade it was advocated that gross national product, rather than income, be used as a measurement.

The United States, which had been giving 2 percent of its gross national product at the height of the Marshall Plan, was down to 0.75 in 1960, 0.65 in 1968. The United Kingdom dropped from 1.21 in 1960 to 0.83 in 1968. On the other hand, Canada increased from 0.39 to 0.49 and Germany increased from 0.88 to 1.24.[24]

In the 1960's there were many people in the ecumenical movement who felt that in a rapidly changing world the World Council needed to do some intensive work in providing an ecumenical social ethic appropriate for this world. The conference at New Delhi had not had time to give adequate attention to this. It was time for another conference like Oxford which would give its full attention to social ethics. Thus, the plans were laid for the study conference on Church and Society in 1966. Study volumes were prepared involving scholars from all over the world. Their titles were: *Christian Social Ethics in a Changing World, Responsible Government in a Revolutionary Age, Economic Growth in World Perspective,* and *Man in Community.*

In the foreword to the first volume, John C. Bennett discussed the new mood in ecumenical theology as reflected in the chapters of the book. It was one that reflected a greater hope for man's historical future than had been present in recent years. There was a mood of expectancy in new nations, a relaxing of the rigid positions taken by people on both sides of the cold war, a more hopeful outlook in Western Europe due in part to the recovery of prosperity, and a chastened attitude among Americans partly as a result of the Vietnam war.

There has been some melting of frozen positions. The fear of nuclear destruction remains, but it is vaguer and less inspired by the fact of conflict between the two major nuclear powers. There is a fluid situation by which one feels less imprisoned than was the case with the world that the churches confronted from Amsterdam (1948) to New Delhi (1961).[25]

The conference was interested particularly in two revolutions and the relation of theology and ethics to them. One was the technological revolution, which was bringing about all kinds of changes in society and even in man himself. Emmanuel G. Mesthene, executive director of the Program on Technology and Society at Harvard University, said: "We no longer wait upon invention to occur accidentally. We foster and force it, because we see it is a way out of the heretofore inviolable constraint that physical nature has imposed upon us in the past."

The other revolution was the social revolution (the struggle for justice), and this evoked greater interest and debate than the first. As some leaders of the Third World pointed out, the technological revolution may simply make the gap between rich and poor nations greater. "For to him who has will more be given."

One of the most discussed addresses at the Geneva conference was given by Bola Ige, a young lawyer from Nigeria and a former general secretary of the Student Christian Movement of Nigeria. He said:

There can be no peace in the world where 75 nations have their economic (and therefore their political) future dictated by the narrow self-interest of Europe and America. There can be no peace where the Soviet Union and the United States arrogate to themselves the monopoly of directing the future of the world and of other nations. And there can be no peace as long as there is any colony in the world, and as long as neo-colonialism remains more vicious than its parent—colonialism.[26]

NORTH-SOUTH CONFLICT

One of the points that became increasingly clear throughout the conference was the fact that the North-South conflict now overshadowed the East-West conflict. The widening gap between rich nations (mostly in the northern hemisphere) and the poor nations (mostly in the southern hemisphere) was the central social, political, and economic problem of the time.

The conference report spoke often about the responsibility of using technology for "human" purposes, and of the need for Christian theology to define more clearly the "human." It discussed many aspects of the development question. On population it said:

> The very real spectre of hunger and the waste of human resources is ever present. Hence there is an urgent need for the rapid dissemination of birth control information and techniques.[27]

At the same time the report observed that not all churches agreed on this question and that it is important for people to be faithful to their consciences and the teachings of their churches.

Other factors in development included food and agricultural productivity, international transfer of capital and skills, internal reforms, and improved trade relations. On trade it observed:

> The political and economic bargaining power of most raw material producing countries is weak. This results in unsatisfactory relations in international trade conferences, in the giving and receiving of aid, and in trade relations.[28]

The Geneva conference called upon the WCC, possibly in cooperation with the Roman Catholic Church, to engage in study and action on development issues. The specific recommendations of a working group on "The Church's Action in Society" were:

> that the World Council of Churches take immediate and effective steps towards *a*) providing an ecumenical forum for continuing conversation on international economic issues; *b*) expressing the concern of the churches for international economic justice; *c*) helping churches in the affluent societies to quicken the conscience of their nations to increase their efforts for international aid up to a target of at least 2% of the gross national product and to improve the existing trade systems and capital investments so they are more conducive to

economic growth and justice in developing nations; *d*) helping Churches in the developing countries to encourage the growth of the viable economic structures required for rapid economic growth; and *e*) making common cause with other international bodies in developing more just international economic structures and relationships.[29]

Positive Approach Taken Toward Secular Society

On "Man in a Secular Society," the conference said:

Secularization is a process whereby man becomes freed from the presuppositions of metaphysical and religious ideology and attempts to understand and live in the various realms of the world on their own terms. In contrast with the society in which a particular religious ideology sets limits to a genuine search for truth, the secular society not only permits the diversity of religious ideas but also encourages the pursuit of a sincere and open understanding of the factual reality of the universe.[30]

The conference report on secularization reflects a development of great significance in the 1960's. Churchmen were taking a more positive attitude toward the idea of a secular or neutral society. In the experiences of the younger churches, it was apparent that a neutral society was more promising than a Moslem state or a Communist state. They favored a pluralistic society in which each group could contribute toward nation-building and would be free to worship and practice in its own way. Also Western nations, traditionally Christian, were not only recognizing their increasing secularity but also the positive aspects of it. Many factors contributed to this. America's experience with pluralism was positive. The writings of Dietrich Bonhoeffer of Germany on "holy worldliness" and "religionless Christianity" in "a world come of age" were influential. An American who reflected Bonhoeffer's influence was Harvey Cox, whose book *The Secular City* made important distinctions between secularization and secularism, taking a positive attitude toward the former and a negative attitude toward the latter. Secularization allows for an open or neutral society, whereas secularism involves the close-minded imposition of some philosophy or religion upon a total society.

Other important factors were the movement toward urbanism all over the world as well as the increased developments in technology. The world was becoming one vast technological, urban, secular society. The positive attitude expressed by ecumenical theologians toward secularization did not mean a change of attitude toward secularism. The ecumenical experience with Nazism and Communism had not been forgotten.

Within Protestant thought in the 1960's there was much emphasis on the church as a servant rather than as the dominator of society, and a similar stress was found in the theology of the Second Vatican Council as it rejected triumphalism (church domination) for servanthood.

For the first time serious consideration was given to the possibility of Christian participation in violent revolutions. A delegate from South America said: "In my country 200 children die every day of malnutrition. This is a sin of violence, and it will go on until we change the structures of power."

As Paul Abrecht pointed out in his report on the conference, some new themes had been introduced into ecumenical thought—theology and revolution, the meaning of "Humanum," worldwide social and economic development. These overshadowed the questions of the "responsible society," the conflict between capitalism and Communism, which had stood in the center of ecumenical social thought.

SODEPAX HOLDS A DEVELOPMENT CONFERENCE

There had been Roman Catholic observers participating in the conference, one of them being Barbara Ward (Lady Jackson), noted British economist, and the conference went on record as favoring further collaboration with Roman Catholics in the pursuit of peace and world development. Out of this proposal emerged an exploratory group who prepared the way for the Committee on Society, Development, and Peace (SODEPAX) jointly sponsored by the WCC and the Pontifical Commission on Justice and Peace. SODEPAX first addressed itself to the problems of world development by holding a major conference on the subject in Beirut, Lebanon, in April 1968. The conference brought together many experts in the field and was cochaired by Jan Tinbergen, chairman of the United Nations Development Planning Committee, and B. T. G. Chidzero, United Nations representative to Kenya.

The conference observed that we live in a world "in which it can seem 'normal' to spend $150,000 millions a year on armaments, yet difficult to mobilize more than $10,000 millions for the works of economic and social cooperation." The conference made recommendations to developing countries, to developed countries, and to the United Nations.

Because some people felt that the theological issues raised at the Geneva conference needed further exploration, a special conference was held in Zagorsk, Russia, in March of 1968 under the sponsorship of the Department on Church and Society and the Commission of Faith and Order of the WCC. Underlying all the current discussions were basic theological questions such as: What is man? What is society? What is progress in the new age?

The conference worked with the subjects of the "humanum" and of revolution, and agreed to recommend to Uppsala that the "humanum" deserves much more careful study. A paper by H. D. Wendland of Germany placed emphasis on the need for humanizing revolutions and for finding a model for the future society with relative freedom and justice. Wendland has consistently manifested an understanding of the social revolutions in the world and has consistently held to the value of the responsible society concept which has been so important in ecumenical history. He believed that it could and should continue to be applied in the contemporary scene. He has won the high regard of men like M. M. Thomas and other Third World churchmen for his ability to relate the truths of the Christian heritage to a rapidly changing world.

Besides the international conferences emerging out of Geneva there were national conferences in various countries of the world. All of these provided a backing or impetus for the

1968 Uppsala conference, confronting it with a host of burning issues. Uppsala, of course, like previous WCC assemblies, had many other topics to handle besides those of social ethics.

Of the four sections at Uppsala two were clearly dealing with social issues. Section III dealt with "World Economic and Social Development" and Section IV with the theme "Towards Justice and Peace in International Affairs."

Uppsala Calls for a Responsible World Society

Uppsala will, no doubt, be remembered for its emphasis on development, for its effort to help Christians think of their responsibility for a responsible world society in a time in which there was a growing gap between rich and poor nations. This aspect of the 1966 Geneva studies which had been further refined at Beirut early in 1968, was especially stressed at Uppsala.

The report from Section III ("World Economic and Social Development") of the 1968 Uppsala Assembly, as adopted, began with a section on "The Christian Concern for Development." It opened with these words:

We live in a new world of exciting prospects. For the first time in history we can see the oneness of mankind as a reality. For the first time we know that all men could share in the proper use of the world's resources. . . .

Then it called attention to the reality of sin manifested in the exploitation of man by man, and proceeded to affirm that

in Christ God entered our world with all its structures and has already won the victory over the "principalities and powers." His Kingdom is coming with his judgment and mercy.

There followed an appeal to Christians to enlarge their sights in regard to Christian social responsibility:

The great majority of men and also of Christians are aware of their responsibility for members of their own national societies who are in need. But few have discovered that we now live in a world in which people in need in all parts of the world are our neighbors for whom we bear responsibility. Christians who know from their Scriptures that all men are created by God in his image and that Christ died for all, should be in the forefront of the battle to overcome a provincial, narrow sense of solidarity and to create a sense of participation in a world-wide responsible society with justice for all.[31]

In a section on "The Dynamics of Development" the report called attention to analyses made in previous ecumenical meetings and in the UN, and, like the Beirut conference, said that

effective world development requires radical changes in institutions and structures at three levels: within developing countries, within developed countries, and in the international economy. . . .

At all three levels it is necessary to instill social and economic processes with a new dynamic of human solidarity and justice. In several developing nations ruling groups monopolize the produce of their economy and allow foreign resources to aid and abet them in such action. In the international economy, the amount received as aid is often neutralized by inequitable patterns of trade, excessive returns on private investment, and the burden of debt repayment.[32]

The Population Problem Is Taken Seriously

In keeping with the recommendations of earlier conferences, Uppsala urged that at least one percent of the gross national product of developed nations be made available as aid to developing nations but insisted that this aid must be seen in the framework of equitable patterns of trade and investment. A subsection on political conditions of world development called attention to the need to reshape political structures, and to bring about revolutionary changes in social structures. Revolution, however, need not be violent. Developed nations would need to make drastic changes in political climate and in priorities. New supranational structures would be needed to deal with regional and world economic policy. A subsection on some human issues of development insisted on the importance of seeing all aspects in relation to effects upon persons. It dealt with discrimination, unemployment and under-employment, and with food and population. On population control it said:

> The implications of the world's unprecedented population explosion are far-reaching with regard to long-range economic planning, the provision of food, employment, housing, education and health services. Many churches are agreed that we need to promote family planning and birth control as a matter of urgency. An ever growing number of parents want to exercise their rights to plan their families. We recognize however that some churches may have moral objections to certain methods of population control.[33]

Thus the WCC issued its first official pronouncement on the subject of family planning and birth control. That it was not a very strong statement can be attributed to at least two factors: (*a*) the difference of opinion among member churches of the WCC, especially between Orthodox and Protestant; and (*b*) the feeling of a number of Third World leaders that many people in developed countries are more inclined to work on the birth control problem than on the more basic economic issues of development.

Churches were given suggestions on how they could be involved in the development program:

> The churches are already engaged in mission and service projects for economic and social development and some of these resources could be used strategically on a priority basis for pioneer or demonstration projects, as an important response to the most acute needs of specific peoples and areas. . . . Every church should make available for development aid such proportion of its regular income as would entail sacrifice, this amount to be in addition to amounts spent on mission and other programmes.

It called upon the churches to engage in the prophetic and critical task, evaluating the structures of society. Furthermore, it urged them to educate their members regarding responsible citizenship so that they would urge their countries to take action to meet the challenge presented at Uppsala. For example:

> In agreement with the recommendations of the World Conference on Church and Society and *populorum progressio,* the World Council

of Churches and the Roman Catholic Church, acting together, should enlist the influence of all Christians and men of goodwill in the world to diminish expenditures on armaments and to transfer the resulting savings to development.

The report concluded with a statement on the new theological urgency:

Theology has also to come to grips with the meaning and goal of peoples all over the world who have awakened to a new sense of the human. Indeed the interaction between technology and social justice is a crucial issue of our time.

Theological thought can only meet this challenge if those in administration, industry, and technology join forces with the theologians in working out the response. They must give knowledge and receive vision.

We ask the World Council of Churches to press upon member churches the crying need for such studies within their own structures, to relate with basic studies of the Council—such as that on the Nature of Man.[34]

Section IV, "Towards Justice and Peace in International Affairs," also had a subsection on development, calling attention particularly to the relationship between economic justice and world order. It said:

Unless the relative growth of the developing nations is increased substantially by vigorous international action, it seems certain that outbreaks of disorder will proliferate on an international scale.[35]

The Uppsala report reflected the change in outlook on development that had taken place in the late 1960's. In the previous decade it had been assumed that the problem was that of achieving a greater balance of wealth in the world and that this could be done by encouraging rich nations to share their wealth and experience with poor nations. But all kinds of factors were working against this. Military preoccupations of many nations, political pressures on developing countries, unequal trade opportunities, debt burdens, population explosions, etc., were putting the developing nations farther behind the developed nations than they were before the UN Decade of Development began. The failure of the UN Conference on

Trade and Development (UNCTAD) to bring about more favorable trade policies for the developing nations was an indication of the frustrating failures of the Development Decade. At Uppsala it was clear that development required fundamental structural and institutional changes within the developing countries, in the developed countries, and in the international economy. Clearly, there was going to be no smooth and natural evolution into the realm of world justice.

No Smooth Road to Development

The basic conflicts and contradictions in the area of development were pointed out with particular vividness at Uppsala by an Indian economist, S. L. Parmar, a member of the United Church of North India. He observed that there are parallels between nations and the world, and that one can learn lessons from national efforts to overcome the gaps between rich and poor and apply them on a world scale to overcome the gaps between rich and poor nations. One might move from a welfare society to a welfare world. But he also saw significant differences. In a country there is a state which has the power to tax people and to regulate the economy. This does not exist on a world scale. Within many a nation it has been discovered that it is enlightened self-interest to improve the lot of the poor, for this increases purchasing power. But on a world scale this is not necessarily true. Developed nations can get along economically without improving the lot of the poor nations. Within a nation groups have gained justice by organizing through labor unions, etc. But on a world scale the poor nations do not have the unity or the bargaining power to do this. Unless trends change, he said, the disparity between rich and poor nations will be greater in the year 2000 than it is now. Development will not come about smoothly, not without revolution and disorder, but disorder will undermine development.

Our task is to imbue the revolutionary movements of our time with creativity and divest them of their anarchic content. For neither disorder nor revolution are ends in themselves. So too development. They are means to human betterment and establishment of a society based on justice.[36]

In his writings Parmar has also emphasized the "Trade, Not Aid" theory. He believes that generous trade policies are much more beneficial to developing countries than foreign aid.

The Uppsala report stimulated the thinking of churchmen around the world. All the talk of revolution proved to be bewildering to many people in the industrially developed nations, despite the fact that those nations have had revolutions which enabled them to be what they are, and despite the fact that the rising expectations in the world are a result of the spread of revolutionary ideas about democracy, human rights, efficiency, welfare, etc., from the now developed nations.

Following the Uppsala Assembly the WCC has moved to implement actions taken there. Consultations in various parts of the world explored the ways in which churches might support development programs. A conference in Montreux, Switzerland, suggested characteristics of exemplary and pioneering projects which the churches might undertake as part of their world mission. Guidelines provided by the conference favored projects that develop self-reliance in people, that pursue justice in nonviolent ways, that provide creative community life, or that reconcile estranged groups.[37]

The population question was given further attention after Uppsala. In view of the World Population Year called by the United Nations for 1974, the Central Committee asked several departments to make a study. Their report entitled "Population Policy, Social Justice and the Quality of Life" was commended by the Central Committee in 1973 and made available to the member churches. The report stresses the need to see population problems in relation to development, since economic development often leads to a decline in the birthrate. It also gives a qualified support to government population policies, favoring those which respect human freedom and opposing those which do not.[38]

Symbolic of church concern for world economic justice was

the participation of Pope Paul VI and Eugene Carson Blake, general secretary of the WCC, in the fiftieth anniversary of the International Labor Organization in Geneva in 1969. Pope Paul on that occasion also made a historic visit to the WCC headquarters. In their greetings to each other Dr. Blake and Pope Paul referred to the growing cooperation in a number of areas including development. Dr. Blake said:

> By coming to this house on the same visit you remind the whole world of the rapidly developing joint efforts of the Roman Catholic Church and the World Council of Churches in the interest of justice and peace, being implemented by our joint secretariat, lodged in this centre. We are convinced that this common effort in the study of the basic causes of hunger and poverty in our world and our commitment to the mobilization of the whole people of God towards a more responsible society will deepen and strengthen the efforts for peace of all men of good will. Your coming here is a sign of the re-dedication of all Christians to the affirmation of the prophet Isaiah which our Lord used as a description of his own ministry: "to bring good tidings to the afflicted; to bind up the brokenhearted, to proclaim liberty to the captives, and the opening of the prison to those who are bound." (Isa. 61:1; Luke 4:18.)[39]

SUMMARY

It took many years before the ecumenical movement gave high priority to the development of an international economic ethic. Already in 1928 the Jerusalem meeting of the International Missionary Council, responding to the concerns of Chinese, Japanese and other Christians, made strikingly clear the need for such an ethic. But there was a period between 1928 and 1952 when the process moved rather slowly.

A number of factors account for this. World War II and its aftermath posed its share of problems. The worldwide depression gave Western nations severe economic problems within their own boundaries. The missionary movement itself was divided. Greater impetus for social concern came from some of the younger churches themselves than from the missionary societies, some of which had a strong pietistic orientation. Life and Work tended at first to work with Western problems, leaving to the IMC many of the problems facing the younger churches. Not until the younger churches became independent and joined the World Council of Churches did they have a significant voice in that body.

In the 1950's the WCC began to depart from its Western orientation and to think in truly global terms. Study conferences in Asia prepared the way for a change of direction at the Evanston Assembly of 1954. Studies on rapid social change in the late 1950's involved the churches from Africa, Asia, and Latin America. Thus at New Delhi in 1961 the attention was focused on the problems of emerging nations.

The Geneva conference on Church and Society in 1966 made a special effort to give the Third World an equal voice with the powerful nations of the northern hemisphere. There it became apparent that the widening gap between north and south was of crucial importance, that development meant more than technical assistance, that it meant revolutionary changes in both developing and developed nations, and that technology needed to be harnessed for the betterment of all mankind.

Thus the concept of a responsible society was enlarged to the concept of a responsible world society, where rich and poor nations have responsibilities within their own societies, to each other, and also to international bodies.

The Uppsala Assembly of 1968 gave much attention to development, calling upon churches as well as nations to accord high priority to this purpose in their giving and in their policies and actions.

In pursuing world economic issues the churches also came to grips with the problem of secularism. In 1928 it was recognized that secularism exists everywhere and that there are no Christian nations. The studies of rapid social change carried on during the 1950's helped to develop a positive attitude toward secularization while maintaining a negative attitude toward secularism. The idea of a neutral or secular state allowing pluralistic views within it was viewed favorably, but the idea of a state imposing one ideology on all of its citizens was rejected. The church was not to dominate society but to be a servant people within it.

CORRELATION WITH ROMAN CATHOLIC THOUGHT

Like World Council teachings, Roman Catholic social teachings were dominantly Western in orientation prior to the 1950's and became more universal in scope thereafter. The European experience set the tone for most papal encyclicals from Leo XIII until Pope John XXIII, whereas American experience was just as important as European experience in the development of World Council social thought.

According to two Belgian Roman Catholic scholars, François Houtart and A. Delobelle, papal concern for the underdeveloped countries was first clearly expressed in two encyclicals of Pope Pius XII issued in the 1950's. But, they said, it was Pope John in particular who brought new light on the problem in his encyclicals *Mater et Magistra* and *Pacem in Terris*. Pope John expressed a concern for full development, in which social was just as important as economic development. He emphasized the need for disinterested work. In *Pacem in Terris* he said, "It is vitally important, therefore, that the wealthier States, in providing varied forms of assistance to the poor, should . . . avoid any intention of political domination." He appealed for respect for the characteristics of the individual communities and for the hierarchy of values. In *Mater et Magistra* he wrote that "scientific and technical progress . . . are not . . . the supreme values . . . but are essentially instrumental in character." [40]

Some aspects of development studies were carried out by the WCC sooner than by the Vatican. Through its studies on rapid social change in the 1950's, the WCC addressed itself earlier to the moral issues connected with the birth of new nations in Africa and Asia, the mass migration from rural areas to the cities, the effect of the population explosion, and the influence of these changes upon the churches.

Vatican II, like Geneva and Uppsala, outlined the duties of developed nations to developing nations, condemned current trade practices and urged the change of social structures within nations. Pope Paul VI's encyclical *Populorum Progressio* condemned neocolonialism and unfair trade practices which contribute to the widening gap between rich and poor nations. It recognized the desperation that would lead men to violent revolution but warned against new injustices that could arise from the use of this method. It also recognized the need for an international order capable of taking steps toward world economic justice. Pope Paul said that "the new name for peace is development." *Populorum Progressio* was so favorably received in the ecumenical world that it was a study document for the WCC Assembly in 1968.

Perhaps the most striking difference between World Council of Churches and Vatican thought has to do with population. While the WCC and the Vatican both make efforts to care for the expanding population, and while both are concerned about increasing the understanding of responsible parenthood, the Vatican has limited the means of contraception to natural means—rhythm. Pope Paul's encyclical *Humanae Vitae* caused a worldwide controversy when it reaffirmed traditional Catholic thought on this issue rather than modifying it as many had hoped it would do. On the subject of abortion the difference has not been so great. The Vatican has been strongly opposed to abortion. The World Council officially said nothing, though an unofficial study report of 1959 took a stand against abortion. WCC member churches are divided, with Europeans generally opposing abortion and a number of English and American churches taking stands in support.

In their underlying approach to development, WCC and Vatican statements are quite similar, both stressing that development is something more than the increase of material goods. It ought to enable man to reach a fuller humanity. Thus there has emerged a great interest in a theology of development.

The cooperation on development begun in the Beirut conference of 1968 has continued in the joint Committee on Society, Development, and Peace (SODEPAX). Edward Duff, author of *The Social Thought of the World Council of Churches* and one of the Roman Catholic consultants at the Geneva conference, observed:

> There exists therefore in SODEPAX an organized effort on the part of the Roman Catholic Church and the World Council constituency to examine the social evils that darken human existence. The programme, modest though it is, expresses the intention of the Third Assembly of the World Council of Churches (New Delhi, 1961) "that we do separately only those things which we cannot do together. . . ."
>
> Clearly, then, there is a convergence in the social thinking, particularly on world economic justice, of the Roman Catholic Church and the World Council of Churches.[41]

At the end of the experimental three-year period (1968–1971) the SODEPAX program was continued for another three-year period, but under changed conditions. Both sides had increased their development programs, but SODEPAX was given a more limited role, partly due to Roman Catholic hesitations about encouraging the growth of an office which would not have clear responsibility to the head of the church. Thus, in 1974, cooperation is limited to projects agreed to in advance. The budget has been reduced and there are only two staff persons. Still it can be said that Vatican-WCC cooperation in development continues.

VIII

The Church in the World

In the 1970's the World Council is continuing to grapple with worldwide social and ethical issues and to stimulate Christian concern. Among current issues at the forefront of study and action are the population explosion, threats to the environment, racism, theologies of liberation, and technology. In June 1974 the World Conference on Science and Technology for Human Development was held in Bucharest, Rumania. Preparations are being made for the next assembly scheduled for Djakarta, Indonesia, in the summer of 1975.

The old debate as to whether Christians should become involved in social action as well as in evangelism has continued to the present and was given special attention in the conference on "Salvation Today," held in Bangkok, Thailand, in 1973 under the sponsorship of the Commission on World Mission and Evangelism. Probably no statement shows more clearly how concerns for personal salvation and social action flow from the same gospel than the "Affirmation on Salvation Today" produced by that conference:

With gratitude and joy we affirm again
our confidence in the sufficiency of our crucified and risen Lord.
We know Him as the one who is, who was and who is to come,
the sovereign Lord of all.
To the individual He comes with power
to liberate him from every evil and sin,
from every power in heaven and earth,
and from every threat of life or death.
To the world He comes as the Lord of the universe,

with deep compassion for the poor and the hungry,
to liberate the powerless and the oppressed.
To the powerful and the oppressors He comes
in judgment and mercy.
    We see God at work today,
both within the Church and beyond the Church,
towards the achievement of His purpose,
that justice might shine on every nation.
    He calls His Church to be part of His saving activity,
both in calling men to decisive personal response to his Lordship,
and in unequivocal commitment to the movement and works
by which all men may know justice,
and have opportunity to be fully human.
    In joyous trust in Christ's power and victory,
we can live with freedom and hope,
whatever the present may be.
    The Lord is at hand.[1]

The search for a responsible world society goes on, involving Christians of many nationalities and confessions, contributing through a common effort to a deeper unity and a deeper insight. One ecumenical consultation expressed it in this way: "The discovery of their unity *transcending without destroying the ecclesiastical limitations and national loyalties of Christians* throughout the world gives churches *a new perspective* from which they may come to a more objective judgment of the conflicts of our time." [2] This has been the experience of the past half century. The many members of the body of Christ have contributed to the effective functioning of the whole body.

CHURCHMEN LEARN FROM EACH OTHER

    As churchmen from many parts of the world struggled with social issues, they learned from each other. The ecumenical social teachings were made possible by distinctive contributions from individuals, confessions, and nations. While all cannot easily be identified, some of them are quite noticeable. The following comments are meant to be illustrative; there is no attempt here to make a thorough appraisal of the contributions of individuals or confessions.

The American influence is evident first of all in the activism and enthusiasm which helped to get the Christian social action movement started at Stockholm and which manifested itself in continued support. Drawing upon their own tradition, they contributed many human rights concepts to ecumenical social thought. Christian realists Reinhold Niebuhr and John C. Bennett helped bridge the American-European differences by combining American activism with Reformation theological perspectives.

From the Anglican tradition, exemplified in William Temple, came the emphasis on natural law and the positive view of the state as an instrument of justice. Temple also helped develop the middle axiom approach.

According to Nils Ehrenström, an ecumenical scholar, the Reformed tradition has exerted the greatest influence on the ecumenical movement. It has always been activistic and deeply concerned about politics and economics. The first two general secretaries of the WCC stand in this tradition—W. A. Visser 't Hooft from the Netherlands, a member of the Reformed Church, and Eugene Carson Blake from the United States, a Presbyterian. Two Swiss Reformed theologians, Karl Barth and Emil Brunner, exerted considerable influence on ecumenical social thought.

From the German church (primarily Lutheran, secondarily Reformed) have come a number of contributions, an important one being that provided by the Confessing Church movement in its struggle against Hitler. The theme of the Oxford conference, "Let the Church Be the Church," reflected the direct experience of the Confessing Church. German scholars have contributed a great deal. Through his writings while in prison, Dietrich Bonhoeffer, a leader in the Confessing Church, also influenced the later thinking of the ecumenical movement in its approach to the secular world. H. D. Wendland helped to incorporate Anglo-Saxon thinking on democracy and human rights into German social thought, and later served as a mediator between Western churches and younger churches. When considering the Lutheran tradition, it is important to recognize Scandinavian Lutherans, among whom Archbishop Nathan Söderblom, founder of Life and Work, stands out.

The free churches (Baptist, Congregationalist, Quaker, and Methodist), as well as the International Missionary Council, can take credit for contributing much from their heritage and experience to an understanding of religious liberty, thereby enabling the WCC to take a progressive and consistent stand on this subject.

In the 1950's, the churches of Asia, especially in India, initiated the study on rapid social change, thereby helping the WCC to move from a Western orientation to a more universal outlook. M. M. Thomas of India did very creative thinking on these problems. When Thomas in 1968 succeeded Franklin Clark Fry, a Lutheran leader from the United States, as chairman of the Central Committee, there was, one might say, an official recognition of the leadership being provided by Christians from the Third World. The churches of Africa and Latin America followed the lead of the Indian churches. In the 1960's the Latin American experience provided illumination for the extensive discussions of a theology of revolution. Black and white churchmen from southern Africa and from the United States took the lead in ecumenical thinking on racism.

Members of the peace churches (Brethren, Quakers, Mennonites) and pacifists in other churches constantly reminded the ecumenical movement of the value of the pacifist witness. Already at Oxford in 1937 they enabled it to recognize the pacifist position as a valid Christian position. Thus the Life and Work movement supported the rights of the conscientious objector twenty-seven years before the Vatican did so. Pacifists, though a minority, provided constant prodding to the churches subscribing to the "just war" theory, forcing them to reexamine many of their assumptions. At Uppsala in 1968 the peace churches gave strong support to the establishment of a worldwide study on nonviolent methods of social change.

In the ecumenical movement Eastern Orthodox churchmen have generally shown more interest in Faith and Order than in Church and Society. Yet as they have become more involved in the life of the WCC, they have made important contributions also in the social realm, as is evidenced by the writings of several Orthodox scholars in a volume analyzing the Geneva and Uppsala statements.[3] One of their emphases has been the need to see all of human action in relationship to the Eucharistic community. Sharply critical of humanistic trends in ecumenical thinking, they have stressed the distinctive quality and contribution of the church, the mystical body of Christ.

Protestant churches of eastern Europe have helped the churches in the rest of the world to realize the supranational and supra-ideological character of the Church. Again and again Josef Hromádka of Czechoslovakia and others emphasized that Christianity is not to be identified with any political or social system, and that each church has to serve the Lord in its own situation. Like the Confessing Church in Germany, they have demonstrated what it means to be faithful under duress.

CONFLICT THREATENS CHRISTIAN FELLOWSHIP

Throughout the period under study, there have been moments of real tension. The desire to maintain a universal Christian fellowship on the one hand and the necessity of standing for justice on the other led to a number of crises or near-crises. Two of them led to a break in fellowship. WCC action on the Korean war led to the departure of the Chinese Christians. The strong opposition of the WCC to segregation led to the withdrawal from the WCC of three Dutch Reformed churches in South Africa. The Amsterdam statement condemning both Communism and laissez-faire capitalism, and the Program to Combat Racism, launched in 1970, produced strong reactions within the World Council membership and caused severe strains on the movement.

The effect of the WCC's social teachings is very hard to evaluate. Most of the pronouncements depend upon the member churches for their fulfillment. For example, American churches have engaged in significant actions to implement the teachings on racial justice and integration. Third World churches have become deeply involved in the studies of rapid social change and in their consequences.

The WCC itself has been most active in implementing the pronouncements in international relations. It was equipped to do so through its agency, the CCIA. In the work with the UN and related agencies, the CCIA has been particularly effective. It helped bring about the Universal Declaration of Human Rights and helped write the statement on religious liberty in that declaration. It also facilitated steps toward disarmament such as the nuclear test ban treaty (1963) and the nuclear nonproliferation treaty (1968). More recently, the WCC has secured a staff to implement its teachings on racism as well as development. Another tangible result of WCC social action is the new cooperative arrangement for joint efforts with the Roman Catholic Church.

There are obvious weaknesses in the social action program of the WCC. It has a small staff, smaller than that of some individual denominations or national councils. On some issues, there is not sufficient unanimity among the churches to make possible significant action. WCC deliberations on social issues must often be carried out in a relatively short time. There is, of course, a period of study and preparation, but the assemblies themselves last about two weeks. The limited authority of the WCC pronouncements causes them to be less well known than papal encyclicals. Some ideas were expressed in the WCC statements long before they appeared in papal encyclicals or Vatican Council documents; yet it was the latter which received attention.

Visser 't Hooft pointed to a fundamental problem in the communication of ecumenical social ethics when he said prior to the Amsterdam conference: "We must say something clear and definite also about the present world situation. How can that be done in such a way that it will be understood by a generation which has lost the ability to understand any Christian language? We must at least try."

LIMITED LOCAL INVOLVEMENT

Like the whole WCC program, ecumenical social thought has not yet become well known among the laity of the world's churches. This is one of the great tragedies and one of the great challenges of the ecumenical movement. How desirable it would be for Christian laymen struggling with ethical issues to have some encounter with Christians of other nations, races, and experiences, or at least some reading knowledge of their views.

In evaluating these pronouncements, one might be tempted to conclude that they are of little value because they are dated. It is true that they are dated. What was valid for the world of the 1930's is not necessarily valid for the world of the 1970's. But from the way Christians were faithful in confronting the problems of the '30s, one can learn something for confronting the problems of today, just as one can learn something by reading how Christians in the Middle Ages or in Reformation times applied Christianity to their societies.

It should be emphasized that ecumenical social thought includes more than these pronouncements. It includes the ecumenical dialogue that precedes their writing and the influences of the authors in their respective churches and countries. It includes the writings on theology and ethics by theologians and laymen in various lands, and the day-by-day witness of people who attempt to put their Christian ethics into action. One might say that the ecumenical pronouncements are just the tip of the iceberg.

A View to the Future Is Needed

Looking at ecumenical social thought from a sociological and theological perspective, Roger Mehl of France finds it of great importance for the future of Christianity. Christianity, he says, is universal in nature, and to be credible it must demonstrate that universality. It cannot be identified with a feudalistic culture or middle-class values or Western society. He sees an important demonstration of universality in the rapid social change studies and in the efforts of the WCC to identify with the people of the Third World. He also notes the emergence of a universal world culture through technology and believes that the church must learn to relate its message to a technological secular urban society in order to retain its universality and credibility. This challenge confronts Catholic, Protestant, and Orthodox churches and contributes to their awareness of the need for greater Christian unity.[4]

It is this larger and longer perspective that influences the WCC Program to Combat Racism. In the world of the future, the voice of the nonwhite segment of the world's population will be as great or greater than the voice of the white segment. Will the world of the future listen to the church? This will depend in part on the outcome of the church's attempt to identify with the black and yellow and brown people as truly as it identifies with whites.

Thus the experience of the past half century offers a springboard for further action on the problems which will emerge in the future and which, no doubt, will be as great or greater than those of the past.

In surveying the actions of the churches in the midst of the world's conflicts, one sees the truth of the Amsterdam statement that "normally there are Christians on both sides of every frontier" and that this presents the church with a unique opportunity in reconciliation. And one sees new depths of meaning in the Evanston statement:

Their [the churches'] first duty is to fulfill their calling to manifest the Kingdom of God among men. Their fellowship must be a bond of union among all, a bond both more patient and more resistant than any other. The Church must seek to be the kind of community which God wishes the world to become. By virtue of its calling it must act as a redemptive suffering fellowship in the form and manner of its Lord Jesus Christ. Within it differences of sex, class, nation, color, or race are to become a source of mutual enrichment, and not of rivalry or antagonism. Its members must rise above the limitations of nationalism to a truly ecumenical outlook. It must carry into the turmoil of international relations the real possibility of the reconciliation of all races, nationalities and classes in the love of Christ. It must witness to the creative power of forgiveness and spiritual renewal.[5]

In November 1972, Philip Potter, a West Indian Methodist, succeeded Eugene Carson Blake as the general secretary of the WCC. In August of 1973, on the occasion of the World Council's twenty-fifth anniversary, Dr. Potter spoke of the tasks facing the ecumenical movement in the years ahead and said: "The most effective service the churches and the ecumenical movement could render to a divided world would be to live a credible fellowship amidst the conflicts and diversities of peoples and societies of which the churches are a part. A truly multicultural, multilingual, multiconfessional form of conciliarity could become a tremendous source of enrichment, encouragement and of deeper insights into the purpose of God."

While one cannot predict the precise issues that the church will confront in the next half century, one can say that the church's distinctive contribution in the future, as in the past, will be its faith, hope, and love. Believing in one God, who identified himself with man in the incarnation, Christians are concerned to manifest the divine love—a love that transcends all human divisions, that also transcends differing theological and ethical systems.

In expressing this love it is not simply a case of "Doctrine divides, service unites." Uniting in service while confronting the world's conflicts, Christians are led to reexamine their beliefs and to find together their implications for the common problems. Thus service, while uniting, leads into deeper probing into doctrine. Therein lies the hope for the future. The church will best contribute to the solution of the world's problems if everyone heeds the words of the Oxford conference: "Let the Church Be the Church."

Notes

I. The Nature and Purpose of World Council Pronouncements

1. W. A. Visser 't Hooft, "The General Ecumenical Development Since 1948," in *The Ecumenical Advance: A History of the Ecumenical Movement, Volume 2, 1948–1968,* ed. by Harold E. Fey (The Westminster Press, 1970), p. 23.

2. *Man's Disorder and God's Design,* The Amsterdam Assembly series, 5 vols. (Harper & Brothers, 1949). Vol. V, *The First Assembly of the World Council of Churches, Official Report,* ed. by W. A. Visser 't Hooft, p. 128.

3. *The Church and Its Function in Society,* ed. by W. A. Visser 't Hooft and J. H. Oldham (Willett, Clark & Company, 1937), p. 203.

4. "Statement of the Zagorsk Consultation," *Study Encounter* (Division of Studies, World Council of Churches), Vol. IV, No. 2 (1968), p. 71.

5. This criticism is forcefully expressed in the book by Paul Ramsey, *Who Speaks for the Church? A Critique of the 1966 Geneva Conference on Church and Society* (Abingdon Press, 1967).

6. Ronald H. Preston, "A Breakthrough in Ecumenical Social Ethics?" in Ronald H. Preston (ed.), *Technology and Social Justice* (Judson Press, 1971), p. 32.

7. *Ibid.,* pp. 36–37.

II. Trends in Ecumenical Social Thought, 1925–1970

1. *The Stockholm Conference 1925: The Official Report of the Universal Christian Conference on Life and Work,* ed. by G. K. A. Bell (Oxford University Press, 1926), p. 712.

2. *The Oxford Conference* (official report), ed. by J. H. Oldham (Willett, Clark & Company, 1937), p. 2.

3. *Ibid.*, p. 219.

4. *Man's Disorder and God's Design,* Vol. III, p. 195.

5. Paul Abrecht, "The Development of Ecumenical Social Thought and Action," in Fey (ed.), *The Ecumenical Advance,* p. 249.

6. W. A. Visser 't Hooft, "World Conference on Church and Society," *The Ecumenical Review,* Vol. XVIII (October, 1966), p. 421.

7. *Ibid.*, p. 423.

8. *World Conference on Church and Society* (official report), ed. by M. M. Thomas and Paul Abrecht (Geneva: WCC, 1967), p. 191.

9. Robert McAfee Brown, *The Ecumenical Revolution: An Interpretation of the Catholic-Protestant Dialogue.* Rev. and enlarged ed. (Doubleday & Company, Inc., 1969), p. 408.

10. *The Uppsala Report 1968: Official Report of the Fourth Assembly of the World Council of Churches,* ed. by Norman Goodall (Geneva: WCC, 1968), pp. 45–51.

11. Since 1969 study conferences have been held in Geneva (1970), Nemi, Italy (1971), and Cardiff, Wales (1972). The concluding conference on "Science and Technology for Human Development" was held in Bucharest, Rumania, in June 1974.

III. The Political and Economic Orders

1. *The Stockholm Conference: Official Report,* p. 712.

2. *The Christian Mission in Relation to Industrial Problems* (Vol. V of *The Jerusalem Meeting of the International Missionary Council*) (New York, 1928), p. 144.

3. *The Oxford Conference,* pp. 66–67.

4. *Ibid.*, p. 69.

5. *Ibid.*, p. 72.

6. *Ibid.*, p. 67.

7. *Ibid.*, pp. 59–60.

8. *Ibid.*, p. 245.

9. *Ibid.*, p. 115.

10. *Ibid.*, pp. 87–91.

11. *Ibid.*, p. 100.

12. *Ibid.*, p. 101.

13. *Ibid.*, p. 79.

14. *Ibid.*, pp. 111–112.

15. John W. Turnbull, *Ecumenical Documents on Church and Society, 1925–1953* (Geneva: WCC, 1954), pp. 106–107.

16. *Ibid.*, pp. 94–95.

17. *Man's Disorder and God's Design,* Vol. IV, p. 148.

18. *Man's Disorder and God's Design,* Vol. III, p. 192.

19. *Ibid.*, p. 196.

20. *Ibid.*, pp. 192–193.

21. *Man's Disorder and God's Design*, Vol. IV, pp. 226–227.

22. *Ibid.*, p. 225.

23. *Ibid.*, p. 222.

24. Egon Schwelb, *Human Rights and the International Community: The Roots and Growth of the Universal Declaration of Human Rights, 1948–1963* (Quadrangle Books, Inc., 1964), p. 83.

25. *Ecumenical Documents on Church and Society*, pp. 145–146.

26. *Ibid.*, p. 150.

27. *Evanston Speaks: Reports from the Second Assembly of the World Council of Churches, 1954* (Geneva: WCC, 1955), p. 27.

28. *Ibid.*, pp. 28–29.

29. *Ibid.*, p. 29.

30. *Ibid.*, p. 30.

31. *Ibid.*, p. 31.

32. *Ibid.*, pp. 64–65.

33. *Ibid.*, p. 35.

34. *Dilemmas and Opportunities: Christian Action in Rapid Social Change. Report of an International Ecumenical Study Conference, Thessalonica, Greece* (Geneva: WCC, 1959), p. 53.

35. *Ibid.*, p. 54.

36. *The New Delhi Report: The Third Assembly of the World Council of Churches*, ed. by W. A. Visser 't Hooft (Association Press, 1962), p. 106.

37. *Ibid.*, p. 107.

38. *Ibid.*, p. 100.

39. *Ibid.*, pp. 100–101.

40. *Ibid.*, p. 159.

41. *Ibid.*, p. 101.

42. *World Conference on Church and Society*, p. 57.

43. *Ibid.*

44. *Ibid.*, pp. 115–116.

45. "Statement of the Zagorsk Consultation," *Study Encounter*, Vol. IV, No. 2 (1968), p. 77.

46. *The Uppsala Report 1968*, p. 48.

47. *Ibid.*, p. 64.

48. Paul Abrecht, "The Development of Ecumenical Social Thought and Action," in Fey (ed.), *The Ecumenical Advance*, p. 238.

IV. War and Peace

1. *The Stockholm Conference: Official Report*, p. 713.

2. Nils Ehrenström, "Movements for International Friendship and Life and Work, 1925–1948," in Ruth Rouse and Stephen C. Neill

(eds.), *A History of the Ecumenical Movement, 1517–1948* (The Westminster Press, 1954), p. 564.

3. *The Oxford Conference,* p. 162.

4. *Ibid.,* p. 157.

5. *Ibid.,* p. 162.

6. *Ibid.,* p. 158.

7. *Ibid.,* p. 160.

8. Walter Van Kirk, "Cambridge—1946," *The Ecumenical Review* (July, 1956), p. 451.

9. *Man's Disorder and God's Design,* Vol. IV, p. 217.

10. *Ibid.,* p. 218.

11. *Ibid.,* p. 221.

12. *Ibid.,* p. 223.

13. *Ibid.,* p. 220.

14. Commission of the Churches on International Affairs, *Background Documentation on Disarmament and Related Questions* (Geneva: WCC, 1968), p. 2.

15. *Evanston Speaks,* pp. 39–40.

16. *Ibid.,* p. 40.

17. *Ibid.,* pp. 40–41.

18. *Ibid.,* p. 46.

19. *Ibid.,* p. 47.

20. "Ecumenical Chronicle," *The Ecumenical Review* (October, 1958), p. 81.

21. *Ibid.,* p. 80.

22. *The New Delhi Report,* p. 108.

23. *Ibid.,* pp. 280–281.

24. Commission of the Churches on International Affairs, *Background Documentation on Vietnam* (Geneva: WCC, 1968), p. 16.

25. *Ibid.,* pp. 16–17.

26. *World Conference on Church and Society,* p. 128.

27. "Ecumenical Chronicle," *The Ecumenical Review* (October, 1967), p. 458.

28. *The Uppsala Report 1968,* p. 189.

29. *Ibid.,* p. 62.

30. *Ibid.,* p. 63.

31. *The Oxford Conference,* p. 164.

32. *The Uppsala Report 1968,* p. 64.

33. *Ibid.,* p. 70.

34. *Ibid.,* p. 170.

35. *Peace—the Desperate Imperative: A SODEPAX Report,* (Geneva: WCC, 1970), p. 39.

36. *The Social Teachings of the Church,* ed. by Anne Fremantle (The New American Library of World Literature, Inc., 1963), p. 300.

37. *The Documents of Vatican II,* ed. by Walter M. Abbott (Association Press, 1969), p. 294.

V. COMMUNISM

1. Heinz Eduard Tödt, "Die Marxismus—Diskussion in der ökumenischen Bewegung," *Marxismusstudien,* Sechste Folge (Tübingen, 1969), p. 6.
2. N. N. Alexeiev, "The Marxist Anthropology and the Christian Conception of Man," in T. E. Jessop *et al., The Christian Understanding of Man,* Vol. II, The Official Oxford Conference Books (Willett, Clark & Company, 1938), p. 137.
3. J. H. Oldham, *Church, Community and State: A World Issue* (Harper & Brothers, 1935), pp. 9–11.
4. *The Oxford Conference,* pp. 85–86.
5. *Ecumenical Documents on Church and Society,* pp. 91–92.
6. For this account and for several other accounts of events in this chapter the writer owes credit to Klaus Spennemann, whose doctoral dissertation for Heidelberg University in Germany was written on the ecumenical movement and Russian Communism.
7. *Ecumenical Documents on Church and Society,* pp. 114–115.
8. *Man's Disorder and God's Design,* Vol. III, p. 195.
9. *Ibid.,* Vol. III, pp. 193–194.
10. *Ibid.,* Vol. IV, pp. 219–220.
11. *Statements of the World Council of Churches on Social Questions* (Geneva: WCC, 1956), pp. 39–40.
12. *Ecumenical Documents on Church and Society,* pp. 139–140.
13. *Ibid.,* p. 147.
14. *Ibid.,* p. 149.
15. *Evanston Speaks,* p. 34.
16. "Ecumenical Chronicle," *The Ecumenical Review* (October, 1956), p. 45.
17. *Ibid.,* p. 47.
18. "Ecumenical Chronicle," *The Ecumenical Review* (January, 1957), p. 162.
19. *The New Delhi Report,* pp. 105–106.
20. "Ecumenical Chronicle," *The Ecumenical Review* (January, 1962), p. 232.
21. *World Conference on Church and Society,* p. 140.
22. Fremantle (ed.), *The Social Teachings of the Church,* pp. 100, 102.
23. *Ibid.,* p. 310.
24. "Pastoral Constitution on the Church in the Modern World," in Abbott (ed.), *The Documents of Vatican II,* p. 219.

VI. Racial and Ethnic Relations

1. Daisuke Kitagawa, " 'Racial' Man in the Modern World," in Egbert de Vries (ed.), *Man in Community* (Association Press, 1966), p. 142.

2. J. H. Oldham, *Christianity and the Race Problem* (London, 1924), pp. 4–5.

3. *Missions and Race Conflict* (Vol. IV of *The Jerusalem Meeting of the International Missionary Council*) (London, 1928), p. 195.

4. *The Oxford Conference,* pp. 60, 213, 214.

5. *Ibid.,* p. 214.

6. *Ibid.,* p. 215.

7. *Ibid.,* p. 217.

8. *Ecumenical Documents on Church and Society,* p. 97.

9. *Ibid.,* p. 113.

10. *Man's Disorder and God's Design,* Vol. I, p. 208.

11. *Man's Disorder and God's Design,* Vol. V, p. 161.

12. B. J. Marais, *Colour: Unsolved Problem of the West* (Cape Town, 1952), p. 326.

13. David P. Gaines, *The World Council of Churches: A Study of Its Background and History* (Richard R. Smith Company, Inc., 1966), p. 662.

14. *Evanston Speaks,* p. 53.

15. *Ibid.,* p. 54.

16. *Ibid.*

17. *Ibid.,* p. 55.

18. *Ibid.,* p. 56.

19. *Ibid.,* p. 57.

20. Gaines, *The World Council of Churches,* p. 672.

21. *Ecumenical Statements on Race Relations* (Geneva: WCC, 1965), p.23.

22. Commission of the Churches on International Affairs, *Background Documentation on Africa* (Geneva: WCC, 1968), p. 4.

23. *The New Delhi Report,* pp. 102–103.

24. *Ibid.,* p. 103.

25. *Ibid.,* p. 148.

26. *Ibid.,* p. 150.

27. *Ecumenical Statements on Race Relations,* pp. 37–39.

28. *Ibid.,* p. 38.

29. *Christians and Race Relations in Southern Africa* (Geneva: WCC, 1964), pp. 5, 13.

30. *Ibid.,* p. 19.

31. *World Conference on Church and Society,* pp. 175–176.

32. *The Uppsala Report 1968,* pp. 65–66.

33. John J. Vincent, *The Race Race* (London: SCM Press, Ltd., 1970), p. 41.

34. *Ibid.,* p. 105.

35. Fremantle (ed.), *The Social Teachings of the Church,* p. 90.

36. *Ibid.,* p. 298.

37. Abbott (ed.), *The Documents of Vatican II,* pp. 665–666.

38. *Peace—the Desperate Imperative: A SODEPAX Report,* p. 53.

VII. Economic and Social Development

1. *The Christian Mission in Relation to Industrial Problems* (Vol. V of *The Jerusalem Meeting of the International Missionary Council*) (New York, 1928), p. 42.

2. *Ibid.,* p. 138.

3. *Ibid.,* p. 109.

4. *Ibid.,* pp. 145–148.

5. *The Christian Life and Message in Relation to the Non-Christian Systems of Life and Thought* (Vol. I of *The Jerusalem Meeting of the International Missionary Council*) (New York, 1928), p. 412.

6. *The Oxford Conference,* pp. 84–85.

7. *Ibid.,* p. 170.

8. *Ibid.,* pp. 183–184.

9. *Ecumenical Documents on Church and Society,* p. 97.

10. *Ibid.,* p. 92.

11. Paul Abrecht, *The Churches and Rapid Social Change* (Doubleday & Company, Inc., 1961), p. 137.

12. Kenneth Scott Latourette and William Richey Hogg, *Tomorrow Is Here* (Friendship Press, 1948), p. 54.

13. M. M. Thomas, "The Situation in Asia—II," in *Man's Disorder and God's Design,* Vol. III, pp. 78–79.

14. *Man's Disorder and God's Design,* Vol. III, p. 190.

15. *Ibid.,* Vol. IV, p. 220.

16. Norman Goodall (ed.), *Missions Under the Cross* (London: International Missionary Council, 1953), p. 224.

17. *Evanston Speaks,* p. 35.

18. *Ibid.,* pp. 42–43.

19. Commission of the Churches on International Affairs, *Background Documentation on Economic and Social Development,* p. 13.

20. "A Report on Responsible Parenthood and the Population Problem," *The Ecumenical Review,* Vol. XII, No. 1 (October, 1959), p. 89.

21. *Ibid.,* p. 91.

22. *Dilemmas and Opportunities,* p. 36.

23. *The New Delhi Report,* pp. 94–95.

24. Lester B. Pearson *et al., Partners in Development* (Frederick A. Praeger, Inc., Publishers, 1969), p. 145.

25. *Christian Social Ethics in a Changing World,* ed. by John C. Bennett (Association Press, 1966), pp. 18–19.

26. *World Conference on Church and Society,* p. 18.

27. *Ibid.,* p. 72.

28. *Ibid.,* p. 81.

29. *Ibid.,* p. 210.

30. *Ibid.,* p. 158.

31. *The Uppsala Report 1968,* p. 45.

32. *Ibid.,* pp. 47–48.

33. *Ibid.,* p. 50.

34. *Ibid.,* pp. 51–55.

35. *Ibid.,* p. 67.

36. *Ibid.,* p. 43.

37. *Fetters of Injustice* (Geneva, 1970), p. 110.

38. "Population Policy, Social Justice and the Quality of Life," *Study Encounter,* Vol. IX, No. 4 (1973).

39. "Ecumenical Chronicle," *The Ecumenical Review,* Vol. XXI, No. 3 (July, 1969), p. 265.

40. François Houtart and A. Delobelle, "The Roman Catholic Church and Economic Planning—at the National and International Level," in Denys L. Munby (ed.), *Economic Growth in World Perspective* (Association Press, 1966), pp. 349, 359, 360.

41. Edward Duff, "The Common Christian Concern," in Preston (ed.), *Technology and Social Justice,* p. 57.

VIII. The Church in the World

1. M. M. Thomas, "Report of the Chairman of the Executive Committee," *The Ecumenical Review,* Vol. XXV (October, 1973), pp. 412–413.

2. M. M. Thomas, "Report of the Executive Committee by the Chairman," *The Ecumenical Review,* Vol. XXIII (April, 1971), p. 96.

3. Preston (ed.), *Technology and Social Justice.*

4. Roger Mehl, *The Sociology of Protestantism,* tr. by James H. Farley (The Westminster Press, 1970), Ch. IX, "Sociology of Ecumenism."

5. *Evanston Speaks,* pp. 47–48.

Selected Bibliography

Abrecht, Paul. *The Churches and Rapid Social Change*. Doubleday & Company, Inc., 1961.

Brown, Robert McAfee. *The Ecumenical Revolution: An Interpretation of the Catholic-Protestant Dialogue*. Rev. and enlarged ed. Doubleday & Company, Inc., 1969.

Christian Social Ethics in a Changing World: An Ecumenical Theological Inquiry. Ed. by John C. Bennett. Association Press, 1966.

The Church and Its Function in Society. Ed. by W. A. Visser 't Hooft and J. H. Oldham. Willett, Clark & Company, 1937.

de Vries, Egbert. *Man in Rapid Social Change*. Doubleday & Company, Inc., 1961.

Dilemmas and Opportunities: Christian Action in Rapid Social Change. Report of an International Ecumenical Study Conference, Thessalonica, Greece. Geneva: WCC, 1959.

The Documents of Vatican II. Ed. by Walter M. Abbott. Association Press, 1966.

Duff, Edward. *The Social Thought of the World Council of Churches*. Association Press, 1956.

Economic Growth in World Perspective. Ed. by Denys L. Munby. Association Press, 1966.

The Ecumenical Advance: A History of the Ecumenical Movement, Volume 2, 1948–1968. Ed. by Harold E. Fey. The Westminster Press, 1970.

The Evanston Report: The Second Assembly of the World Council of Churches, 1954. Ed. by W. A. Visser 't Hooft. Harper & Brothers, 1955.

Foundations of Ecumenical Thought (the official report of Oxford, 1937). Ed. by J. H. Oldham. Fortress Press, 1966.

Fremantle, Anne. *The Social Teachings of the Church: The Key Pronouncements of the Catholic Church on Social Issues*. The New American Library of World Literature, Inc., 1963.

Gaines, David P. *The World Council of Churches: A Study of Its Background and History.* Richard R. Smith Company, Inc., 1966.

Goodall, Norman. *The Ecumenical Movement: What It Is and What It Does,* 2d ed. Oxford University Press, 1964.

A History of the Ecumenical Movement, 1517–1948. Ed. by Ruth Rouse and Stephen C. Neill. The Westminster Press, 1954.

Hogg, William Richey. *Ecumenical Foundations: A History of the International Missionary Council and Its Nineteenth-Century Background.* Harper & Brothers, 1952.

Hudson, Darril. *The Ecumenical Movement in World Affairs.* The National Press, Inc., 1969.

Man in Community: Christian Concern for the Human in Changing Society. Ed. by Egbert de Vries. Association Press, 1966.

Man's Disorder and God's Design. The Amsterdam Assembly series. 5 vols. Harper & Brothers, 1949.

Mehl, Roger. *The Sociology of Protestantism.* Tr. by James H. Farley. The Westminster Press, 1970.

Muelder, Walter. *Foundations of the Responsible Society.* Abingdon Press, 1959.

The New Delhi Report: The Third Assembly of the World Council of Churches. Ed. by W. A. Visser 't Hooft. Association Press, 1962.

The Oxford Conference (official report). Ed. by J. H. Oldham. Willett, Clark & Company, 1937.

Ramsey, Paul. *Who Speaks for the Church? A Critique of the 1966 Geneva Conference on Church and Society.* Abingdon Press, 1967.

Responsible Government in a Revolutionary Age. Ed. by Z. K. Matthews. Association Press, 1966.

The Stockholm Conference 1925: The Official Report of the Universal Christian Conference on Life and Work. Ed. by G. K. A. Bell. Oxford University Press, 1926.

Technology and Social Justice. Ed. by Ronald H. Preston. Judson Press, 1971.

The Uppsala Report 1968: Official Report of the Fourth Assembly of the World Council of Churches. Ed. by Norman Goodall. Geneva: WCC, 1968.

Vatican II: An Interfaith Appraisal. Ed. by John H. Miller. University of Notre Dame Press, 1966.

Vincent, John J. *The Race Race.* London: SCM Press, Ltd., 1970.

Visser 't Hooft, W. A. *Memoirs.* The Westminster Press, 1973.

World Conference on Church and Society (official report). Ed. by M. M. Thomas and Paul Abrecht. Geneva: WCC, 1967.

Index

Brink, C. B., 168
British Commission on Christian
  Social Responsibility, 97
Brown, Robert McAfee, 48
Brunner, Emil, 36, 55, 129, 227
Bucharest 1974, conference on
  Science and Technology for
  Human Development, 51n11,
  225
Bulgakov, Sergius, 123

Calvin, John, 33, 52, 83
Capitalism, 52–55, 59–63, 67–68,
  75, 81, 86, 126, 131, 132, 192
Cardenas, Gonzalo Castillo, 147
Carnegie, Andrew, 31
Chao, T. C., 43, 136
Chidzero, B. T. G., 213
China, admittance to UN, 111,
  115, 142, 145
Christian-Marxist dialogue, 148–
  149
Christian Peace Conference, 143–
  144
Christian realism, 37, 55, 60, 94
Christian social action, bases for,
  17–20, 65, 225–226
Christian Social Union, 31
Church, distinctive role, 37, 95,
  160, 233
Church and state, 57–60, 80
Church Peace Union, 31
Churchill, Winston, 129
Civil disobedience, 167
Colonialism, 187–188, 189–190,
  192, 195, 196
Commission of the Churches on
  International Affairs (CCIA):
  founding, 40–41, 97–98; action
  on human rights including re-
  ligious liberty, 66, 70–71, 100;
  action in crises, 103, 118; dis-
  armament, 106–108; Vietnam
  war, 109; Middle East, 112;

changes made at Uppsala, 116;
  WCC pronouncements, 118; on
  China, 142, 145; on Angola,
  170; on population, 202–205
Commission on a Just and Dura-
  ble Peace, 97, 102, 127, 195
Communism, 61, 67–68, 86, 87,
  121–154
Confessing Church, Germany, 36,
  96, 129, 161, 164, 227, 229
Congar, Yves, 184
Congregationalists, 58, 228
Conscientious objection, 19, 92,
  96, 105, 119, 228; selective, 114,
  119
Constantine, 18, 93
Convergence of economic sys-
  tems, 81–82
Cottesloe Report, 170, 173
Cox, Harvey, 211
Cuban missile crisis, 146
Czechoslovakia, statement of
  WCC officers on, 116

Davis, J. Merle, 192
Davos 1955, Department on
  Church and Society, 43
Dawood, Naway, 179
Delobelle, A., 222
Democracy, 52, 53, 66, 78, 79, 205
Devanandan, Paul D., 198
Development, economic and so-
  cial, 43–49, 148, 186–224
de Vries, Egbert, 207
Dialectical theology, 35
Dibelius, Bishop Otto, 139
Disarmament, 91, 103–109, 113,
  119, 120
Divini Redemptoris, encyclical,
  152
Duff, Edward, 11, 224
Dulles, John Foster, 41, 97, 127,
  130, 131